The United States, Russia, and China

The United States, Russia, and China

Confronting Global Terrorism and Security Challenges in the 21st Century

Edited by
Paul J. Bolt, Su Changhe,
and Sharyl Cross

PSI Reports

PRAEGER SECURITY INTERNATIONAL
Westport, Connecticut · London

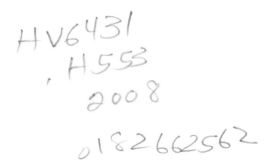

Library of Congress Cataloging-in-Publication Data

The United States, Russia, and China : confronting global terrorism and security challenges in the
    21st century / edited by Paul J. Bolt, Su Changhe, and Sharyl Cross.
        p. cm.
    Includes bibliographical references and index.
    ISBN-13: 978–0–275–99894–3 (alk. paper)
 1. Terrorism—Prevention—International cooperation. 2. Security, International. 3. United States—
Relations—China. 4. United States—Relations—Russia (Federation) 5. Russia (Federation)—
Relations—United States. 6. China—Relations—United States. I. Bolt, Paul J., 1964– II. Su,
Changhe, 1971– III. Cross, Sharyl.
    HV6431.H553 2008
363.325'17—dc22   2007048122

British Library Cataloguing in Publication Data is available.

Library of Congress Catalog Card Number: 2007048122
ISBN-13: 978–0–275–99894–3

First published in 2008

Praeger Security International, 88 Post Road West, Westport, CT 06881
An imprint of Greenwood Publishing Group, Inc.
www.praeger.com

Printed in the United States of America

The paper used in this book complies with the
Permanent Paper Standard issued by the National
Information Standards Organization (Z39.48–1984).

10 9 8 7 6 5 4 3 2 1

We dedicate this book with the shared hope of advancing security & peace among our countries & the broader community of nations . . .

Contents

Preface

This book explores international dimensions of the global terrorist challenge and critical contemporary and emerging security issues from the perspectives of three major powers in the twenty-first-century global community, the United States, Russia, and China. Developments among these three nations, with very different historical experiences, cultures, and traditions, will undoubtedly be of vital significance to shaping the twenty-first-century global security environment.

Contributors to this volume explore possibilities for the evolving U.S.-Russia-China security relationship. Authors advance assessments concerning the factors likely to shape the future relationship among these three countries as either "rivals," "competitors," or "partners." Contributors also offer views concerning the potential consequences of the trilateral U.S.-Russia-China relationship for the domestic security of each country, as well as examining implications for security of the broader global community. Authors further attempt to define similarities and differences among these three major powers regarding assumptions with respect to countering terrorism and international security challenges, as well as strategies for responding to the global terrorist threat. Authors thus explore both traditional (i.e., weapons proliferation) and nontraditional (i.e., environmental and energy) international security challenges.

A major objective of this book is to produce a genuinely U.S.-Russian-Chinese collaborative collection capturing exchanges between specialists of the three countries. Thus, each chapter is coauthored by participants from at least two of the three countries. The contributors gathered for a three-day conference sponsored by Fudan University in Shanghai, China, in May 2006. The conference provided the opportunity for authors to present working papers soliciting feedback from all participants.

Authors continued to confer throughout the various phases of the writing process. Such a collaborative work could not have been achieved by simply compiling existing essays or articles produced in isolation from the collective review process. In the end, we hope that by enlisting specialists representing all three countries, we have provided a more comprehensive treatment of these critical global security issues.

We also believe readers will benefit by the range of views represented in this collection. Specialists are not only products of different cultural backgrounds, academic traditions, and professional experiences, but we also included both senior researchers and contributors recently completing graduate study to provide multi-generational perspectives on these critical security issues. We have encouraged authors to offer forward-oriented, creative, and innovative approaches in examining possible responses to the complex challenges of the emerging security environment.

The United States, Russia, and China: Confronting Global Terrorism and Security Challenges in the 21st Century is primarily intended for use in university courses and graduate seminars. However, the wealth of primary source material contained within this book, as well as analysis of contemporary policy issues, suggests that it should be of interest to the policy communities and general public as well.

This project was initiated in 2005 by faculty of the Fudan University Department of International Politics in Shanghai and the U.S. Air Force Academy in Colorado Springs, Colorado. The editors and contributors would like to express our appreciation to the several universities and academic centers in the United States, Europe, Russia, and China that provided institutional and/or travel support for participants in the project. The editors and contributors would like to thank Ms. Hilary Claggett, Mr. Robert Hutchinson, and Mr. Sean Greaney of Praeger/Greenwood and Matthew Van Atta of BeaconPMG for supporting the project. We are especially grateful to our colleagues of Fudan University, Department of International Politics, for hosting the conference of contributors held in Shanghai in 2006.

This book represents the culmination of a two-year effort of our contributors who share the common objective of heightening awareness and enhancing understanding of U.S.-Russia-China security challenges in the context of the terrorist threat. We thank each of our colleagues who participated in this project for taking time from demanding schedules to prepare the contributions contained in this book. The fact that American, Russian, and Chinese specialists managed to overcome the cultural, linguistic, and distance barriers in preparing this book demonstrates that cooperation is possible when a shared commitment to enhancing security and peace exists.

Paul J. Bolt
Su Changhe
Sharyl Cross

Part I ————————————————————

United States, Russia, and China: Building Cooperative Approaches

Introduction

Sharyl Cross and Paul J. Bolt

The twenty-first-century international security environment presents daunting challenges and responsibilities for nation-states, especially major powers. As a result of the continually increasing economic globalization of the world community, never have the fates of nations been so mutually dependent for continued prosperity. Furthermore, as a result of the increasing power of nonstate actors to inflict horrific damage through acts of terrorism, never have states been so mutually dependent for their continued security. Policymakers must respond effectively in a complex security environment linked by a nexus of associations transcending borders. No nation, even the United States, possessing unprecedented power by every traditional measure, can expect to begin to meet the most pressing security challenges facing humanity without cultivating reliable partnerships.

While the growing prevalence and capacity of transnational terrorists have altered the rules of warfare and led to reconsideration of the elements of "power" in the international arena, the sovereign nation-state will undoubtedly continue to constitute the dominant agent of influence in world politics for the foreseeable future. Nation-states must constantly strive to create better approaches for building cooperation in addressing issues of terrorism, weapons proliferation, failed states, crime, and a host of additional security concerns. Managing the earth's resources and preserving the environment will also require sustained consultation and compromise throughout the global community of nations.

The United States, Russia, and China obviously possess differing capabilities and priorities affecting prospects for mutual cooperation in addressing security challenges. Among many concerns, Islamist-motivated terrorism has been a higher priority for the United States, and also even for Russia. While there was no single assault in Russia resulting in the loss of thousands of lives, such as the attacks of September 11, 2001, in New York and Washington, Russia has suffered a series of terrorist incidents over the past several years that culminated in the tragic school siege in Beslan in September 2004, an incident that carries similar cultural resonance in Russia to that of the 9/11 attacks in the United States. While the United States initiated a well-resourced worldwide campaign to combat terrorism following the 9/11 assault, Russia has focused primarily on the threat emanating from Chechen separatism. Although Chinese officials express concern regarding violent religious extremism or the spread of radical Islamism in the western province of Xinjiang, other issues such as ensuring continuing economic growth and the status of Taiwan consume far greater attention. However, even given differing priorities, it is not insignificant that Russia and China have provided intelligence and other forms of cooperation in support of U.S. and other multilateral initiatives to counter terrorism since 9/11.

Many uncertainties exist in defining the relationship among these three major powers as the post–Cold War international system is being shaped. Since the collapse of the Soviet empire, the system appears to have transitioned from a well-defined bipolar order to a unipolar order in which the United States has assumed a predominant role as well as enormous responsibility. Demonstrating determination to resist any suggestion of U.S. hegemony in the emerging system, leaders in Russia and China have repeatedly asserted the desirability of a multipolar world community that relies on international institutional organizations as central mechanisms for governing the world system. Both Russia and China strongly oppose the Iraq war, and both countries have attempted to cultivate greater cooperation with the European Union (EU). The promotion of newly instituted regional organizations, such as the Shanghai Cooperation Organization (SCO), and Russian and Chinese objections to key U.S. actions within the UN Security Council clearly illustrate divergence of objectives and resolve on the part of both the Russian and Chinese leadership to refrain from supporting, and sometimes even to challenge, U.S. policies deemed counter to their national or global interests. U.S. policymakers have openly criticized recent reversals of democratic reform in Russia and speculate on whether China's growing power could be directed against fundamental American interests and influence in the future. While Russia has become a major energy and arms supplier for China, the Moscow leadership is at the same time concerned that dwindling population growth and control of the Far East could leave the region increasingly vulnerable to penetration by China that further threatens the territorial integrity of the Russian Federation.

Almost two decades after the end of the Cold War, the United States, Russia, and China remain ambivalent regarding each others' future ambitions or intentions. The policy communities in Washington, Moscow, and Beijing remain skeptical over the possibility that a triangular relationship characterized by a benign posture among the three countries is likely for the future. Furthermore, there are concerns that allying too closely with one or the other nation could result in being drawn into a dispute with the third country.

At the same time, in spite of the fact that the three countries have a history of mutual distrust, the United States, Russia, and China share important economic ties and common security interests. China constitutes the fastest-growing export market for U.S. products, with total exports increasing 150 percent since China was admitted to the World Trade Organization (WTO) in 2001. The United States ranks second only to the European Union among China's largest trading partners. In addition to Russia supplying energy to China, a range of economic ties exist between Russia's Far East and China in trade, investment, labor, and tourism. The United States, Russia, and China all seek to prevent a return to an international climate akin to the Cold War that could consume or divert much needed resources for continued economic growth and entail grave risks. These major powers share interests in countering terrorism, halting the proliferation of weapons of mass destruction, managing energy resources, limiting crime, combating poverty and infectious disease, and protecting the environment and climate from further degradation. The three countries would all benefit by preventing further conflict or deterioration in Iraq, Afghanistan, Iran, North Korea, Taiwan, Central Asia, the Caucasus, the Balkans, and other regions of shared interest.

In the coming decades, the United States would be well served to cede greater responsibility for ensuring the security and stability of the world community to other major powers and clusters of nations by working more vigorously through multilateral organizations. Any nation that would attempt to assume a disproportionate share of the burden for attempting to manage these security challenges might risk significant dissipation of resources, affecting its own standard of living and security.

Both Russia and China will be positioned to assume even greater leadership and responsibility in world diplomacy, and should be prepared to assume a larger share of the burden as major powers in addressing pressing international problems. There is no question that both countries must devote considerable resources toward continued modernization, economic growth, infrastructure development, and improving conditions for so many citizens that still suffer in poverty and lack access to adequate health care and education. Essential domestic needs notwithstanding, given current growth rates, projections indicate that China will likely possess the world's largest economy within the first half of this century. Although China has focused resources on economic modernization and elects to assume a modest orientation toward the world, stressing that it remains a "developing nation," the enormous growth of China's economy and military capacity must inevitably be accompanied by a more assertive and engaged role in global affairs. In spite of Russia's diminished status following the collapse of the Soviet empire, the Moscow leadership and Russian society maintain a perception of a national identity based on "great power" status. Russia remains a huge nation straddling two continents and is emboldened by its role as a major energy power.

Since the collapse of the Soviet empire, and particularly in response to the 9/11 attacks, U.S. policymakers have been consumed with counterterrorism and preoccupied with Iraq and instability resulting from the implosion of smaller failed states. It would behoove the American policy community to focus greater attention on the potential of major power centers, particularly Moscow and Beijing, where the consequences of policy decisions will be so significant for the stability of the entire world community. If the United States can manage to develop productive and cooperative relationships with these two giants, it will go a long way toward enabling America to meet the challenge from terrorism, bring about a favorable outcome in Afghanistan and Iraq, and help advance many critical priority issues.

The need for greater levels of trust, better communication, and cultural understanding among nations of the twenty-first century cannot be underestimated for governing a complex and interdependent security environment. The relationships among the United States, Russia, and China—three nations possessing vastly differing historical experiences and cultural traditions—will be pivotal for the emerging international security order that will regulate world politics well into the twenty-first century.

The following chapters set forth major security priorities and unique perspectives for all three countries. Authors affiliated with the strategic policy and academic communities of the United States, Russia, and China have collaborated to explore the options available for the three countries in responding to a range of transnational security challenges and regional issues. As the chapters indicate, there are both barriers to and opportunities for greater collaboration.

Chapter 1 examines the security policies of China, the United States, and Russia, focusing on the nature of the terrorist challenge to each state and the different responses of each state. In the next section of the book, "Transnational Security Issues and Challenges," Chapter 2 explores policies regarding nuclear weapons. A remnant of the Cold War struggle, nuclear weapons continue to play an important role in relations between China, the United States, and Russia, although their role in combating terrorism is less clear. Chapter 3 examines energy security, a particularly timely issue as the U.S. continues to consume vast amounts of energy and China's energy demand is increasing rapidly, while Russia is becoming a vital energy supplier. Chapter 4 looks at the problem of environmental degradation in China and the ways in which the United States and Russia can cooperate with China to ameliorate this global problem. Chapter 5 brings us back to terrorism, particularly focusing on countering its ideological support. Here we find important differences in policy, particularly tied to the American emphasis on democratization as a means to combat terror. Chapter 6 also focuses on terrorism, approaching it from the perspective of internal security and comparing it to the potential effects of a deadly epidemic similar to the "Spanish flu" of 1918.

The final section of this volume, "Regional Security Issues and Challenges," examines interactions between China, the United States, and Russia on four regional issues. Chapter 7 focuses on the complex triangular relations between the United States, Russia, and Europe. Chapter 8 explores the complementary and divergent interests of China, Russia, and the United States in Central Asian states eager to establish themselves in the world. Chapter 9 succinctly summarizes security challenges in the Middle East from American and Russian perspectives, while Chapter 10 compares American and Chinese approaches to the North Korean nuclear issue. All chapters thus directly and indirectly explore barriers to and opportunities for greater collaboration among the United States, China, and Russia.

1

Chinese, American, and Russian Security Policies: The Response to Terrorism[1]

Paul J. Bolt, Su Changhe, Robin L. Bowman, and David H. Sacko

Security is a foremost objective of all states. However, threats can change rapidly, and state security policies must adjust. In the past two decades, the threats and opportunities for China, the United States, and Russia have changed markedly. As a result, security policies have changed as well. The first major shock was the end of the Cold War (although as noted below, China's security policies began a major transformation as early as 1979). The second major shock was 9/11 and the ensuing terrorist threat. However, each of these shocks meant different things to China, the United States, and Russia, and each has responded differently.

This chapter examines the security environments and policies of China, the United States, and Russia in the post–Cold War world. Particular emphasis is placed first on the nature of the terrorist challenge to each state. Although terrorism threatens each country, and each country justifies its policies in terms of the terrorist threat, the nature of that threat is quite different for China, the United States, and Russia. We also emphasize the response to terrorism of China, the United States, and Russia, focusing on the extent to which these responses are unilateral or multilateral.[2] Clearly the struggle against terror has opened new avenues of cooperation. However, all three states also reserve the right to take unilateral action, ignoring international criticism, when they see such action as necessary to their security.

CHINA'S RESPONSE TO TERRORISM

From Bystander to Stakeholder: China's Security Doctrine in Quiet Evolution

The sudden terrorist attacks on the United States on September 11, 2001 represented a turning point in world politics in the post–Cold War era. Before 9/11, the great powers had been perplexed as to how to adjust their relations. The collapse of the Soviet Union left the United States as the sole superpower in world politics. Thus the direction of the respective bilateral relations among China, the United States, the EU, Russia, and Japan were very uncertain. In particular, the Sino-American relationship was bedeviled by the Taiwan issue, trade disputes, and human rights issues, as well as arms sales over the decade before the 9/11 incidents. Sino-American relations were difficult due to the fact that the strategic consensus had disappeared with the dissolution of the Soviet Union.

However, China took the lead in going beyond Cold War thinking in order to meet the new global security challenges. It is widely accepted that the shock of 9/11 propelled China forward to become involved in global antiterrorism cooperation, and made it possible for China and the United States to find a new strategic consensus. There is some truth to this, but it is not the complete story.

Changes in China's foreign policy can actually be traced to the early 1990s, when China began to rethink its strategic security environment, and urgent problems emerged at the very beginning of the new century that challenged China's traditional thinking and practice of security. One of the conspicuous features in Chinese diplomatic transformation is that a new concept of security is gradually prevailing in Chinese foreign relations. In the isolated system before 1979, when China began to implement the Open Policy, China's economy was mostly independent from the world. Communication between China and the world was minimal, which enabled China to maintain its autonomy in domestic and foreign policy decision-making. As a result, domestic and international issues could be easily differentiated because of the weak linkages between domestic and international issues. Additionally, China was likely to select unilateral or radical policies, since the importance of trade and investment was quite small in its overall economy and the costs of its political and economic decision-making were much lower. Obviously, the implementation of the Open Policy has brought about a transformation in China's diplomacy.

Furthermore, with the end of the Cold War and the ensuing dramatic change in international structure, the life-or-death struggle of the past no longer characterized the relations between China and other great powers. Instead, common security and cooperative security became the new wave in international politics. In an interdependent world, as explained by liberal international relations theory, the threat or use of military power is discouraged in resolving problems. Table 1.1 illustrates that China was involved in many military conflicts, directly or indirectly, in its neighboring areas before 1979, while after 1979 there have been no military conflicts

Table 1.1   The Decline of Military Factors in Relations Between China and Its Neighboring Countries

Bilateral Relations	Military Events (1949–1979)	Issues (1979–2007)
Korean Peninsula	Korea War (1950)	Six-party talks
Sino-India	Border military conflict (1962)	Unresolved
Sino–Soviet Union/Russia	Border military conflict (1969)	Border demarcation finished
Sino-Vietnam	Military aid to Vietnam	Border conflict (1979–1989), land border demarcation projected in 2008
Sino-Japan		Unresolved issue of Diaoyu Islands
Sino–ASEAN countries		Declaration on South China Sea in 2001

between China and its neighboring countries except for the Sino-Vietnam border conflict from 1979 to 1989. This does not mean that China was inclined to use military action to resolve border disputes in the independence phase before 1979, but it does emphasize that the relevance of traditional border disputes in overall Chinese foreign relations is declining with China integrating into the world economy. Theoretically, with the strengthening of economic interdependence and transnational issue-linkages, military factors will gradually be constrained in resolving bilateral and multilateral relations.[3]

Compared to the retreat of bilateral issues, regional transnational public issues linking China and its surrounding countries have become more important since 1979. Tables 1.2 and 1.3 list regional transnational public issues between China or China's subregions and surrounding countries from 1979 to the present. China and its neighboring countries face three categories of transnational public issues.

Table 1.2   Transnational Public Issues Between China and its Neighboring Countries (1979–2007)

Category	Issues
Security	Nuclear proliferation, terrorism
Trade and financial	Asian financial crisis, regional economic cooperation, regional integration
Environment	Air pollution, acid rain, water pollution, fishing resource depletion
Public health	AIDS, SARS, bird flu
Public security	Potential refugees, transnational crime, drug trafficking, illegal immigration

Table 1.3 Transnational Issues between Chinese Subregions and Neighboring Countries

Chinese Subregions	Transnational Issues	Neighbor Involved
Northeast	Acid rain, air pollution, water pollution, illegal immigrants, potential refugees, transnational crime, spread of WMD	Russia, DPRK, South Korea, Japan, Mongolia
Northwest	International terrorism	Russia, Afghanistan, Central Asia
Southeast, Southwest	Terrorism, drug trafficking, illegal immigrants, environmental pollution, disease control, piracy	South Asian countries, ASEAN

The first is regional security issues, including the spread of weapons of mass destruction (WMD) and counterterrorism. The second is regional economic development, such as reducing tariffs, expanding mutual investment, and making regional monetary arrangements. The third encompasses regional social development, such as drug trafficking, environmental protection, and disease control. One point we should notice is that if we see China as consisting of several subregions, Table 1.3 illustrates that the priorities of transnational issues are different in the case of different Chinese subregions.

Global public issues have characteristics of transparency, connectiveness, and commonality. Transparency means that these issues cross territorial borders, with every country dealing with them. Connectiveness means these issues blur the border of domestic and international politics. Commonality means that these issues are relevant to each nation's interests, thus states need to make collective decisions. It is evident that regional transnational issues are playing an increasingly important role in Chinese foreign relations if we compare the two periods of Chinese foreign relations after 1949. One of the most important reasons for this phenomenon is that policy adjustments in China since 1979 integrate China's domestic economy and society into international society. As a consequence, multilateral diplomacy and international organizations play increasingly important roles in Chinese foreign relations.

In sum, the fact that China lives in an interdependent world prompts China to rethink and adjust its diplomacy and international relations. The new security concept was gradually put forward by decision-makers and has been a guiding principle for international security cooperation. Some points about the new security concept need to be explained. First, it underlines the importance of common security, which holds that countries cannot maintain security at the expense of their neighbors' security. Second, it focuses on the value of comprehensive security, which insists on the multidimensional aspect of security including human security, social security, economic security, and world security, as well as traditional military security. Third, it holds that security can be reached only through mutual confidence, mutual benefit, equality, and coordination. Lastly, it maintains that international disputes should be resolved by peaceful means.[4]

China and the Threat of Terrorism

The increased threat of terrorism faced by China is reflected in the recent change in official discourse. This is evident in China's National Defense White Papers.[5] The first and second White Papers in 1998 and 2000 assert that terrorist activities are a new form of danger and a threat to international security. But the two papers just touch on this problem; the word "terrorism" is used only once, with the assertion that it will take a long time for international society to remove the danger of terrorism. However, there are differences between the first two White Papers and the latest three in terms of terrorism. First, terrorism is highlighted much more in the 2002, 2004, and 2006 White Papers. In particular, the 2002 White Paper gives wide coverage to international antiterrorism cooperation, and the latest three White Papers delve deeply into terrorism and China's position on terrorism. Second, the White Papers since 2002 began to differentiate between traditional and nontraditional security threats. The three papers since 2002 recognize that the terrorist threat to international security is increasing, and China is not immune to this new form of threat. In addition, Chinese officials and scholars have begun to place more stress on terrorism as a nontraditional security issue since 2002. Third, papers since 2002 assert that China is also a victim of international terrorism, especially from East Turkistan terrorist activities.

The frequency and strength of terrorist activities against China have intensified recently. The real terrorist threats to China following 9/11 could be categorized as international terrorist organizations and individual terrorists, East Turkistan and Tibet independence movement terrorists at home and abroad, and potential terrorist dangers from cults and criminal gangs.[6]

The major illegal activities of international terrorist organizations and individual terrorists in China are focused on money laundering, population trafficking, narcotics trafficking, and kidnapping. These activities are increasingly a threat to social stability and public and private property. Structurally, terrorists from abroad often collude with Chinese domestic underground criminal gangs; in terms of subregions in China, these types of terrorist activities are mainly concentrated around the southeast coastal area, southwest China, and northeast China, and the development of these activities has been gradually extended to China's interior.

The most serious threat to China from terrorism is from East Turkistan terrorist groups. These groups maintain close training and financial links with the Taliban and al Qaeda, and they are widely seen as part of international terrorism, even though their activities mainly take place in northwestern China and Central Asia. The East Turkistan Islamic Movement was listed as an international terrorist organization by the UN Security Council in 2002. However, other East Turkistan terrorist

organizations are still not defined as such by international society, even though they
have conducted many terrorist activities in China and Central Asia. The most recent
possible terrorist threat to China is from radical organizations, such as the Tibet
Youth Congress (TYC), that advocate taking violent action to separate Tibet from
China. The TYC has undertaken many terrorist activities against the government
and innocent persons in Tibet in recent years.

Cult terrorism, such as Falungong and other extreme criminal gangs, is seen by the
Chinese government as a new form of terrorism that endangers Chinese domestic
society. Some assert that religious cults are likely to turn to terrorism, and in many
instances, cults and terrorist groups share chilling similarities.[7] Though cults and
extreme criminal gangs are not easily differentiated from normal criminals, they
could be described as soft terrorists. The Falungong cult has been described as a typical terrorist organization whose thinking and activities poisoned thousands of persons in China over the last decade. Mafia activities are another form of soft
terrorism in China that jeopardizes public security. The mafias' activities are rising
in China, and their membership is estimated to be at least one million. Although
Chinese officials never use the word *mafia* or officially recognize the existence of
mafias, this phenomenon is described as "criminal gangs with the mafia's characteristics" in official discourse.[8]

The range of terrorist activities against China is still evolving. Many terrorist
attacks against China occurred at home before 2000. However, with more and more
Chinese people and companies going abroad, terrorist attacks against Chinese are rising rapidly. Additionally, China's overseas interests are threatened by terrorists. One
such interest threatened by terrorists is energy security. Recent riots and terrorist
bombings in Indonesia, Sudan, Afghanistan, and Nigeria directly damaged the business of Chinese multinational corporations. Undoubtedly, these terrorist attacks
against overseas Chinese people and companies will grow dramatically in the future.
In response to increasing incidents overseas, the Chinese Foreign Affairs Ministry
established a new External Security Affairs Bureau in 2004. The new bureau aims
to strengthen coordination in dealing with overseas emergencies.

China's Multilateral Response to Global Terrorism

Zhao Yongchen, one of the leading cadres from the Anti-Terrorism Bureau of the
Chinese Public Security Ministry, elaborated on China's viewpoint on the war
against terrorism when he attended the 22nd Congress on the Law of the World in
Shanghai in 2005. First, terrorism is a threat to world peace and security, having negative international effects. China is firmly against any forms of global terrorism.
International society should take collective action and necessary legislative, adminis-
trative, and judicial measures to strike against terrorism. Second, double standards
should be discarded in the global war against terrorism, since any form of terrorism
is detrimental to world peace. No country, party, or other organization should
employ double standards due to its self-interest or ideology. Third, measures taken
by international society should be in the interest of world peace and be beneficial

in reducing regional disputes rather than aggravating tensions in terms of ethnic discrimination, religious hostility, or civilizational conflict. Fourth, international efforts at counterterrorism should operate in the framework of the UN Charter and basic principles of international law. The UN Security Council should play a key role in fighting terrorism. Fifth, China is against linking the causes of terrorism with specific ethnic and religious issues. It is not appropriate for international society to resolve conflicts of civilizations through drastic antiterrorism measures, including military strikes. Lastly, terrorism should be treated by looking into both its root causes and symptoms. Every country should take comprehensive measures (including political, economic, diplomatic, military, and legal measures) rather than only use force to deal with terrorism. Great powers should discard unilateralist thinking and make efforts to reduce the economic gap between developed and developing countries and construct a just international order through political dialogue, economic cooperation, and cultural exchange.[9]

China prefers to take a multilateral approach to the increasing terrorist threat. The multilateral response to terrorism conforms with China's new diplomacy since the end of the Cold War. One of the distinguishing features of Chinese diplomatic transformation is that China gradually accepts principles of multilateralism and behaves more and more multilaterally.[10] Obviously, China's approach to counterterrorism is also influenced by Chinese diplomatic transformation during the post–Cold War timeframe.

China has participated in most current international conventions on antiterrorism. China has been a member of 10 out of 12 international conventions on antiterrorism. China also takes positive actions in the UN Security Council Counter Terrorism Committee. In the 2001 Asia-Pacific Economic Cooperation (APEC) Shanghai meeting, which followed the 9/11 attacks, the Chinese government responded quickly and successfully facilitated a member declaration on antiterrorism.

China also supports the Shanghai Cooperation Organization (SCO), which was established in 2001 to build up a permanent body in countering terrorism. The SCO's members consist of China, Russia, and the Central Asian countries. One of its major aims is to deal with increasing transnational terrorist activities among member states. In 2001, the six member countries of the SCO in Shanghai signed the *Shanghai Convention on Combating Terrorism, Separatism and Extremism* and the *Agreement Between the SCO Member Countries Concerning the Regional Counter-Terrorism Agency.* The SCO also has conducted many joint antiterrorism military exercises. The latest exercise, code-named Peace Mission 2007, was held in August 2007. It was the largest joint antiterrorism exercise with participation of all the SCO member states. The purpose of this exercise was to attack assumed terrorists. The exercise indicates "the endorsement of the common strategic interests existing among the six states: cracking down on the three evil forces such as the violent terrorist forces, national secessionist forces and extreme religious forces, safeguarding regional security and stability, and promoting regional development and prosperity."[11]

The ASEAN Regional Forum (ARF) is another example of Chinese cooperation with a multinational organization. China and the Association of Southeast Asian Nations (ASEAN) issued the Joint Declaration on Non-traditional Security Cooperation in November 2001. This declaration attempted to strengthen information exchanges, personnel training, and research in the field of nontraditional security cooperation. Additionally, China has also engaged in joint bilateral nontraditional security exercises with Thailand, Pakistan, and India over the past few years.

China also values the role of multilateral financial institutions in cracking down on terrorism. In coordinating multilateral financial attacks on terrorism, China has built up an interdepartmental joint action unit (including 23 domestic departments) in just two years to deal with money laundering and to cut off terrorist financial sources. In 2005, the Law of Anti-Money Laundering was approved by the Chinese Congress.[12] China also insists on fulfilling the International Convention for the Suppression of the Financing of Terrorism. China recently made efforts to join the Financial Action Task Force On Money Laundering (FATF). It was invited to be a FATF observer in 2005, and is expected to become a member of this institution in coming years.

Domestically, the Chinese Ministry of Public Security established an Anti-Terrorism Bureau in 2002 to research, plan, coordinate, and guide national antiterrorism actions. Accordingly, at the local level, many large cities in China also are making efforts to improve their antiterrorism infrastructure. It is reported that the Beijing municipal administration is even planning to establish a special antiterrorism bureau in 2007 for the upcoming Olympic Games.

THE AMERICAN RESPONSE TO TERRORISM

American Security Doctrine: Consistent Goals, Changing Tactics

Unlike China in 1979, there has been no single turning point in American politics that shifted American policy from being radical and inward-focused to one that looked toward global engagement. Instead, as a former colony, the United States has always had important trade and diplomatic links with Europe. As the United States grew over time, it became more and more engaged in international commerce and politics throughout the world, including Asia. Its security interests expanded as well.

Like China, the United States is linked by regional transnational issues to its neighbors, particularly Canada and Latin America. In the security arena, broadly defined, the United States and Canada are North Atlantic Treaty Organization (NATO) allies and are both concerned about securing the common border against terrorist infiltration while not inhibiting commerce. On its southern border, the United States focuses on illegal immigration and drug smuggling, while Mexican leaders seek to ensure that Mexicans can continue to work in the United States. In terms of commerce and investment, the United States, Mexico, and Canada are closely linked through the North American Free Trade Agreement (NAFTA). The

United States sent almost 37 percent of its exports to Canada and Mexico in 2005, while receiving nearly 27 percent of its imports from its NAFTA partners.[13] The United States also shares environmental concerns with its neighbors, particularly in terms of air pollution. However, while transnational issues are important, American concerns are also global. Thus the primary security concern comes from terrorist groups that are based in the Middle East or Southwest Asia, but may use Canada or Mexico (and other areas as well) as transit routes for weapons or personnel.[14]

As a regional and global force, the United States is closely involved with multilateral institutions. However, as a result of history and geography, Americans have held conflicted attitudes toward these institutions. With only two neighbors, neither of which poses a threat to the United States, and oceans to the east and west, as well as a sense of uniqueness, Americans have sometimes been reluctant to engage in long-term cooperative efforts. Nothing illustrates this better than the aftermath of World War I. While President Wilson was a primary architect of the League of Nations, the U.S. Senate failed to ratify its charter and join the League. American leadership was instrumental in drafting the United Nations during World War II; but contrary to the vision of its founders, the UN quickly became a Cold War battleground in which the United States and the Soviet Union promoted their own agendas. Throughout the Cold War, multilateral institutions such as NATO were created to serve Cold War purposes. In fact, some have argued that during the Cold War, multinational institutions such as the UN were used to subvert American constitutional processes. For example, President Truman relied on UN authority rather than a declaration of war by Congress to fight the Korean War.[15]

Nevertheless, in spite of the relative stability in American policy compared to China's 1979 turnaround, within the last 20 years there have been two major paradigm shifts in American conceptions of security. The fall of the Berlin Wall in November 1989 marked the first. No longer was the West fighting against the Soviet threat; new security issues and challenges emerged. It was hoped that this new era would be safe and marked by cooperation among states, allowing for a reduction in military spending and a "peace dividend." However, this "new world order," as coined by President George H. W. Bush, was not as peaceful or easily managed as many hoped, as illustrated initially by the Gulf War. While the United States was well aware of its changed environment, articulating post–Cold War doctrine and policies proved to be a challenge. According to Richard Haass, the Bush administration's approach to this new order never came to fruition, and post-1989 foreign policy continued to focus "mostly on managing relations among the great powers, protecting those few U.S. interests deemed vital, and promoting open trade."[16]

The Clinton administration, which held power from 1993 to 2001, also tried to respond to this new security environment. Over the course of his eight years in office, President Clinton released three separate National Security Strategies,[17] each recognizing that while the Soviet danger had passed, the security challenges of the post–Cold War environment were far more diverse: ethnic conflict and regional instability, proliferation of WMD, large-scale environmental degradation, and dramatic demographic changes. But despite these growing threats, the tone of the Clinton Doctrine of engagement and democratic enlargement presented an optimistic outlook, celebrating "unparalleled opportunities to make our nation safer and more prosperous" through increased globalization and technological connections, the spread of democracy, peaceful conflict resolution, and a stronger international community to address global issues.[18] Clinton believed there was a connection between supporting the growth of free states after the collapse of the Soviet Union and securing a more prosperous and peaceful international environment.[19] Thus, in this emerging unipolar order with new security challenges, President Clinton's grand strategy to secure national interests was to promote developing democracies, as well as open and free market economies, in order to foster peace and security.

Moreover, the Clinton Doctrine championed multilateral approaches to employing hard and soft power, especially the diplomatic, economic, and military arenas, to meet these national security objectives. On the diplomatic front, President Clinton emphasized that the United States must pay its dues to the United Nations. He advocated enlargement of NATO into the former Soviet satellites of Central and Eastern Europe, as well as strengthening NATO-Russian and U.S.-Russian diplomatic relations, goals that proved to be somewhat incompatible. On the economic front, the president turned his attention to such multilateral economic cooperation as NAFTA, APEC, and the General Agreement on Tariffs and Trade (GATT).

Arguably, with the end of the Cold War, the military instrument of power also became much easier for the United States to employ absent any threat of retaliation by the Soviet Union. Thus, the Clinton administration engaged the U.S. military in various types of operations. Often these were in accord with the multilateral spirit, such as the UN peacekeeping mission in Somalia. However, they also included air strikes over Kosovo, approved by NATO in lieu of UN Security Council approval, which Russia would not grant. The United States was also willing to strike unilaterally, as in cruise missile attacks against Afghanistan and Sudan.

The United States and the Threat of Terrorism

The second major paradigm shift came with the 9/11 attacks. The United States was certainly a target of terrorists long before 9/11. There are numerous examples of al Qaeda–associated attacks on Americans or American interests. For example, in February 1993, six people were killed in a World Trade Center bombing that unsuccessfully sought to bring the towers down. In 1996, a truck bombing at Khobar Towers in Saudi Arabia killed 19 Americans. In August 1998, the U.S. embassies in Kenya and Tanzania were bombed, killing 12 Americans and 212 others. In December 1999, an Algerian was captured attempting to smuggle explosives into the United States from Canada, with the purpose of wreaking havoc at the millennium celebrations in Seattle.

However, nothing compared to the attacks of September 11, 2001. These coordinated attacks on the World Trade Center in New York and the Pentagon in Washington, along with a plane that crashed into the fields of Pennsylvania, resulted in nearly 3,000 dead, both Americans and citizens from around the world. These attacks were strategic in every sense of the word, striking at the symbols of American commercial prowess and military power and bringing true terror to America itself. As such, they brought about a strategic response. American security policy changed dramatically, particularly in terms of methods. While the end of the Cold War left many questions regarding the direction of American security policy but a general sense of well-being, 9/11 resulted in greater insecurity but also brought a grand strategy with demonstrable coherence.

Three features of the 9/11 attacks in particular have shaped American policy. First, the homeland itself was attacked in a way that brought mass casualties. A corollary is that there is now an expectation of future attacks. For instance, a July 2007 National Intelligence Estimate stated that "the U.S. Homeland will face a persistent and evolving terrorist threat over the next three years," in part due to a "regenerated" al Qaeda.[20] In August 2007, Vice Admiral (ret.) John Scott Redd, head of the National Counterterrorism Center, stated that another attack on the United States is bound to occur.[21] It is simply too difficult to stop every plot. There is great concern that the next attack will utilize WMD, making the results especially horrific.

A second feature of the 9/11 attacks is that they created great soul-searching as to why a country with the resources of the United States could not prevent them. For example, the 9/11 Commission Final Report noted numerous failures throughout the U.S. government and provided recommendations on major reforms of government policy and structure.[22] One particular problem was that the United States still had the mind-set of state actors being the greatest threat. The shift to fight extremely motivated and adaptive nonstate actors is difficult for a state that has achieved great power status by following the old rules. Much of the changed security strategy of the United States is intended to help make that shift. Moreover, the threat is still not fully understood, meaning that American strategy continues to evolve.[23]

A third feature of the terrorist challenge to the United States sets it apart from the threats faced by China and Russia. The threat to the United States comes primarily from outside the country. Most of the 9/11 terrorists, for instance, were Saudi nationals. While the fear of homegrown terrorists is very real, the main threat since 9/11 has come from the Middle East and Southwest Asia.

The American Response to Global Terrorism

The American response to global terrorism has utilized both unilateral and multilateral approaches. The strategy outlining this American response is most clearly summarized in the *National Security Strategy of the United States of America* (NSS), first published in September 2002, then updated in March 2006, and the *National Strategy for Combating Terrorism,* first published in February 2003 and revised in September 2006.[24] There are five main elements to U.S. security strategy as outlined in these doctrines and seen in American practice.

The first element is a declaration that "America is at war."[25] This is a common theme in discussions of the terrorist challenge, expressed in phrases such as the "war on terror" and "long war." More concretely, the United States is engaged in wars in Afghanistan and Iraq. It has also used its military in a variety of places in the fight against terrorism, ranging from support to the Philippine military in battling Abu Sayyaf, an attack from a drone on suspected terrorists in Yemen, to fighter patrols over American cities. Moreover, the NSS of 2002 and 2006 both proclaim a doctrine of preemption, in effect proclaiming that the United States will use military force against a threat before an attack on the United States occurs.[26]

However, American security doctrine sees the war on terror in a much broader sense than merely a military conflict. The struggle against terror is also viewed as a battle of ideas and ideologies, expressed in part in forms of government. Thus, a very important piece of American strategy is the promotion of freedom, the protection of human dignity, and democratization.[27] This is one explanation for the Iraq war—the administration hoped that a successful conclusion would create a bulkhead of democracy in the Middle East. This element of the strategy rests on the premise that authoritarian states provide the breeding ground for terrorism, while democracies provide healthier outlets for frustration. Likewise, the American strategy also touts the importance of free markets and economic development in order to reduce poverty. Another element in the battle of ideas is defining Islam. Official American statements are careful to state that the war on terror is not a battle against Islam. Instead, it is a fight against those extremists who have distorted and exploited Islam for their own purposes.

A third element in the American response to global terrorism is domestic institutional reform. This takes place first through the strengthening of laws to give greater powers to government. The Patriot Act and changes to the 1978 Foreign Intelligence Surveillance Act are examples. A second component of this is the reorganization of bureaucratic organizations charged with domestic security, most notably the creation of the Department of Homeland Security. Similarly, the United States has worked to enhance domestic interagency cooperation with the creation of the National Counterterrorism Center and the Office of Director of National Intelligence.

There are other steps the United States has taken to cripple terrorist networks as well. These include disrupting terrorist financing by working closely with international banks and financial institutions, working to limit the proliferation of WMD, and putting pressure on "rogue states" believed to support terrorism for their own national goals.

Finally, the United States has endeavored to work with a variety of international organizations to combat terrorism. In this regard, Washington asserts that the United States must take the lead and inspire action because "only when we do our part will others do theirs."[28] The American strategy has been to work within existing international organizations to shift their focus to terrorism. For instance, the United States has been involved in developing 12 universal conventions and protocols against terrorism in the United Nations, in addition to resolutions in the Security Council. The United States has worked with the Group of Eight in developing counterterrorism standards, and the war in Afghanistan is being fought in partnership with NATO. The United States has cooperated with multilateral organizations including the International Maritime Organization and the International Civil

Aviation Organization, as well as regional organizations such as the Asia-Pacific Economic Cooperation, the Organization of American States, the African Union, and ASEAN. The United States also supports ARF. ARF is important to the United States in that it legitimizes the role of the United States in Asia, provides a forum to coordinate responses to terrorism and other issues, and allows for confidence building between regional actors.

There is a wide variety of other policy areas related to the battle against terror in which the United States supports multilateral actions. Examples include reliance on Six Party Talks to resolve the North Korean nuclear issue, multilateral mechanisms for dealing with Iran's nuclear program, close participation with the "Middle East Quartet" (the European Union, Russia, the UN, and the United States) in attempting to resolve the Palestine issue, and leadership in the Proliferation Security Initiative (PSI) to deal with the spread of WMD.[29] Moreover, American public opinion shows strong support for multilateral policy options.[30]

Some have praised American strategy under the Bush administration. According to John Lewis Gaddis, the differences between the Clinton and Bush doctrines are stark. He claims that the first Bush NSS is proactive, and "rejects the Clinton administration's assumption that since the movement toward democracy and market economics had become irreversible in the post–Cold War era, all the United States had to do was 'engage' with the rest of the world to 'enlarge' those processes." Gaddis also asserts that "the Bush administration, unlike several of its predecessors, sees no contradiction between power and principles," noting that this administration is "thoroughly Wilsonian." Finally, says Gaddis, the new strategy is candid: "this administration speaks plainly, at times eloquently, with no attempt to be polite or diplomatic or 'nuanced.' What you hear and what you read is pretty much what you can expect to get."[31] Others, however, have been much more critical, asserting that American application of power is too unilateral.

There are reasons for this perception. The National Security Strategies of 2002 and 2006 both proclaim a doctrine of preemption, which in effect blurs the distinction between preemptive war and preventive war.[32] Multilateral institutional approval for such wars is very difficult to obtain. The American campaign in Afghanistan in 2001, while supported by allies, began without sanctioning by any multilateral institution. The 2003 war on Iraq was not explicitly sanctioned by the UN or any other international body, in spite of U.S. efforts to obtain UN approval. Although the United States was supported by a "coalition of the willing," there was widespread international condemnation of the war. Other examples outside the realm of terrorism that demonstrate U.S. unwillingness to abide by widely supported multilateral agreements include rejection of the Kyoto Protocol, rejection of the International Criminal Court, and failure to ratify the Comprehensive Nuclear Test Ban Treaty.

In order to understand the reasons why the United States has sometimes resorted to unilateral action rather than relying on multilateral institutions, one must examine the international context since September 11, 2001. Three factors in particular stand out. The first is the 9/11 attacks themselves. The second factor concerns the failures and limitations of multilateral institutions, and the third is the role of the United States as a world power.

The 9/11 attack was a severe shock to the United States. It was comparable to the Pearl Harbor attack in 1941 in that it fundamentally changed the American view of the world. After a brief honeymoon from the end of the Cold War until 9/11—when it appeared that, at least for the United States, the world was a relatively safe place— it became painfully clear that the American homeland itself was vulnerable to attack. Most dangerous were nonstate actors that must be dealt with in a manner different from traditional state threats. Diplomacy and deterrence could not directly stop them. In this environment, preemption as a principle has widespread political support in the United States, although the specifics might be highly contested. When the safety of the American homeland is at risk, no president can be seen to have his hands tied by international organizations.

Second, the failures and limitations of multilateral institutions in providing security have become painfully clear. From genocide in Rwanda to dealing effectively with Saddam Hussein, the United Nations has often proven ineffective. More specifically, the United Nations has not been out front in the fight against terrorism.[33] As Joachim Krause notes, "A world in which the paramount international security institution is unable to solve or even effectively address the most dramatic and dangerous threats to security is a world on the verge of regressing to a system of self-help."[34] Lastly, there are theoretical reasons why the United States might not fully support multilateral organizations. As the world's foremost military and economic power, the United States has incentives not to be constrained by multilateral organizations.[35]

Clearly, however, most foreign policy goals of the United States require multilateral action to be achieved, and often the participation of multilateral institutions is also necessary. For instance, stabilizing Iraq cannot be achieved by the United States alone. More broadly speaking, nation building requires efforts by the international community. Similarly, preventing proliferation cannot be achieved unilaterally. Thus the United States has worked through the UN, Russia, China, and its European allies to try to halt Iran's nuclear weapons program. Preventing terrorism clearly requires multilateral cooperation from all states. Other goals, including spreading democracy, promoting human dignity, defusing regional conflicts, and expanding development almost by definition require multilateral cooperation.

Most importantly, the effective exercise of American power in the world requires legitimacy. While there is some agreement within the United States that preemption may be a necessary option, the unilateral exercise of power may stimulate a fear of American strength abroad. Such fear makes it difficult for the United States to achieve its purposes, pointing to the need for legitimacy to elicit cooperation.[36] Legitimacy is gained in part by working through international institutions. Therefore, the United States needs to work to strengthen international bodies so that they have the power to effectively fight against terrorism and other twenty-first-century security threats.

RUSSIA'S RESPONSE TO TERRORISM

From Pariah to Partner? A Different Perception of Russia's Security Doctrine

After the collapse of the Soviet Union, Russia faced serious challenges in both the domestic and international arenas. The most pressing challenge was to build strong, accountable political institutions and a productive, market-based economy. Tied to this challenge was a renewed debate on Russia's relations with the West. Would Russia become a part of the West or continue to have a separate identity in the world? Within Russia itself, solutions to these challenges shifted with changing political dynamics.[37] President Boris Yeltsin's administration protested yet largely accommodated U.S. and NATO enlargement and the U.S.-NATO air war against the Serbs with the longer view of peaceful and beneficial cohabitation with the West. The Second Chechen War in 1999, led by Prime Minister Vladimir Putin, represented a marked departure in this philosophy with the weakening of Mr. Yeltsin within his own government. President Putin's ascendancy represented the rise of a "Russia First" philosophy that squarely set Russian national interest in front of any agreement with the West (Europe and the United States), or even the East (China) or South (India and Iran).

To this end, Russia has advocated a multipolar international system with an emphasis on the importance of the UN Security Council, where Russia has veto power. As the National Security Concept of the Russian Federation notes, Russia will "facilitate the development of an ideology of the creation of a multipolar world."[38] Russia has also consistently emphasized the importance of state sovereignty, reacting strongly against what it sees as outside interference in its internal affairs and governance. The Second Chechen War highlighted this concern.[39] After the renewed Russian offensive in October 1999, the U.S. State Department criticized Russian tactics as indiscriminate and contradictory to Russia's obligations as a signatory of both the Geneva Conventions and Code of Conduct of the Organization for Security and Co-operation in Europe (OSCE).[40] Russia's conduct in Chechnya both under the Yeltsin and Putin administrations (Putin became acting president following Boris Yeltsin's resignation on December 31, 1999) was criticized roundly by the West throughout the entire conflict. At no point, however, were economic sanctions or any significant political sanctions ever employed. The West considered Russia's use of force against civilians to be untoward and was seen in stark contrast against the U.S.-NATO's careful and meticulous planning of its air campaign against Serbia. The Global Salafist Jihadi attack against the United States on September 11, 2001 would change the U.S. perception of Russia's actions in Chechnya. While still sometimes critical, the American perspective was more sympathetic to the Russian cause.

After 9/11, Russian policy was quite pragmatic. On issues of major importance to the United States, Russia has backed the United States or failed to raise significant opposition. However, in issues vital to Russia but less important to the United States, Russia has gone its own way. Examples include Russian policy toward ex-Soviet republics, weapons sales to China, and domestic reforms to strengthen and centralize central government.[41] Russia and the United States share many common interests in combating terrorism, but there are also significant areas where the two countries diverge, such as Russia's strong objection to U.S. intervention in Iraq. Russians have also expressed bitterness at perceived Western attempts to take advantage of Russian weakness through the expansion of the EU and NATO, as well as through criticism of human rights violations that are often seen as self-serving or hypocritical.[42] Western attitudes toward Russia were not always positive before 9/11, nor were they always negative afterwards. In other words, Russia was not a pariah, nor is it seen as an interconnected partner now. Russia is, however, perceived as a country that has shared the experience of the psychological dislocation of major incidents of terror. This has inextricably altered American perceptions of Russia's security doctrine.

Russia and the Threat of Terrorism

Physical security against nonstate actors was rarely if ever a concern for Russians during the Soviet era. On the rare occasion that Soviet diplomats were targeted internationally, such actions were met with the full force of Soviet diplomatic and intelligence capabilities such that future acts of terrorism were quite often deterred.[43] Within Russia itself, security was assured. A hallmark of life in Russia was the safety the Soviet system brought to the average citizen, at least from *random* violence. Following the Soviet Union's dissolution, perceptions of what constituted a threat for the Russian citizenry naturally increased—all varieties of crime that were previously unheard of now seemed common in the emergence of the Russian state. The Russian sense of security would be most affected, however, by the terrorist incidents following the conclusion of the first Chechen war in 1997, caused by dissatisfaction among some Chechen separatists with the terms of the peace agreement.

Problems began in Chechnya but quickly spread into other parts of Russia. In May 1998, Valentin Vlasov, Yeltsin's personal representative in Chechnya, was kidnapped and held for six months. Later in the year, four engineers from Britain and New Zealand were kidnapped and murdered. The following year, in March 1999, General Gennadiy Shpigun, Moscow's top envoy to Chechnya, was kidnapped from the airport in Grozny. His corpse was later found in Chechnya in March 2000. In September 1999, Chechen terrorists shockingly killed 300 people in a bomb attack on Russian military housing in Dagestan and a series of apartment block bombings elsewhere in Russia. As a result of these terrorist incidents, the war resumed in October 1999.

After the Russian conventional offensive in Chechnya began anew, Chechen terrorism was largely suspended until the October 2002 Dubrokvka theater incident. Here Chechen rebels seized a theater and held about 800 people hostage. Most of the rebels and some 120 hostages were killed when Russian forces stormed the building. Later that year in December, Russian government offices in Grozny were attacked by a suicide bomber and 80 people were killed. In May 2003, over 50 people were killed in yet another suicide bombing of a Russian government building in the north of the republic. Each terrorist incident brought a Russian conventional response that incurred more civilian collateral damage. The following year, in May 2004, President Akhmad Kadyrov and many of his staff were killed in a Grozny bomb blast. Two passenger airlines were brought down by Chechen women suicide bombers in August 2004 in addition to a series of subway bombings the same month. The following September, the siege at a school in Beslan captured international attention. Hundreds of Russian citizens were killed or wounded— many of them young students—when it ended in violence. Thus, in sum, Russia did not experience the sudden catastrophic loss of life and property as was experienced by the United States on 9/11. Its horror was spread out over several years.

Russia's Multilateral Response to Global Terrorism

The terrorist threat to Russia is primarily from within—Chechen fighters with international support. Still, this represents an internal issue that has become vastly more complex given the availability of international training and support—a complex problem that requires a multilateral response. Russia well understands that foreign cooperation is necessary for a resolution of its own security threat. As stated in its *National Security Concept* in 2000, "to fight [terrorism] requires unification of efforts by the entire international community . . . there must be effective collaboration with foreign states and their law enforcement agencies, and also with the international organizations tasked with fighting terrorism . . . broad use must be made of international experience in dealing with this phenomenon and there must be a well coordinated mechanism for countering international terrorism."[44]

In the wake of the terrorist attack on the United States on September 11, the Russian National Security Concept seems quite prescient. A new understanding between Russia and the United States was forged instantaneously in the fires of that day. The American Global War on Terror (GWOT) would be fought in Central Asia against the Chechens' allies, and the Russian battleground in Chechnya was assumed to also be an American battlefront, although no Russian troops would deploy to Afghanistan again, just as no U.S. forces were sent to Chechnya. An understanding and a level of cooperation not seen since World War II, however, was spawned.

U.S.-Russian cooperation in counterterrorism has reached unprecedented levels since 9/11. The U.S-Russia Working Group on Counter Terrorism serves as the primary bilateral mechanism for facilitating cooperation. The United States and Russia have worked closely in the Global Initiative to Combat Nuclear Terrorism, and in 2007, American Deputy Secretary of State John Negroponte praised Russia for working with the U.S. in countering terrorism.[45]

In addition, Russia has also worked with multilateral bodies. For instance, the NATO-Russia Council has fostered cooperation in countering terror, including working to ensure greater intelligence sharing between Russia and NATO. Russia has also been an integral part of SCO efforts to combat terrorism, including participation in major military exercises in China. This raises Russia's status and provides a Eurasian counterweight to the United States and NATO.

Most recently, Russia has shown much greater confidence in foreign affairs, fueled in part by healthy energy export revenues. This has sometimes led to conflicts with international organizations. For example, Russia has clashed with the OSCE on elections in Belarus, Ukraine, and Azerbaijan, and Russia has had sharp disagreements with the Council of Europe on human rights issues. In July 2007, Russia also suspended all participation in the Treaty on Conventional Arms in Europe. Russia has further clashed with states in Europe. For example, Britain and Russia expelled each others' diplomats over the investigation of the poisoning of a former Soviet spy in London, while Russia has battled Poland and the Czech Republic over American plans for antimissile defense systems. Russia has further extended the reach of its military patrols.

This does not mean that Russia now stands firmly against the West, or that we are entering another Cold War. Russia continues to be an ally in the war on terror. However, it does mean that Russia is no longer trying to join the West, if it ever was. It is establishing its own identity and sphere of influence. As one Russian ambassador expresses it, Russia's geopolitical position puts it at the center between the West, the Muslim world, and Asia. Russia will serve as a bridge, following its own interests, rather than becoming an appendage of the West.[46] This will bring cooperation with multilateral institutions on some issues and opposition on others.

CONCLUSION

Our analyses have pointed to similarities between China, the United States, and Russia in their responses to post–Cold War security challenges and, in particular, the threat of terrorism. All three states have highlighted the threat of terrorism in their official doctrines, and have made adjustments both in domestic and foreign policies to deal with terrorism. All three states cooperate in the fight against terrorism, to a degree that would have surprised observers before 9/11, and use terrorism as a rhetorical common enemy. China, the United States, and Russia have also worked to strengthen multilateral cooperation against terror.

However, there are also noteworthy differences. First is the definition of terrorism. China, the United States, and Russia all view al Qaeda and its affiliated groups as terrorists. However, China takes a more expansive view of terrorist groups than the United States, including a variety of cults, separatist groups, traffickers, and criminal organizations. While before 9/11 the United States was sometimes critical of the treatment by Russia and China of domestic groups that Russia and China considered to be threats, since 9/11 American criticism has been quieter.

Second, the nature of the terrorist threat faced by China, the United States, and Russia differs. China faces growing terrorist attacks on its citizens outside China, and China also must prepare for the danger of international terrorism at the 2008 Olympics.[47] However, for China and Russia, the source of terrorism is primarily domestic separatists or other domestic parties opposed to government policies. Groups using violence in Xinjiang and Chechen rebels are most prominent. While these groups seek outside aid and are linked with al Qaeda, they are often motivated by nationalism. The threat to the United States has come primarily from outside the country. None of the 9/11 terrorists was an American citizen, and the goals of terrorists attacking the United States are geopolitical and tied to American foreign policy and the shape of the Muslim world.

Finally, the policy responses to terrorism of China, the United States, and Russia have varied. The United States has used extensive military force in the GWOT along with numerous other policy tools, including the effort to counter ideological support for terrorism. Furthermore, the struggle against terrorism defines American foreign and security policies. Defeating terrorism is the main goal. This is not true of China and Russia. While fighting terrorism is important, China's primary goal continues to be building its economy and increasing its influence in the world. Russia, while using military force extensively in Chechnya, also seeks to strengthen its own government and economy, in the process regaining a more prominent position in world politics. For all three states, the fight against terrorism is tied to continued jockeying for position in the world. This leads to both cooperation and competition, as will be outlined in greater detail in subsequent chapters.

NOTES

1. The opinions in this paper are those of the authors alone and do not represent the policies or positions of any government or institution.

2. While multilateralism is almost always thought of in a positive light, states have very different reasons for promoting multilateralism. For an analysis of the views of Germany, France, and Britain, see Joachim Krause, "Multilateralism: Behind European Views," *Washington Quarterly* 27, no. 2: 48–53. For an analysis on the different perspectives of the United States and Europe toward unilateral and multilateral action, see Robert Kagan, *Of Paradise and Power* (New York: Alfred A. Knopf, 2003).

3. This does not mean that China was inclined to use force to resolve bilateral disputes. China makes serious efforts to resolve territorial disputes with its neighboring countries.

4. On details of the new security concept, see the 16th Communist Party of China Congress Report by Jiang Zemin.

5. On China's National Defense White Papers in 1998, 2000, 2002, and 2004, see http://www.chinamil.com.cn/site1/gfbps/gfbps.htm. On the full text of China's 2006 National Defense White Paper, see http://news.sina.com.cn/c/2006–12–29/123911916415.shtml.

6. Zhang Jiadong, *Lun kongbu zhuyi (On Terrorism)* (Beijing: Shishi chubanshe, 2007).

7. See James Long, "Cults and Terrorist Groups Share Chilling Similarities," *Oregonian*, November 9, 2001, http://www.rickross.com/reference/alqaeda/alqaeda25.html.

8. Zhang Jingping, "Cracking Down on Underground Criminal Gangs Must Counter Corruption in Advance," *Saohei bixu xian fanfu (Chinese Newsweek)*, October 24, 2000.

9. "Gongan bu guanyuan chanshu Zhongguo fankong lichang" ("Official from Public Security Ministry Elaborates on Chinese Standpoints in Countering Global Terrorism"), http://www.china.com.cn/chinese/MATERIAL/961632.htm. Chinese official standpoints on anti-terrorism can also be found in China's 2004 National Defense White Paper, section 6; see http://www.chinamil.com.cn/site1/database/2004-09/30/content_26806.htm.

10. See Su Changhe, "Faxian Zhongguo xin waijiao" ("Rediscovering Chinese Diplomacy"), *Shijie jing yu zhengzhi (World Economics and Politics)* no. 4, 2005.

11. Weiwei, "Ruhe jiedu Shanghai hezuo zuzhi 2007 heping shiming junshi yanxi" ("How to Read SCO Joint Anti-Terrorism Military Exercise 'Peace Mission 2007'"), *Jiefangjun bao* (*People's Liberation Army Daily*), May 22, 2007, http://english.pladaily.com.cn/site2/news-channels/2007–05/22/content_822538.htm.

12. "Gonganbu fankongju guanyuan tan Zhongguo fankong cuoshi" ("Official from Public Security Ministry Talks on China's Measures to Counter Terrorism"), *Jiefangjun bao* (*People's Liberation Army Daily*), August 27, 2006.

13. World Trade Organization Country Profiles at http://stat.wto.org/Home/WSDBHome.aspx?Language=.

14. Nevertheless, homegrown American threats without explicit links to al Qaeda are still a problem as well. See Josh Meyer, "Small Groups Now a Large Threat in U.S.," *Los Angeles Times,* August 16, 2007, http://www.latimes.com/news/nationworld/nation/la-na-homegrown16.1aug16,1,2233111.story?ctrack=1&cset=true.

15. See Louis Fisher, "The War Power: No Checks, No Balance," in *Congress and the Politics of Foreign Policy,* ed. Colton C. Campbell (Upper Saddle River, NJ: Prentice Hall, 2003), 1–21.

16. Richard N. Haass, "Fatal Distraction: Bill Clinton's Foreign Policy," *Foreign Policy* 108 (Fall 1997): 112.

17. *A National Security Strategy of Engagement and Enlargement* in February 1995, *A National Security Strategy for A New Century* in October 1998, and *A National Security Strategy for A Global Age* in December 2000.

18. *A National Security Strategy of Engagement and Enlargement* (February 1995), i, available at http://www.au.af.mil/au/awc/awcgate/nss/nss-95.pdf.

19. Douglas Brinkley, "Democratic Enlargement: The Clinton Doctrine," *Foreign Policy* 106 (Spring 1997): 110–27.

20. National Intelligence Estimate, "The Terrorist Threat to the U.S. Homeland," July 2007, http://www.dni.gov/press_releases/20070717_release.pdf.

21. Mark Hosenball and Jeffrey Bartholet, " 'We are Going to Get Hit Again,' " *Newsweek,* September 10, 2007, http://www.msnbc.msn.com/id/20466414/site/newsweek.

22. National Commission on Terrorist Attacks Upon the United States, *The 9/11 Report* (New York: St. Martin's Press, 2004).

23. For the need to more clearly conceptualize the threat, see David J. Kilcullen, "New Paradigms for 21st Century Conflict," *eJournal USA,* May 2007, http://usinfo.state.gov/journals/itps/0507/ijpe/kilcullen.htm.

24. Much of the following material comes from *National Security Strategy of the United States of America* (September 2002), http://www.whitehouse.gov/nsc/nss.pdf; *National Security Strategy of the United States* (March 2006), http://www.whitehouse.org/nsc/nss/2006/nss2006.pdf; and *National Strategy for Combating Terrorism* (September 2006), http://www.whitehouse.gov/nsc/nsct/2006/nsct2006.pdf.

25. *National Security Strategy,* 2006, i. These are also the first four words of the *National Strategy for Combating Terrorism.*

26. For instance, President Bush's introduction to the 2002 document states "We will cooperate with other nations to deny, contain, and curtail our enemies' efforts to acquire dangerous technologies. And, as a matter of common sense and self-defense, America will act against such emerging threats before they are fully formed." *National Security Strategy,* 2002, v.

27. The 2006 *National Strategy for Combating Terrorism* states "The long-term solution for winning the War on Terror is the advancement of freedom and human dignity through effective democracy," 9.

28. *National Security Strategy of the United States,* 2006, ii.

29. See Colin L. Powell, "A Strategy of Partnerships," *Foreign Affairs* 83, no. 1 (January–February 2004), Ebscohost; "Win Some, Lose Some," *Economist,* June 5, 2004, Ebscohost; and "The New Multilateralism," *Wall Street Journal* (Eastern Edition), January 8, 2004, A22.

30. See Alexander Todorov and Anesu N. Mandisodza, "Public Opinion on Foreign Policy: The Multilateral Public that Perceives Itself as Unilateral," *Public Opinion Quarterly* 68, no. 3 (Fall 2004): 323–48.

31. John Lewis Gaddis, "A Grand Strategy," *Foreign Policy* 133 (November 2002): 53–54.

32. President Bush's introduction to the 2002 document states "We will cooperate with other nations to deny, contain, and curtail our enemies' efforts to acquire dangerous technologies. And, as a matter of common sense and self-defense, America will act against such emerging threats before they are fully formed." *National Security Strategy,* 2002, v.

33. For a European perspective outlining the failures of multilateral action, see Krause, "Multilateralism," 45–48.

34. Krause, "Multilateralism," 57.

35. For an overview of some of the theoretical writing on this, see Evelyn Goh, "The ASEAN Regional Forum in United States East Asian Strategy," *Pacific Review* 17, no. 1 (March 2004): 48–49.

36. See John Lewis Gaddis, "Grand Strategy in the Second Term," *Foreign Affairs* 84, no. 1 (January–February 2005), Ebscohost.

37. For an example of the changes among Russia's liberals alone, see Eduard Solov'ev, "The Foreign Policy Priorities of Liberal Russia," *Russian Politics and Law* 44, no. 3 (May–June 2006): 52–72.

38. National Security Concept of the Russian Federation, Approved by Presidential Decree on December 17, 1999. English translation text from http://www.fas.org/nuke/guide/russia/doctrine/gazeta012400.htm. See also S. Neil MacFarlane, "The 'R' in BRICs: Is Russia an Emerging Power?" *International Affairs* 82, no. 1 (2006): 48–49.

39. Hostilities in Chechnya date to the December 1994 Russian military response to the Chechen independence movement following the breakup of the Soviet Union and the 20-month prolonged military intervention. After a peace agreement was signed in May 1997 between President Yeltsin and Chechen rebel chief of staff Aslan Maskhadov, irregular hostilities continued until Russia's reengagement in 1999.

40. Barnaby Mason, "West Critical But Cautious on Chechnya," *BBC News,* November 19, 1999, http://news.bbc.co.uk/1/hi/world/europe/514489.stm.

41. See MacFarlane, "The 'R' in BRICs," 49–53.

42. Mikhail Maiorov, "On Moral Principles and National Interests," *International Affairs: A Russian Journal of World Politics, Diplomacy, and International Relations* 53, no. 2 (2007): 36–44.

43. The example here is the October 1, 1985 kidnapping of four Soviet diplomats and the subsequent killing of one in Beirut, Lebanon. The Soviet Union pressed Syria while dispatching paramilitary KGB forces that struck hard at the terrorists. These forces kidnapped several Islamic fundamentalists tied to the kidnappers and reportedly sliced off their fingers and sent them to the fundamentalist leadership implying that more pieces would be forthcoming. After

the KGB threatened to go in shooting, the three living captives were released and no more Soviet citizens were kidnapped in Lebanon.

44. National Security Concept of the Russian Federation, quoted from Sharyl Cross, "Russia's Relationship with the United States/NATO in the U.S.-Led Global War on Terrorism," *Journal of Slavic Military Studies* 19 (2006): 175–92, quote on 177.

45. "Transcript: Powell Says Terrorist Arrests Illustrate U.S., Russian Cooperation," http://www.fas.org/asmp/campaigns/MANPADS/Powell13Aug03.htm; United States Department of State, "U.S.-Russia Cooperation Touted for Reducing Nuclear Threat," http://usinfo.state.gov/xarchives/display.html?; United States Department of State, "U.S.-Russia Joint Fact Sheet on the Global Initiative to Combat Nuclear Terrorism," http://www.state.gov/r/pa/prs/ps/2006/69016.htm; and Cross, "Russia's Relationship," 185–89.

46. Maiorov, "On Moral Principles and National Interests." See also Dmitri Trenin, "Russia Leaves the West," *Foreign Affairs* 85, no. 4 (July–August 2006), Ebscohost; and Andrew C. Kuchins, "New Directions in Russian Foreign Policy: Is the East Wind Prevailing Over the West Wind in Moscow?" Paper presented at "Russia, the G-8 Chairmanship, and Beyond," http://www.cdi.org/russia/johnson/9314–27.cfm.

47. See Zhu Zhe, "Terrorism 'Big Threat' to Olympics," *China Daily,* September 11, 2007, http://chinadaily.com.cn/olympics/2007–09/11/content_6095748.htm.

Part II ⎯⎯⎯⎯⎯⎯⎯⎯⎯⎯⎯⎯⎯⎯⎯⎯

Transnational Security Issues and Challenges

2

Nuclear Weapons in a Changing Threat Environment

Pavel Podvig, Fred Wehling, and Jing-dong Yuan

While China, Russia, and the United States have begun to adapt their nuclear forces to the strategic and political challenges of the new century, the size and structure of those forces and the doctrines for their employment remain little changed from the Cold War era. Beijing, Moscow, and Washington all acknowledge that terrorist attacks using weapons of mass destruction or regional nuclear contingencies in the Middle East, South Asia, or Northeast Asia are now more likely than nuclear war between the major powers. Nevertheless, the three largest nuclear powers have not yet made major efforts to reorient their nuclear forces to the emerging global threat environment. This chapter provides an overview of the Chinese, Russian, and U.S. nuclear arsenals, trends in each country toward modernization of forces and doctrine, and the development of policies toward nuclear arms control, disarmament, and nonproliferation.

CHINESE NUCLEAR FORCES

Among the five nuclear weapons states recognized in the Treaty on the Non-Proliferation of Nuclear Weapons (NPT),[1] China claims to maintain the least number of operational nuclear weapons. The most recent publicly available sources estimate that China's current nuclear forces consist of approximately 145 deployed warheads and about 200 additional warheads in its stockpile.[2] China's nuclear doctrine, the size of its nuclear arsenal, and scope and speed of its modernization will depend on a host of politico-strategic considerations, Sino-U.S. relations, and developments in the revolution in military affairs (RMA).[3]

Nuclear Arsenal and Strategic Force Modernization

China's "East Wind" (Dong Feng) series of land-based strategic missiles, operated by the People's Liberation Army's (PLA) Second Artillery Corps (SAC),[4] remain the pillars of China's strategic nuclear deterrent.[5] However, China's currently deployed ICBMs are thought to be vulnerable to both a disarming nuclear attack and conventional precision-guided munitions. Over the past two decades, therefore, China has embarked on serious efforts to upgrade the capabilities of its existing arsenal to enhance its survivability and hence credibility.[6] It is expected that within the next 5–10 years, older missiles will be retired and replaced with a new generation of solid-fueled mobile missiles, the DF-31 and DF-31A. The DF-31 (CSS-X-10), an ICBM with a range of 8,000 km, has been under development since 1985.[7] The DF-31A, a 12,000-km range ICBM, is a modified version of the DF-31 that is being developed to replace China's aging DF-5A ICBMs and may achieve initial operational capability (IOC) by 2010. Once the DF-31A is deployed, China would for the first time have mobile ICBMs capable of reaching targets in all of the United States in addition to Europe and Russia.[8]

China currently has only one SSBN, the *Xia*-class submarine (Type 092). Commissioned in 1981, the *Xia* carries 12 *Julang-1* (Giant Wave) SLBMs and became

Table 2.1 Chinese Nuclear Forces

Type	Delivery systems	Warheads
Strategic		
ICBMs	42	42
SLBMs	12	12
Total strategic		54
Nonstrategic		
Theater missiles	51	51
Bombers	~40	~40
Stockpiled weapons		~200
Total nonstrategic		~291
Total Nuclear Weapons		~345

Sources: Hans M. Kristensen et al, *Chinese Nuclear Forces and U.S. Nuclear War Planning* (Washington, DC: FAS/NRDC, 2006); Robert S. Norris and Hans M. Kristensen, "NRDC Nuclear Notebook: Chinese Nuclear Forces, 2006," *Bulletin of the Atomic Scientists* (May–June 2006), 60–63.

operational in 1988. The *Xia* SSBN has been plagued with technical problems and has rarely left port. Development of a new SSBN, the Type 094, began in the late 1980s and has continued for years without deployment.[9] The May 2007 Department of Defense annual report on the Chinese military confirms progress made in the building and testing of the second-generation *Jin*-class Type 094 SSBN. The Type 094 SSBN will replace the *Xia*-class Type 092 SSBN, and will be armed with JL-2 submarine-launched ballistic missiles (SLBM); the report expects IOC between 2007 and 2010.[10]

China operates about 120 Hong-6 (B-6/BADGER) and 20 Qian-5 (A-5/FAN-TAN) bombers, but only a few dozen are believed to be dedicated to nuclear weapons delivery.[11] These bombers, which have been in service for well over 30 years, do not constitute a credible retaliatory force against adversaries equipped with modern air defenses. Beijing does not appear to be making efforts to upgrade the air leg of its strategic triad; China's 2002 Defense White Paper refers to the nuclear missions of the Second Artillery Corps and the navy's SSBN force, but makes no mention of a nuclear role for the air force.[12]

Nuclear Doctrine and No-First-Use Policy

In general, the Chinese nuclear doctrine and force modernization have been informed and guided by three general principles: effectiveness (*youxiaoxing*), sufficiency (*zugou*), and counterdeterrence (*fanweishe*).[13] While Chinese analysts acknowledge that deterrence underpins China's nuclear doctrine, it is more in the sense of preventing nuclear coercion by the superpower(s) without being coercive itself, and hence it is counter-coercion or counterdeterrence.[14]

Discussion of nuclear strategy in China's 2006 Defense White Paper reaffirms China's no-first-use (NFU) principle. However, there are growing doubts and debates on whether China would uphold this principle under extreme circumstances. In July 2005, PLA Major General Zhu Chenghu provoked considerable controversy when he declared that China should respond with nuclear weapons if the United States intervened with powerful conventional military forces in a confrontation over Taiwan.[15] In the intervening two years since that controversial statement, however, high-level Chinese military officials have disavowed any change to the country's long-standing no-first-use policy, which states that China will not be the first to use nuclear weapons in a conflict.[16] Nonetheless, Zhu's remarks highlight an ongoing debate in China on the issues of nuclear doctrine and the no-first-use policy, reflected by growing and more public discussion of these topics in the Chinese media and academic literature.

For now, no-first-use remains in place as official Chinese policy. Reports of SAC troop exercises strongly hint that the country would not only refrain from using nuclear weapons first, but would also delay a counterattack until after it had absorbed the incoming nuclear strike (*houfazhiren*).[17] Despite this seeming continuity in Chinese doctrine, the pronouncements of retired Chinese military figures and academics suggest that a serious debate on the future of this posture is likely to continue and even intensify in the months and years ahead.

Arms Control and Disarmament

The 2006 Defense White Paper highlights China's commitments to international arms control and nonproliferation agreements. China endorses the principle of nuclear disarmament and opposes the deployment of nuclear weapons on foreign soil. China also supports efforts to start negotiations on a fissile materials cutoff treaty (FMCT) and signed (although has not yet ratified) the Comprehensive Test Ban Treaty (CTBT), with the latter imposing significant constraints on China's ability to develop new nuclear weapons, especially the miniaturization of nuclear warheads for ballistic missiles currently under development. It is believed to have stopped producing weapons-grade, highly enriched uranium (HEU) and military plutonium, although it retains a stockpile sufficient in quantities for future expansion of its nuclear arsenal should the need arise.[18]

The future of Chinese nuclear weapons modernization will likely influence its position on and commitments to international arms control and nonproliferation agreements and vice versa. Interestingly, a 2007 article by a PLA analyst suggests that China may need to boost its nuclear arsenal in anticipation of growing pressure for it to participate in multilateral nuclear disarmament.[19]

Safety and Security

Historically, China's nuclear weapons facilities and national research laboratories were deliberately established in remote locations to keep them secret and reduce the likelihood of direct impacts on populations should nuclear accidents occur. They have also been tightly guarded by the security forces, normally units of the People's Liberation Army. As China is projected to expand its nuclear power capacities in the coming decades, the issues of security and safety against potential terrorist attacks are becoming increasingly salient. While most of China's nuclear weapons facilities are located in remote regions and presumably well guarded, that has not always been the case with civilian- and university-operated facilities. With projected growth in nuclear energy, medicine, and other nuclear dual uses, as well as nuclear research, assessing security threats and developing effective preventive measures against nuclear terrorist theft or sabotage requires closer cooperation between the United States and China.[20] During the late 1990s, the two countries launched the bilateral lab-to-lab exchange programs to introduce the Chinese to the concept and practice of materials protection, control, and accounting (MPC&A). However, the controversial Wen-ho Lee incident and the subsequent release of the Cox Report in 1999 charging Chinese nuclear espionage effectively put the program to an end.[21] In the aftermath of 9/11, Washington and Beijing have resumed limited cooperation and restarted that process, with MPC&A demonstration workshops ("Technology

Demonstration of U.S.-China Physical Protection of Nuclear Materials") held in China over the past few years.[22]

Future Trends

Chinese nuclear weapons policies may be influenced by two aspects of nuclear developments in the United States. The first revolves around the overall strategic orientation of U.S. nuclear forces. Chinese media commentaries argue that the end of the Cold War has resulted in a unique environment in which the United States is gradually achieving unchallenged nuclear dominance, as the result of declining Russian nuclear arsenals and still-limited Chinese nuclear capabilities.[23] Second, Chinese analysts have expressed considerable concern about potential U.S. efforts to develop new types of nuclear weapons and the Bush administration's Reliable Replacement Warheads program (discussed in this chapter's section on U.S. nuclear forces). Chinese analysts argue that these U.S. programs could lead to renewed nuclear arms races between nuclear weapons states, induce threshold states to openly pursue nuclear weapon capabilities, and fundamentally undermine global nuclear nonproliferation efforts.[24]

China faces specific challenges from recent developments in U.S. defense posture and capabilities as the Pentagon continues to push for the RMA and transformation of America's armed forces. One is the ongoing missile defense architectures— national and regional—that could erode the confidence of Chinese nuclear retaliatory capability. The other, the deployment and use of precision-guided munitions, including air- and sea-launched cruise missiles, could directly threaten to disarm a very limited Chinese ICBM arsenal in a first strike. It also undermines the very principle of no first use and puts Beijing in a dilemma with regard to proper responses under such circumstances. These operational concerns, coupled with a generally cautious assessment of U.S. nuclear weapon policy, are sufficient motivations for China to continue, and speed up, its nuclear modernization efforts to ensure the survival, credibility, reliability, and effectiveness of its small nuclear arsenal, particularly in areas that enhance penetration, mobility, and possibly the expansion of the overall numbers of deployed ICBMs or the introduction of multiple warheads.[25]

RUSSIAN NUCLEAR FORCES

In the years after the breakup of the Soviet Union, Russia has undertaken substantial efforts to preserve its strategic nuclear forces and to maintain, as much as is possible, parity with the United States. Russia in 2007 had over 740 strategic delivery systems that can carry about 3,300 nuclear warheads. In addition to this, Russia is believed to have more than 2,000 warheads associated with nonstrategic delivery systems. Table 2.2 presents a summary of the current status of the Russian nuclear arsenal.

Most Russian strategic warheads are deployed on land-based ICBMs. The Strategic Rocket Forces currently have 76 SS-18 heavy missiles (R-36MUTTH and

Table 2.2   Russian Nuclear Forces

Type	Delivery systems	Warheads
Strategic		
ICBMs	489	1,788
SLBMs	173	609
Strategic bombers	79	884
Total strategic		3,821
Nonstrategic		
Missile defense	100	100
Air defense	1,900	600
Aviation	~490	974
Naval	n/a	655
Total nonstrategic		~2,330
Total Deployed Nuclear Weapons		~5,600

Sources: Pavel Podvig, "Current Status of the Strategic Forces," Russianforces.org Web site (http://
russianforces.org/eng/current/ (accessed on August 3, 2007); Robert S. Norris and Hans M. Kristensen, "Russian Nuclear Forces, 2007," *Bulletin of the Atomic Scientists* (March–April 2007), 61–64.

R-36M2 modifications), each carrying 10 warheads; 123 SS-19/UR-100NUTTH
with six warheads each; 243 single-warhead land-mobile SS-25/Topol missiles; and
47 single-warhead SS-27/Topol-M, most of which are deployed in silos.

The strategic fleet includes 12 submarines: six Delta IV/Project 667BRDM, which
carry SS-N-23/R-29RM missiles, and six older Delta III with SS-N-18/R-29R missiles. Eight submarines (six Delta IV and two Delta III) are based at the bases of
the Northern Fleet, and four Delta III are based in the Pacific. Not all submarines,
however, are operational, as three Delta IV ships are currently undergoing overhaul
and the operational status of the Delta III fleet is uncertain.[26]

Strategic aviation includes 79 intercontinental-range bombers, which are
equipped to carry air-launched cruise missiles. Most of the bombers are relatively
old turboprop Tu-95MS aircraft, but Russia also deploys 15 newer Tu-160 super-
sonic bombers.

Force Modernization

Russian strategic forces are currently undergoing transformation, which
will reduce the number of operational launchers and warheads and replace older
strategic systems with new ones. The changes in the land-based intercontinental

missile force will include withdrawal of SS-19 missiles and a significant number of SS-18 (R-36MUTTH version) and SS-25 missiles. These will be partly replaced by newly manufactured SS-27/Topol-M missiles, deployed in silos and on road-mobile launchers.[27] In May 2007, Russia tested a multiple-warhead version of the Topol-M missile, which was designated RS-24. Introduction of this missile, however, would not substantially change the number of ICBM warheads. It is unlikely that by 2015 Russia will have more than 150 ICBMs with about 600 warheads on them.[28]

In the strategic fleet, Russia is developing a new sea-based ballistic missile that will be deployed on submarines of the Borey/Project 955 class, but it is unlikely that Russia will be able to bring the first Borey submarine into operation before 2009. Development of the Bulava missile for this class encountered some problems after three failed flight tests in a row in September–December 2006. The current plan is to build at least eight new submarines, which will replace Delta III and IV boats as they reach the end of their operational lives.

The number of strategic bombers is likely to remain at the current level. The only significant change would be the addition of a new Tu-160 bomber to the force, scheduled for 2007. There are plans to produce a modernized version of the Tu-160 aircraft, but this will not begin before all currently deployed bombers undergo modernization, which would take more than a decade. Tu-95MS aircraft will undergo a similar (but not as thorough) upgrade. Overall, in a decade or so Russia will have in its arsenal about 1,500 operationally deployed nuclear warheads evenly distributed among three legs of the triad.

The future of the Russian nonstrategic nuclear forces is somewhat harder to predict. Even today, very little is known about the number of tactical nuclear warheads and their deployment. Russia is believed to have about 2,300 deployed nonstrategic nuclear warheads. In addition to that, about 4,000 nuclear warheads are stored in reserve.[29] Most of the tactical nuclear weapons seem to have been moved to storage sites rather than deployed with operational units.[30]

It is unlikely that Russia will be ready to undertake serious efforts to reduce its nonstrategic nuclear arsenal, certainly not without concessions from the United States and other NATO countries regarding U.S. nuclear weapons in Europe. In addition to this, according to a view that is quite popular in Russia, tactical nuclear weapons can compensate for the relative weakness of Russia's conventional army.[31]

Doctrinal Issues

According to the military doctrine approved in 2000, "[t]he Russian Federation regards nuclear weapons as a means of deterrence of an aggression, of ensuring the military security of the Russian Federation and its allies, and of maintaining international stability and peace." The doctrine specifies that Russia reserves the right to use nuclear weapons in response to an attack that uses weapons of mass destruction, as well as in the case of a conventional attack "in situations that are critical for the national security of the Russian Federation and its allies." It should be noted that the doctrine specifies that nuclear weapons can be used in either regional large-scale conflict or a global war.[32]

In the years that followed the approval of the 2000 doctrine, the views of the Russian political and military leadership on the nature of threats that are facing Russia have undergone noticeable transformation. To a large extent, this was a response to the terrorist attacks on the United States in September 2001 and to a number of terrorist attacks in Russia. Since then the terrorist threat has become more prominent. Copying the stance taken by the United States, the Russian military announced that it will be ready to strike against terrorist bases outside of Russian territory if necessary. It, however, ruled out nuclear strikes.[33]

Overall, there seems to be a growing understanding that strategic nuclear forces that were built during the Cold War may not be suitable for the more pressing security tasks, in particular for countering terrorism. One result of this understanding is the program to convert strategic bombers to a conventional role and to equip them with precision munitions.

Still, strategic nuclear weapons are considered to play an important role in providing for the security of the Russian state. In a characteristic public statement, Sergei Ivanov, then Russian minister of defense, underscored that Russia's first priority "is to maintain and develop a strategic deterrent capability minimally sufficient for guaranteed repulsion of contemporary and future military threats."[34] At the same time, there is a serious mismatch between the strategic forces' capability and the list of the most important threats, including terrorism, interference by foreign states in Russian internal affairs, and instability in neighboring post-Soviet states.[35] Nuclear weapons are very poorly suited to dealing with these threats, unless, of course, Russia is ready to use them in response to "interference in its internal affairs."

Arms Control and Disarmament

Development of strategic nuclear forces is currently regulated by the START Treaty of 1991. The United States and Russia reached the numerical limits of the treaty some time ago, and right now the main value of the treaty is in the mechanism of transparency, verification, and inspections that is established by it. The treaty, however, will expire in December 2009, and currently there is nothing to replace it in regulating the issues of verification and information exchange.

In 2001–2, Russia and the United States attempted to reach a new arms control agreement that would regulate further reductions of their strategic forces. The result of this attempt was the Treaty of Moscow on strategic offensive reductions (SORT), signed in May 2002. This agreement calls for reduction of the number of operational nuclear warheads to the level of 1,700–2,200 by 2012. This goal will be easily achieved by Russia, which is going to reduce its forces to the level of about 1,500 warheads.

SORT does not contain any verification or transparency provisions, relying instead on the mechanism provided by the START Treaty. However, after START expires in 2009, Russia and the United States will find themselves without an institutional framework for verified reductions of their strategic nuclear arsenals.

It is important to note that, although during the last round of arms control negotiations, which led to the Treaty of Moscow, Russia underscored the importance of equal strategic force levels, strategic parity with the United States is no longer a goal of Russian policy.[36] The modernization program that is being undertaken by Russia is driven mostly by internal considerations. This means that Russia is unlikely to be interested in initiating a new round of arms control negotiations. Equally unlikely is that Russia will follow the United States should it begin reductions of its nuclear warheads arsenal (whether active or in reserve).[37]

Even though some limited opportunities for engagement in arms control negotiations remain—in regard to tactical nuclear weapons in Europe, for example—these issues are not very high on the political agenda either in Russia or in the United States, so no substantial progress should be expected.

U.S. NUCLEAR FORCES

The United States possesses large, robust, and versatile forces of both strategic and nonstrategic nuclear weapons, but it is still in the process of matching the capabilities of this force to current and future security challenges.

Nuclear Force Structure

The U.S. nuclear force structure, summarized in Table 2.3, is heavily weighted toward strategic strike systems. Reliable estimates from open sources indicate that in 2007, the U.S. possessed 5,736 active nuclear warheads and a total stockpile of 9,962 warheads, including inactive weapons and weapons in the responsive force.[38] Consistent with the 2002 Treaty of Moscow, the U.S. plans by 2012 to reduce the number of operationally deployed strategic warheads to between 1,700 and 2,200, with an estimated total stockpile of 5,047.[39]

Although the 2001 Nuclear Posture Review (NPR) declared that U.S. strategic forces were structured in a "new triad" consisting of nuclear and nonnuclear strike capabilities, strategic defenses, and a responsive defense infrastructure,[40] it is clear that the current force structure nevertheless preserves the traditional "triad" of ICBMs, SLBMs, and air-launched weapons developed during the Cold War. The NPR and subsequent documents emphasize that "capability-based planning" rather than a specific target set is used to determine requirements for active forces.[41] While it is not inconceivable that this new mode of force planning will eventually lead to a vastly different future force structure, the large numbers of strategic systems currently fielded evidence a high degree of continuity with Cold War requirements.

Doctrine and Strategy

U.S. doctrine for nuclear operations reflects the difficulty in repurposing nuclear forces to the post-9/11 security environment.[42] The 2001 Nuclear Posture Review

Table 2.3 U.S. Nuclear Forces

Type	Delivery systems	Warheads
Strategic		
ICBMs	500	1115
SLBMs	336	2116
Strategic bombers	115	2005
Total strategic		5236
Nonstrategic		
Tomahawk SLCM	100	100
Bombs	n/a	400
Total nonstrategic		500
Total Nuclear Weapons		5736

Source: National Resources Defense Council, "Nuclear Notebook: US Nuclear Forces, 2007," *Bulletin of the Atomic Scientists* (January–February 2007), 79–82.

represented an important first step toward balancing traditional concerns over the nuclear forces of "peer competitors" (unnamed but clearly understood to be a declining Russia and a rising China) with emerging threats including nuclear proliferators, such as North Korea and Iran, and nonstate actors like the al Qaeda terrorist network.[43] Harshly criticized[44] and vigorously defended,[45] the publicly revealed portions of the classified NPR declared that the mission of U.S. strategic forces is to "dissuade, deter, and defeat" strategic threats. While criticisms that the NPR failed to provide justification for maintaining forces at near–Cold War levels have merit, the shift away from deterrence as the primary role for nuclear weapons and the emphasis on conventional strategic strike systems signaled a noteworthy attempt to respond to new strategic priorities.

Further indications of the evolution of U.S. nuclear doctrine were given in the 2006 Quadrennial Defense Review, which called for significant reductions in strategic nuclear delivery systems and recommended conversion of four SLBMs to conventional strategic strike systems armed with new conventional warheads for the Trident D-5 SLBM.[46] As a 2004 Defense Science Board report points out, the requirement for enhanced conventional strike systems stems from the need to strike urgent targets identified through operations against terrorists or insurgents, which move too quickly to be struck by U.S.- or theater-based aircraft.[47] While it cannot be said that U.S. doctrine has definitively moved "beyond deterrence" as envisioned in the 2001 NPR, a gradual but continuing shift from the traditional deterrent role for U.S. nuclear forces to an emergent strategy for leveraging strategic systems to strengthen capabilities to fight regional conflicts and prosecute a global war on terror is clearly evident.

Safety and Security

Concerns that terrorists might acquire and use nuclear weapons promoted renewed attention to the safety and security of nuclear weapons and material.[48] U.S. officials and independent analysts have found no evidence of significant vulnerabilities in the safety or security of active, reserve, or dismantled U.S. nuclear warheads, but a few security issues with weapons laboratories and other elements of the U.S. nuclear weapons complex were identified in the wake of the 9/11 attacks.[49] It is probably safe to assume that these potential vulnerabilities have since been addressed according to the Design Basis Threat for nuclear weapon facilities revised by DOE and the National Nuclear Security Administration (NNSA) in 2003. While all U.S. weapons include Permissive Action Links (PALs) and other sophisticated devices to prevent unauthorized use, some observers note that gravity bombs stored on the territory of U.S. allies face greater security challenges, and for this reason, consideration should be given to redeploying these weapons onto U.S. soil.[50]

Force Modernization

U.S. discussions on force modernization focus on warheads rather than delivery systems. As part of an overall effort to build the responsive infrastructure called for in the 2001 NPR, NNSA has requested continued funding for the Reliable Replacement Warhead (RRW) program, a research effort designed to develop "replacements for existing weapons that can be more easily manufactured with more readily available and more environmentally benign materials."[51] Critics charged that NNSA's plans to design cleaner and greener weapons actually masked its long-term intentions to resume nuclear testing and develop new warheads, and congressional opposition to the new U.S. warhead could increase under the Democratic majority elected in 2006.[52]

Efforts toward the development of low-yield warheads and Robust Nuclear Earth Penetrators (RNEPs), popularly called "mini-nukes" and "bunker-busters," have been even more controversial. Support for research on new nuclear weapons was strengthened by the repeal of the Spratt-Furse Amendment in 2003, but while the Bush administration has successfully persuaded Congress to fund research on the Advanced Concepts Initiative (for low-yield weapons) and RNEPs, bipartisan congressional opposition to a resumption of nuclear testing remains strong.[53] The primary justification presented for the development of new weapons is counterproliferation—specifically, to gain the capability to destroy superhardened facilities for production and storage of nuclear, chemical, and biological weapons while minimizing collateral damage.[54]

The Bush administration has consistently stated that research on RNEPs would not require development of new physics packages (nuclear components) for these weapons, but nevertheless continues to make gradual preparations for a resumption of nuclear testing. Measures that would reduce the time required for a nuclear test to 18 months are included in "Complex 2030," the strategic plan for the U.S. weapons complex proposed in April 2007.[55] While Complex 2030 and other programs to make the U.S. defense industry more responsive to emerging threats have attracted relatively little controversy to date, the political costs (both at home and internationally) of a decision to resume nuclear testing are likely to keep advanced warhead concepts confined to the design stage unless Iran or other potential U.S. adversaries test nuclear weapons.

Arms Control, Disarmament, and Nonproliferation

Nonproliferation remains a top foreign policy priority for the United States, second only to combating terrorism, and these two goals overlap in many areas. The United States continues to demonstrate strong commitment to cooperative programs to reduce and secure Russia's inventory of nuclear weapons and to the Global Threat Reduction Initiative (GTRI), an ambitious multilateral program to lower the vulnerability of HEU to theft or diversion by terrorists on a worldwide basis.[56] While few doubt the sincerity of the U.S. commitment to nuclear nonproliferation, the March 2006 U.S-Indian agreement on civil nuclear cooperation suggests that with India, as with Israel, the United States is willing to put the development of strategic and political relations with allies ahead of the formal nonproliferation regime.[57]

The Treaty of Moscow commits the United States and Russia to major, if potentially short-lived, reductions in strategic nuclear forces.[58] Both countries pledge to reduce their strategic arsenals to between 1,700 and 2,200 operationally deployed warheads (excluding reserves) by the end of 2012, but timetables for cutting forces to those levels are not specified, and the treaty expires immediately after the date on which the reductions must be completed. Thus, the treaty will be in full force for only one day, December 31, 2012. Moreover, the treaty lacks verification or transparency provisions and does not provide for the irreversibility of the mandated reductions, forcing the conclusion that the accord was negotiated primarily for political atmospherics rather than for structural arms control.[59] The U.S. and Russia will remain bound by the terms of START I, in force since 1994, and although this treaty will expire in 2009, it seems almost certain that the parties will renew the treaty, as neither side currently contemplates returning to strategic nuclear force levels greater than those specified in SORT.

Future Trends

While the technical challenges for restructuring U.S. nuclear forces are relatively modest, the political difficulties of realigning forces and recasting doctrine to meet new security threats should not be underestimated.[60] The continuing threat of terrorism is likely to lower the importance of nuclear forces, and raise that of conventional strategic strike systems, in U.S. strategy. Programs for research on advanced concept nuclear weapons and RNEPs appear on track to continue up to, but not cross, the threshold of nuclear testing, regardless of the results of the 2008 presidential elections. However, in the event of an Iranian nuclear test or a North Korean test with a yield greater than the device tested in October 2006,[61] it seems unlikely that any president of any party could resist the pressure to order a resumption of nuclear testing. Nevertheless, even if these new nuclear threats are realized, the trend toward lower numbers of nuclear weapons deployable on more versatile strategic systems is likely to continue.

CONCLUSIONS

The structure of Chinese, Russian, and U.S. nuclear forces and doctrines for their employment will continue to be shaped by a complex interplay of internal and external factors. In spite of shifts in strategic focus toward counterterrorism, counterinsurgency, and nation building, nuclear weapons continue to play vital roles in Chinese, Russian, and U.S. national security. While all three share concerns over the possible terrorist use of nuclear weapons, and the United States and Russia are working with the International Atomic Energy Agency and other partners to prevent this nightmare scenario, questions remain over the security of some Russian tactical weapons, and the extent to which China has addressed security threats to its nuclear arsenal is unclear. One consolation is that China's nuclear weapons facilities are small in numbers, remote in location, and tightly guarded by the military.[62]

As before, increases in the size or capability of one force, such as the deployment of new-generation Chinese ICBMs and SLBMs or U.S. moves toward testing RNEPs or advanced concept weapons, are likely to prompt responses from the other two parities. Increasingly, however, force planners in Washington, Moscow, and Beijing are responding to nuclear developments in Pyongyang, Tehran, Islamabad, and New Delhi. As a result, unless the three nuclear giants can align their goals and strategies for nuclear nonproliferation, they will find it increasingly difficult to realign their nuclear forces, still largely products of the Cold War, to meet the security challenges of the early twenty-first century.

NOTES

1. The Treaty on the Non-Proliferation of Nuclear Weapons (NPT) defines a nuclear-weapon state as one that has manufactured and exploded a nuclear weapon or other nuclear explosive device prior to January 1, 1967 (Art. IX, § 3). The five states that meet this internationally agreed definition are China, France, Russia, the United Kingdom, and the United States.

2. Hans M. Kristensen, Robert S. Norris, and Matthew G. McKinzie, *Chinese Nuclear Forces and U.S. Nuclear War Planning* (Washington, DC: Federation of American Scientists/ Natural Resources Defense Council, 2006), latest updates on May 2, 2007, at http:// www.nukestrat.com/china/chinareport.htm (accessed July 21, 2007); Shannon N. Kile, Vitaly Fedchenko and Hans M. Kristensen, "World Nuclear Forces," *SIPRI Yearbook 2006:*

Armaments, Disarmament and International Security (Oxford: Oxford University Press, 2006); The Nuclear Information Project, "Status of World Nuclear Forces 2007," May 2, 2007, http://www.nukestrat.com/nukestatus.htm (accessed July 21, 2007).

3. See Jeffrey Lewis, *The Minimum Means of Reprisal: China's Search for Security in the Nuclear Age* (Cambridge, MA: The MIT Press, 2006).

4. The SAC or *di'er paobing* is also known as the Strategic Missile Force (SMF, *zhanlue daodan budui*).

5. Robert S. Norris and Hans M. Kristensen, "Chinese Nuclear Forces, 2006," *Bulletin of the Atomic Scientists* (May/June 2006): 60–63, http://thebulletin.metapress.com/content/1w035m8u644p864u/fulltext.pdf (accessed July 27, 2007).

6. Kristensen et al., *Chinese Nuclear Forces,* chapter 2.

7. Robert S. Norris and William Arkin, "NRDC Nuclear Notebook: Chinese Nuclear Forces, 2001," *Bulletin of the Atomic Scientists* 57, no. 5 (September–October 2001): 71–72; Howard Diamond, "Chinese Strategic Plans Move Forward With Missile Test," *Arms Control Today* 29 (July–August 1999): 27; Global Security.org, "DF-31," http://www.globalsecurity.org/wmd/world/china/df-31.htm (accessed July 27, 2007).

8. Norris and Arkin, "NRDC Nuclear Notebook," 75–76.

9. John Wilson Lewis and Xue Litai, *China's Strategic Seapower: The Politics of Force Modernization in the Nuclear Age* (Stanford, CA: Stanford University Press, 1994), 115–22; *Jane's Fighting Ships 1993–94* (New York: McGraw Hill, 1993), 110.

10. Office of the Secretary of Defense, *Annual Report to Congress: Military Power of the People's Republic of China* (Washington, D.C.: Department of Defense, May 2007), 3, 19.

11. Kristensen et al., *Chinese Nuclear Forces,* 93–97.

12. Information Office of the State Council of the People's Republic of China, *China's National Defense in 2002,* December 2002, http://www.nti.org/db/china/engdocs/whpandef_2002.htm (accessed July 27, 2007).

13. "Summary of Key Findings," Conference on U.S.-China Strategic Nuclear Dynamics, Beijing, June 20–21, 2006, http://www.csis.org/media/csis/events/060620_china_nuclear_report.pdf (accessed July 27, 2007).

14. Wu Zhan, "Heweishe" ["Nuclear Deterrence"], *Meiguo yanjiu [American Studies]* (Spring 1988): 16–22.

15. Joseph Kahn, "Chinese General Threatens Use of A-Bombs if U.S. Intrudes," *New York Times,* July 15, 2005, http://www.nytimes.com/2005/07/15/international/asia/15china.html.

16. Al Pessin, "China Says It Will Not Use Nuclear Weapons First," VOA.com, October 19, 2005, http://www.voanews.com/English/2005-10-19-voa18.cfm (accessed July 27, 2007); "China's Nuclear Chief Makes No-First-Use Pledge," *Philadelphia Inquirer,* October 20, 2005.

17. Dong Jushan, "Zhuzao xinzhongguo heping zhidun: zhanlue daodan budui jueqi jishi" ["Building New China's Shield of Peace: The Rise of the Strategic Missile Force"], *Zhongguo qingnianbao [Chinese Youth Daily],* July 1, 2001; Xinhua News Agency, "Licheng: erpao chengwei juyou hefanji nengli de zhanlue daodan budui" ["Second Artillery Corps Becoming a Strategic Missile Force with Nuclear Counter Attack Capabilities"], July 31, 2005.

18. David Albright and Corey Hinderstein, "Chinese Military Plutonium and Highly Enriched Uranium Inventories," ISIS, June 30, 2005; David Albright, Frans Berkhout, and William Walker, *Plutonium and Highly Enriched Uranium 1996: World Inventories, Capabilities, and Policies* (Oxford: Oxford University Press, 1997), 76–78.

19. Wang Zhongchun, "Nuclear Challenges and China's Choices," *China Security* 3, no. 1 (Winter 2007): 52–65.

20. Zou Yunhua, "Preventing Nuclear Terrorism: A View from China," *The Nonproliferation Review* 13, no. 2 (July 2006): 253–73.

21. Nancy Prindle, "U.S.-Chinese Lab-to-Lab Technical Exchange Program," *The Nonproliferation Review* 5, no. 3 (Spring–Summer 1998): 111–18.

22. Nathan Busch, "China's Fissile Material Protection, Control, and Accounting: The Case for Renewed Collaboration," *The Nonproliferation Review* 9, no. 3 (Fall–Winter 2002): 89–106; Bureau of International Information Program, Department of State, "U.S., China Team Up To Enhance Nuclear Material Security," October 25, 2005, at http://usinfo.state.gov (accessed on August 14, 2007).

23. "A Look at U.S. Nuclear Hegemony," *Dongfang Junshi,* March 9, 2006.

24. Dingli Shen, "Upsetting a Delicate Balance," *Bulletin of the Atomic Scientists* 63, no. 4 (July–August 2007): 37; "U.S. Develops Nuclear Blueprint to Implement Strategy of Preemption," China International Institute for Strategic Studies, April 12, 2006, http://www.chinaiiss.org (accessed April 14, 2006).

25. For a more detailed discussion of the various scenarios that could affect the size of China's future nuclear arsenal, see Phillip C. Saunders and Jing-dong Yuan, "Strategic Force Modernization," in *China's Nuclear Future,* ed. Paul J. Bolt and Albert S. Willner (Boulder, CO: Lynne Rienner Publishers, 2006), 79–118.

26. Hans Kristensen, "Russian Nuclear Submarine Patrols," The Nuclear Information Project, http://www.nukestrat.com/russia/subpatrols.htm (accessed January 23, 2006).

27. The number of silo-based Topol-M missiles would probably be limited to 60. See http://russianforces.org/eng/blog/archive/000678.shtml (accessed January 23, 2007).

28. Pavel Podvig, "Missiles Old and New," http://russianforces.org/blog/2007/02/missiles_old_and_new.shtml (accessed July 30, 2007).

29. Robert S. Norris and Hans M. Kristensen, "Russian Nuclear Forces, 2007," *Bulletin of the Atomic Scientists* (March–April 2007): 61–64.

30. Joshua Handler, "The September 1991 PNIs and the Elimination, Storing and Security Aspects of TNWs," Presentation for "Time to Control Tactical Nuclear Weapons" Seminar, UNIDIR, United Nations, New York, September 24, 2001.

31. For an overview of issues related to reduction of nonstrategic nuclear weapons, see Anatoli Diakov, Eugene Miasnikov, and Timur Kadyshev, *Non-Strategic Nuclear Weapons Problems of Control and Reduction* (Center for Arms Control, Energy and Environmental Studies at the Moscow Institute of Physics and Technology, Dolgoprudny, 2004).

32. Nikolai Sokov, "Russia's 2000 Military Doctrine," NTI Nuclear and Missile Database, October 1999 (revised July 2004), http://www.nti.org/db/nisprofs/over/doctrine.htm (accessed on February 22, 2006).

33. "General Staff: Russia Will Be Preventively Attacking Terrorists All Over the World," Lenta.ru, http://lenta.ru/russia/2004/09/08/baluevski/ (accessed March 5, 2006).

34. Sergei Ivanov, "Russia Must Be Strong," *Wall Street Journal,* January 11, 2006.

35. Ibid.

36. See, for example, "Russia 'Renouncing Military Parity with U.S.': Baluyevsky," *Defense News,* April 3, 2006, http://www.defensenews.com/story.php?F=1661844&C=europe (accessed May 1, 2006).

37. On the U.S. plans to accelerate dismantlement, see Walter Pincus, "U.S. to Step Up Disassembly of Older Nuclear Warheads," *Washington Post,* May 4, 2006, A11.

38. Estimate by Robert Norris, National Resources Defense Council (NRDC), quoted in John Fialka, "U.S. Nuclear-Weapons Stockpile To Be Cut Nearly in Half by 2012," *Wall Street Journal*, June 4, 2004, A8.

39. Robert S. Norris and Hans Kristensen, "New Estimates of the U.S. Nuclear Weapons Stockpile, 2007 and 2012," NRDC Web site, (accessed August 2, 2007).

40. Unclassified excerpts from the classified 2001 Nuclear Posture Review Report (NPR) are available on the Globalsecurity.org Web site at http://www.globalsecurity.org/wmd/library/policy/dod/npr.htm (accessed March 8, 2006). Keith B. Payne discusses the NPR's objectives and rationale in "The Nuclear Posture Review and Deterrence for a New Age," *Comparative Strategy* 23 (2004): 411–19, and "The Nuclear Posture Review: Setting the Record Straight," *Washington Quarterly* 28 (2005): 135–51.

41. Capability-based planning is outlined in Payne, "Deterrence for a New Age" and "Setting the Record Straight"; and analyzed in David S. Yost, "The U.S. Nuclear Posture Review and the NATO Allies," *International Affairs* 80 (2004): 705–29; and H. M. Kristensen, "The Role of U.S. Nuclear Weapons: New Doctrine Falls Short of Bush Pledge," *Arms Control Today* (September 2005), http://www.armscontrol.org/act/2005_09/Kristensen.asp (accessed February 2, 2006).

42. The most authoritative statement of U.S. nuclear doctrine to date is U.S. Department of Defense, *Doctrine for Joint Nuclear Operations* (Joint Publication 3–12, Final Coordination 2, March 15, 2005), available at http://www.globalsecurity.org/wmd/library/policy/dod/jp3_12fc2.pdf (accessed February 2, 2006). For a thorough discussion of the emerging U.S. doctrine, see James J. Wirtz and Jeffrey A. Larsen, eds., *Nuclear Transformation: The New U.S. Nuclear Doctrine* (New York: Palgrave Macmillan, 2005).

43. NPR, 2001.

44. Criticisms of the 2001 NPR are eloquently summarized in Bruce G. Blair, et al., *Toward True Security: A U.S. Nuclear Posture for the Next Decade* (Washington, DC: Federation of American Scientists, Natural Resources Defense Council, Union of Concerned Scientists, June 2001).

45. Payne, "Deterrence for a New Age"; and Payne, "Setting the Record Straight."

46. U.S. Department of Defense, *Quadrennial Defense Review Report* (February 6, 2006), 49–50, http://www.defenselink.mil/qdr/report/Report20060203.pdf (accessed March 8, 2006).

47. U.S. Department of Defense, Office of the Under Secretary of Defense for Acquisition, Technology, and Logistics, *Report of the Defense Science Board Task Force on Future Strategic Strike Forces* (February 2004), 5–10, http://www.acq.osd.mil/dsb/reports/fssf.pdf (accessed February 23, 2006).

48. Noteworthy among the many works discussing this issue are Graham Allison, *Nuclear Terrorism: The Ultimate Preventable Catastrophe* (New York: Times Books, 2004); Graham Allison, ed., *Confronting the Specter of Nuclear Terrorism* (Boulder, CO: Sage, 2006), and Charles D. Ferguson and William C. Potter with Amy Sands, Leonard S. Spector, and Fred L. Wehling, *The Four Faces of Nuclear Terrorism,* rev. ed. (New York: Routledge, 2005).

49. Potential security issues with the U.S. nuclear weapons complex are discussed in Project on Government Oversight, "U.S. Nuclear Weapons Complex Security at Risk," POGO Report, October 2001; U.S. General Accounting Office, "Nuclear Security: Lessons to be Learned from Implementing NNSA's Security Enhancements," GAO-02-358, March 2002; and U.S. Congress, House of Representatives, Subcommittee on National Security, Emerging Threats, and International Relations, "Nuclear Weapons Security," Testimony of

Robin M. Nazzaro, Director, Natural Resources and Environment Team, June 24, 2003, and Testimony of Linton F. Brooks, Under Secretary for Nuclear Security and Administrator, National Nuclear Security Administration Committee on Government Reform, Subcommittee on National Security, Emerging Threats, and International Relations Hearing on Nuclear Security: Can DOE Meet Physical Facility Security Requirements, Tuesday, April 27, 2004, http://www.nnsa.doe.gov/docs/congressional/2004/2004-Apr-27_Shays_testimony.pdf (accessed March 8, 2006).

50. Ferguson and Potter, *The Four Faces of Nuclear Terrorism,* 95.

51. Jonathan Madelia, "The Reliable Replacement Warhead Program: Background and Current Developments," Congressional Research Service Report for Congress, Order Code RL32929, updated May 29, 2007; and "Design Selected for Reliable Replacement Warhead," NNSA press release, March 2, 2007, http://www.nnsa.gov/docs/newsreleases/2007/PR_2007-03-2_NA07-06.htm (accessed April 9, 2007).

52. For more on the RRW program, see Hugh Gustafson, "Understanding the Reliable Replacement Warhead," *Bulletin of the Atomic Scientists Online,* March 26, 2007, http://www.thebulletin.org/columns/hugh-gusterson/20070326.html (accessed April 9, 2007); and "The Next Generation of Nuclear Weapons," *Bulletin of the Atomic Scientists* (July–August 2007): 30–50.

53. Wade Boese, "U.S. Weighing Nuclear Stockpile Changes," *Arms Control Today* (May 2005), http://www.armscontrol.org/act/2005_05/Brooks.asp (accessed February 23, 2006).

54. The effectiveness and desirability of RNEPs for counterproliferation purposes is hotly debated. For technical aspects of the issue, see National Research Council, *Effects of Nuclear Earth-Penetrating and Other Weapons* (2005); Robert W. Nelson, "Low-Yield Earth-Penetrating Nuclear Weapons," *Science & Global Security* 10 (January 2002): 5–10; and Michael May and Zachary Haldeman, "Effectiveness of Nuclear Weapons against Buried Biological Agents," *Science & Global Security* 12 (January–August 2004): 91–114. For viewpoints on the strategic and political utility of RNEPs, see Charles L. Glaser and Steve Fetter, "Counterforce Revisited: Assessing the Nuclear Posture Review's New Missions," *International Security* 30 (2005): 84–126; Christopher E. Paine et al., "Countering Proliferation, or Compounding It? The Bush Administration's Quest for Earth-Penetrating and Low-Yield Nuclear Weapons" (Washington, DC: Natural Resources Defense Council, May 2003); and Sidney Drell, James Goodby, Raymond Jeanloz, and Robert Peurifoy, "A Strategic Choice: New Bunker Busters Versus Nonproliferation," *Arms Control Today* (March 2003).

55. "Statement of Thomas P. D'Agostino, Deputy Administrator for Defense Programs. National Nuclear Security Administration, Before the House Armed Services Committee Subcommittee on Strategic Forces, April 5, 2006," http://www.nnsa.doe.gov/newreleases/2006/PR_2006-04-05_NA-06-09.htm (accessed April 9, 2007).

56. GTRI's objectives are articulated in "Remarks by Energy Secretary Spencer Abraham on the Global Threat Reduction Initiative," May 26, 2004, http://vienna.usmission.gov/_index.php?cmd=cmdFrontendSpeechesAndRelatedDocumentsDetail&speechid=40 (accessed March 8, 2006).

57. Center for Nonproliferation Studies, "Nonproliferation Issues Raised by U.S.-India Nuclear Deal," March 2, 2006, http://cns.miis.edu/pubs/week/060302.htm (accessed March 8, 2006).

58. U.S. Department of State, Bureau of Arms Control, "Treaty Between the United States of America and the Russian Federation On Strategic Offensive Reductions," May 24, 2002, http://www.state.gov/t/ac/trt/18016.htm (accessed March 7, 2006).

59. See Nikolai Sokov, "No SORT of Verification," *Trust & Verify* (July–August 2002), http://www.vertic.org/tnv/julaug02/july_aug02.pdf (accessed March 8, 2006).

60. The contributors to Wirtz and Larsen, *Nuclear Transformation,* discuss these difficulties in detail.

61. Daniel A. Pinkston and Shin Sungtack, "North Korea Likely to Conduct Second Nuclear Test," CNS Web site, January 8, 2007, http://cns.miis.edu/pubs/week/pdf/070108.pdf (accessed April 9, 2007).

62. See Matthew Bunn and Anthony Wier, "Securing the Bomb 2006." Project on Managing the Atom, Belfer Center on International Affairs, July 2006, http://www.nti.org/securingthebomb (accessed August 13, 2007).

Toward Building Cooperation in Energy Security[1]

Dianne Barton, Mikhail V. Margelov, and Sharyl Cross

INTRODUCTION

Energy is a global commodity. Improvements in developing more secure, dependable, and efficient global energy networks for the world community will require solutions grounded in international cooperation and collaboration. As the world's leading producers and consumers of energy, China, Russia, and the United States are in the best position to lead the world in establishing robust energy systems and energy policies that will counter the threat of terrorist attacks on energy infrastructure networks.

As individuals and as part of a global community of nations, we depend on energy infrastructure systems to provide essential services that support economic prosperity and quality of life. These systems are vulnerable to malevolent acts by terrorist groups whose aim is to disrupt, to destroy, and to instigate conflict. Because of the highly interdependent nature of the modern global energy market, attacks in one part of the world have far-reaching effects on a network that has little spare capacity to handle disruption.

This chapter will review terrorist attacks on the world's energy infrastructure and will discuss current energy security challenges for China, Russia, and the United States. We will present some measures to support the development of more robust international energy networks and energy markets in the context of an increasing threat of terrorist attack. In particular, we will focus on the need to encourage investment in improving energy efficiency and in developing modern nuclear technologies.

Timely investment in these areas could provide the levels of energy needed to meet growing demand and increase the spare capacity of the system, thereby minimizing the potential damage caused by deliberate attack or natural disruption.

ENERGY SECURITY AND THE TERRORIST CHALLENGE

Safeguarding the energy infrastructure from deliberate attack has always been a consideration for energy producers, but recently there is a new emphasis on the possibility of increased disruptions caused by terrorist groups. There are over 400 commercial nuclear power generation plants in the world, and although they are generally very well guarded, they are not without their vulnerabilities. The severity of a successful attack on a nuclear power plant resulting in the release of significant radiation into surrounding areas, as well as the possibility of theft of enriched uranium or plutonium to produce nuclear weapons, makes nuclear power plants attractive targets to terrorists. But nuclear power plants are not the only terrorist target.

Al Qaeda has threatened to focus terrorist attacks on oil infrastructure. In a December 2004 audio message, Osama Bin Laden explicitly called for attacks in the Gulf region, the Caspian Sea, and on all sectors of the oil industry.[2] Al Jazeera reported in February 2007 that a Saudi wing of al Qaeda, in their online magazine, *Sawt al-Jihad,* called for increased attacks on the oil facilities of nations such as Canada, Venezuela, and Mexico, which supply oil to the United States.[3] Al Jazeera reports that the al Qaeda publication called for "targeting oil interests including production wells, export pipelines, oil terminals and tankers that can reduce U.S. oil inventory, forcing it to take decisions it has been avoiding for a long time and confuse and strangle its economy."[4] In contrast to nuclear facilities, the global oil infrastructure is much more difficult to protect, because it consists of tens of thousands of miles of pipelines, sea lanes with vulnerable choke points like the Strait of Malacca, the Strait of Hormuz, and the Suez Canal; rail systems; and refinery complexes.

Terrorist attacks, even if not successful, can cause panic buying and selling, which act as multipliers when a product like oil is in short supply with little swing capacity. Currently about $75 per barrel, experts argue that the price of oil would be between $49 and $54 per barrel except for the premium caused by the anticipation of a terrorist attack.[5] In addition, some experts predict that if terrorists could successfully disrupt just 4 percent of the oil flow, prices could rise to over $160 per barrel.[6]

The Memorial Institute for the Prevention of Terrorism (MIPT) maintains a database that provides in-depth information on terrorist incidents. Over the period 1998–2006, MIPT reports incidents of worldwide terrorist attacks on utilities, including the oil sector.[7] Their data indicates that the number of attacks on utilities has increased dramatically in the last three years, primarily because of attacks in Iraq, but also from an increase in attacks elsewhere as well (Figure 3.1).

Noteworthy in these attacks was a failed attempt by suicide bombers to strike Abqaiq, Saudi Arabia's largest oil processing facility.[8] The Abqaiq facility processes more than six million barrels of oil per day. Although the terrorist attack was

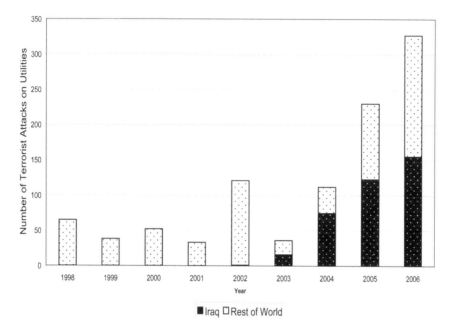

Figure 3.1 **The number of terrorist attacks on utility targets, including energy infrastructure. Attacks in Iraq are shown separately. Data is from the MIPT Terrorism Knowledge Base, "Terrorist Incident Reports: Incidents by Target."**

a failure, it resulted in an immediate increase in the world's oil price by $2 per barrel. The market was nervous because Abqaiq is the central node of the Arabian oil industry.[9]

In addition to the difficulties inherent in protecting the physical security of the oil and gas infrastructure network, the system is also vulnerable because there is little spare oil production capacity outside of Saudi Arabia that would allow the network to dampen the effect of a disruption. In addition to limited production capacity, it is difficult to store significant amounts of natural gas as a buffer to disruption. From a business perspective, it makes no sense to invest in production or storage capacity that is to be left idle. Consequently, the motivation to build more robust networks by developing spare capacity is nonexistent for market-focused oil companies. As a result, terrorist threats pose special challenges to the global oil market because it is limited in its ability to adapt to disruptions.

Globalization has resulted in an increasing interdependence between energy producing, consuming, and transiting nations. As interdependency grows and markets become increasingly integrated, the threat of cascading impacts from an attack in one region to another will increase. This global interdependence requires a multinational approach that is focused on strong communication and cooperation to protect the world's energy infrastructure.

GROUP OF EIGHT SUMMIT ON ENERGY SECURITY

Recognizing the world's growing demand for energy and the increasing energy import dependence of many countries, the 2006 Group of Eight (G8) summit in St. Petersburg took on the challenge of addressing energy security as its main theme. Several market-based energy security issues were discussed, such as the need for increasing the transparency, predictability, and stability of global energy markets and the need for promoting effective legal and regulatory mechanisms to support contract obligations and sustain international investments.[10] Implementation of these market-focused security action items will play a significant role in ensuring sufficient and reliable supplies of energy at reasonable prices. These changes would foster a market environment in which investors would be encouraged to make the necessary investments to ensure that energy supply will meet expected demand. The International Energy Agency (IEA) estimates that $17 trillion in year 2004 U.S. dollars will need to be invested in the entire energy chain by 2030 in order to meet an anticipated 150 percent increase in energy demand.[11]

In addition to supporting measures aimed at building competitive and stable energy markets, the G8 leaders also proposed that investments be made to improve the resiliency of energy infrastructure to disruption from political instability, natural disasters, or other threats such as terrorism. Part of the St. Petersburg plan of action to improve energy security also included a call to promote the development of diverse energy sources, which could reduce the impact of an attack on the current global energy network. The G8 leaders pledged to implement wider use of alternative energy sources and to introduce innovative technologies, including safe and secure nuclear power systems. During a press conference at the summit, Russian President Vladimir Putin and U.S. President George W. Bush announced that their two countries would soon open negotiations on a formal agreement permitting cooperation in the peaceful uses of nuclear energy.[12] The agreement will allow cooperation on a wide range of issues, including the development of advanced reactor technologies, production of mixed-oxide fuel, and the possible reprocessing in Russia of spent nuclear fuel from the United States. The agreement would also advance the Global Nuclear Energy Partnership (GNEP), a U.S. initiative announced in February 2006 to promote the use of nuclear energy as a carbon-free alternative to fossil fuels, while limiting the spread of certain types of nuclear facilities that pose significant nuclear weapon proliferation risks.

The G8 leaders also support efforts to enhance energy efficiency and energy saving. They proposed encouraging the development of best-practice energy-efficiency labeling, the adoption of stringent efficiency standards, and the implementation of financial and tax incentives to promote energy-efficient technology. Efforts to improve energy efficiency would contribute greatly to lowering the energy intensity of economic development, thus strengthening global energy security.[13] Increased energy efficiency and conservation will reduce stress on an infrastructure that operates at nearly maximum capacity. The successful implementation of these actions would serve to improve the security of the energy infrastructure and harden it to disruption by terrorist organizations.

ENERGY SECURITY CHALLENGES: CHINA, RUSSIA, AND THE UNITED STATES

Understanding the current energy status and energy security challenges faced by China, Russia, and the United States is a critical first step in providing a perspective on where a cooperative effort between these three nations might lead. The current focus on global energy security is not related to any sudden increase in energy demand. World energy consumption per capita has not changed significantly and remains about 2.3 – 2.35 tons of oil equivalent (TOE).

Figure 3.2 illustrates how energy consumption per capita changed relative to consumption levels in 1992. While the United States and the rest of the world show little change, Russia's per capita energy consumption has decreased, while China's has escalated. It is significant that 2004 total energy consumption per capita in the United States is seven times higher than it is in China. Russia's 2004 energy consumption per capita is about four times higher than China's.

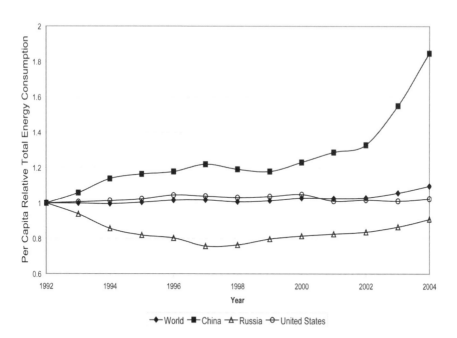

Figure 3.2   Per capita total energy consumption relative to 1992. Data derived from Energy Information Administration, International Energy Annual 2004, Table E. 1, available from http://www.eia.doe.gov/emeu/iea/Notes%20for%20Table%20E_1.html.

In 2004, China, Russia, and the United States were the leading producers as well as the leading consumers of world energy. Together these three countries produced 40 percent and consumed 43 percent of the world's total energy.

The IEA predicts that energy consumption will increase 150 percent by 2030, given no change in demand habits. As the world's leading producers and consumers of energy, China, Russia, and the United States can effect positive change in the security of world energy supplies if they can work together to foster new, globally based energy policies and partnerships. The following sections present a brief review of the major energy security concerns in China, Russia, and the United States.

China—Net Energy Importer, World's Leader in Manufacturing

China is the world's most populous country, its gross domestic product growing strongly at a rate of about 10 percent per year. China is now the second-largest energy consumer after the United States, and in 1993, China became a net energy importer. As the world's manufacturing hub, China's demand for energy is surging rapidly, and its economic growth will have far-reaching consequences for world energy markets. Although China is able to meet more than 90 percent of its energy requirements with domestic supplies, it imports almost half of the oil it consumes (see Figure 3.3). The demand for oil increased suddenly in 2004 when China began to use oil to generate electricity in response to widespread power shortages caused by bottlenecks in coal production. As a result, international energy prices rose to 20-year highs. Oil is also required to power the military, where inadequate supplies could hamper China's efforts to protect its national interests. By 2020, oil imports to China are expected to double when compared to levels in 2005.

China has succeeded in achieving high competition for its energy market and has a wide range of potential suppliers. In addition to Arab countries, China buys oil from Iran, while Uzbekistan, Turkmenistan, and Kazakhstan are ready to enter the Chinese market. In southern China, where oil is supplied by Arab and Iranian imports, energy requirements are growing faster than in northern China. Russia also regards China as a prospective long-term customer for oil produced from eastern Siberian deposits. China is within a minimum transport distance of these deposits, and the development of overland oil supply pipeline routes will become increasingly important to China. In turn, expanding Russian oil exports to China could promote social and economic development of the far east of Russia. Mikhail Margelov discusses in great detail how the dynamics of the global hydrocarbon markets have shaped foreign policy and strategic political and economic relationships between China and Russia, as well as the rest of the world.[14]

In addition to participating in international energy markets as a consumer, Chinese oil companies carry out oil and gas acquisitions in several directions: Russia, Kazakhstan, the Middle East, North Africa, and Latin America. Chinese national oil companies (NOCs) are investing in countries where international oil corporations are not willing to invest because of the risk of low returns on their capital or because of political instability. Foreign investment by Chinese NOCs represents

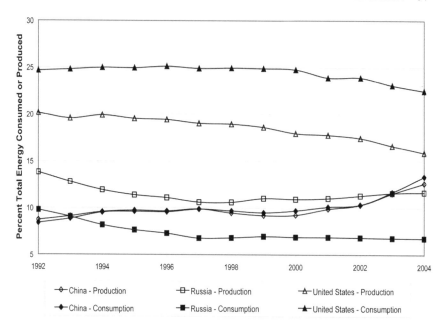

Figure 3.3 Percentage of world total primary energy consumed or produced. Data derived from Energy Information Administration, International Energy Annual 2004, Table E.1, available from http://www.eia.doe.gov/emeu/iea/Notes%20for%20Table% 20E1.html, and Table F.1, available from http://www.eia.doe.gov/emeu/iea/Notes% 20for%20Table-%20F1.html.

complementary state and corporate interests to acquire oil and gas assets abroad, which they hope will improve overall national energy security. The idea that foreign-owned investments enhance energy security is rooted in the expectation that, in times of crisis, China's NOCs will prioritize national above corporate interests, sending oil to China that is currently being sold outside of China in the international energy market. Nevertheless, Chinese investment in the development of new energy supplies is to be welcomed, as it is in the world's best interest that they are able to continue to register fast economic growth to lift their huge population out of poverty. The hope is that energy shortfalls will not derail this growth. Indeed, their investment in developing new energy supplies means that there will be more energy available to international markets as well.

Over the past decade, China has struggled to reform its energy policymaking system.[15] China's leadership has committed to placing equal emphasis on demand moderation and supply expansion. However, poor coordination and conflicting bureaucratic objectives have impeded the development of a single national energy strategy. While the National Development and Reform Commission set a target to reduce energy intensity by 2010, the government has yet to devote resources to meet this goal.[16] Despite China's public rhetoric in support of efficiency and energy conservation, investment as a percentage of the total energy investment has declined in importance, from a high of about 13 percent of energy supply in 1993 to about 4 percent in 2003.[17] This is one of the indications that policy commitments to energy conservation in China have weakened considerably during China's transition to a more market-based economy. Consequently, after managing to keep energy growth well below economic growth for the last two decades of the twentieth century, China has witnessed rapid growth in energy and electricity use since 2001.

Russia—Energy Exporter in a Period of Economic Transition

Russia is important to the security of world energy markets because it holds the world's largest natural gas reserves, the second-largest coal reserves, and the eighth-largest oil reserves. Russia is the world's largest exporter of natural gas and the second-largest oil exporter. At current production rates, its oil reserves are equivalent to 22 years of consumption, its natural gas reserves equivalent to 80 years, and its coal and uranium reserves equivalent to several centuries.

The dynamics of the global hydrocarbon market have contributed to the shaping of foreign policy in today's Russia. Russia's position in the modern global hydrocarbon market has strengthened the Russian economy and led to the development of renewed influence in world politics. This allows Russian diplomacy to effectively pursue solutions to global oil and gas security and supply problems. Political decisions in the area of oil and gas supply can also significantly affect the evolution of developments in social, ecological, political, and other spheres of life. As an example, the oil crisis of the 1970s served as a starting point for the formation of modern relations between countries as the globalization of world energy markets developed. The oil crisis was also the main reason why the United States became a global actor-coordinator of the world's energy markets. Hydrocarbon pipelines and transit paths are a physical representation of the interconnectedness of the world's financial and global relations.

Forecasts predict that in the next two decades, Russia will maintain or increase its high hydrocarbon export rates. Russia is looking to the increasing demand for energy from China to absorb increases in production. Chinese markets can be the most cost-effective options for Russian energy production, although diversification of its consumer base through Pacific Ocean transit routes is also a priority to gain additional competitive advantages. Russia might also benefit from allowing Chinese companies to invest in eastern Siberia, which might support the building of regional infrastructure, benefiting overall regional development.

Interest in investing in Russia by both Russian and foreign businesses is currently focused on the highly profitable hydrocarbon extraction and transport industry. While this interest supports current economic growth, it also discourages investment in alternative value-added industrial development. The Russian economy shows signs of the so-called Dutch Disease, an economic phenomenon in which the discovery and exploitation of natural resources deindustrializes a nation's economy.[18] With Dutch Disease, the value of the country's currency rises, which makes manufactured goods less competitive; imports increase; and nonresource exports decrease. In addition, the availability of energy at below market value discourages efficiency and the ability to compete in the world's free markets. The Russian government has made decoupling economic growth from commodity exports a priority. Alexei Arbatov suggests that if Russia acts only as a commodity exporter, it will be left by the wayside of global progress. Arbatov believes that Russia needs to enact political and economic reforms that will set Russia on the path toward an innovation-based industrial system.[19] To attract additional investment, Russia is opening up its electricity industry to competition, hoping to attract 70 billion of investments to the sector by 2010 to upgrade infrastructure and boost power output. Power companies will be offered an opportunity to invest in companies or build new plants to sell power at free-market prices.

History shows the Soviet Union did not draw a lesson from the 1970s oil crisis, and the country's economy remained energy intensive. In this regard, the Russian Federation and Kazakhstan feature two of the most energy-intensive industrial profiles in the world. The new Russia also fell heir to this legacy. Russia remains among the world's most inefficient energy users because Russia's recent economic recovery primarily affects energy-inefficient industries such as the fuel and power sector, metallurgy, and fundamental and organic chemistry. Growth rates of technological energy saving due to deployment of energy efficiency are 1.5 times lower than was planned for in Russia's Energy Strategy of 2002.[20] In addition, there have been no efficiency gains in the communal household and transportation sectors. If the current trend continues, in 2015 the domestic economy will need an additional 70 Mtoe (millions of tons of oil equivalent) of energy.[21] While Russia's Energy Strategy up to 2020 calls for drastic reduction of energy intensity, there is no governmental institution responsible for energy-efficiency policies. The last energy-efficiency program expired in 2005 without achieving its targets. These failures threaten not only the energy security of Russia, but also of those countries whose economies strongly depend on energy imports from Russia. Russia must renew efforts to encourage structural changes to its economy and implement energy-saving technologies in the power sector, housing utilities, and manufacturing and construction sectors.

United States—Net Energy Importer, Strong Economy

The United States is facing a new era in energy acquisition. The United States' notions of energy security are currently focused on the difficult-to-attain goal of energy independence. At the same time, there has been a dramatic shift in the ownership and control of the world's oil reserves that has further threatened the perceived security of the United States' access to free and open energy markets. World energy markets were once controlled primarily by U.S. and Western-based international oil companies (IOCs). Now, emerging hybrid state-owned/private firms, together with traditional state monopolies like those in the Middle East, control the vast majority of proved oil and gas resources that remain for future exploration and development.[22] By comparison, Western IOCs now control less than 10 percent of the world's oil and gas resource base.

NOCs, particularly in China, have the capital to acquire equity participation in foreign fields and a national policy to cut deals and make new alliances to provide energy to their economy. Governments will often use the income from NOCs to achieve socioeconomic policy objectives. While these objectives are in themselves worthwhile undertakings, any noncommercial obligation will impose costs on the NOCs that can dilute the incentive to maximize profits and hinder their ability to raise external capital and to compete at IOC performance standards. The result could be a stagnation in the ability to grow sufficient oil production capacity to meet anticipated world demand. In addition, many NOCs subsidize the cost of domestic fuel in an effort to redistribute proceeds to the general population. In certain cases, artificially low domestic energy prices have led to skyrocketing energy consumption and inefficiency in both the transportation and industrial sectors of oil-producing economies. Long-term effects of these policies have led some oil-rich countries like Iran and Indonesia to import expensive refined petroleum products from the international market.

Energy independence for the United States is not likely to be achieved in the near future. Therefore, the United States will need to distinguish between economic and strategic concerns in dealing with NOCs.[23] Although the United States might fear that a cartel of powerful countries could disrupt oil supplies, the reality is that they would be doing so at the risk of losing the U.S. market and the associated revenue. However, there is also little evidence that having U.S.- or Western-based IOCs engaged in drilling and oil production around the world decreases the threat of oil disruption from unstable regions.[24] Therefore, rather than relying on a false sense of security created by depending on IOC oil production, the United States needs to accept the new paradigm of NOC-controlled energy markets. The United States should begin to encourage or provide incentives for NOCs to reinvest in oil exploration and production through technology-sharing initiatives to those NOCs that supply energy to the United States. In addition, the United States should advocate that nations with NOC wealth utilize social programs that build competitive economic conditions for their citizens rather than redistribute wealth through energy subsidies that limit world market competitiveness and foster inefficient energy practices.

The United States should consider how current market practices contribute to recent volatility in energy pricing. The Senate Committee on Homeland Security's Subcommittee on Investigations found that speculative purchases of oil futures contracts on the New York Mercantile Exchange and on over-the-counter energy commodities markets by large financial institutions and hedge funds have had the effect of adding as much as $25 per barrel to the price of oil, while speculators have made tens and perhaps hundreds of millions of dollars in profits by trading in energy commodities.[25] While speculative trading can, in effect, finance the production and storage of energy, in the short term it can lead to increased price volatility, which terrorists might use to political advantage. The subcommittee recommends that energy commodity markets be subject to regulations that ensure that prices reflect the laws of supply and demand rather than manipulative practices or excessive speculation.

In addition to market reform, the United States should create a more comprehensive domestic energy policy that would encourage or institute serious measures to curb domestic energy consumption. The United States, with the largest per capita consumption of energy in the world, must take responsibility in leading the international community in the adoption of rigorous standards to promote efficient transportation technologies and shift consumption to non-oil fuels. In addition, the United States should engage in cooperative international energy strategy planning with China and Russia.

ENERGY SECURITY BENEFITS OF IMPROVED INTERNATIONAL RELATIONS—NUCLEAR ENERGY

One action plan that the G8 summit supports is renewed cooperation in the area of nuclear energy. Nuclear power is a nongreenhouse-gas-emitting power source that can supplement fossil fuels and help satisfy a growing global demand for energy. Developing diverse energy sources and continuing to maintain reasonable levels of excess power capacity would make the entire global energy infrastructure more able to withstand disruption and will improve security throughout the network.

China, Russia, and the United States all currently have nuclear energy generation capacity. China is actively promoting nuclear power, and experts forecast that China will add between 15 and 20 GW of new nuclear capacity by 2020.[26] Although Russian nuclear technology has stagnated since the collapse of the Soviet Union, the government plans to develop nuclear technology and renew production facilities.[27] Russia plans to have 33 GW of total nuclear capacity by 2015, raising the share of nuclear power in total generation to 30 percent by 2030. Russia is also in the process of constructing traditional pressurized, light-water reactors for the international market in India, China, and Iran. Although the United States has the most nuclear capacity of any nation, no new commercial reactor has come on line since May 1996.[28] The United States no longer has the capability to forge major nuclear reactor components and depends on foreign sources for more than 80 percent of its enriched uranium requirements. Nevertheless, U.S. commercial nuclear capacity has increased in recent years through a combination of license extensions and upgrading of existing reactors,[29] and public support for nuclear technology is growing.

International cooperation is absolutely essential to providing the investment needed to establish and implement a new vision for nuclear energy. In July 2006, the Generation IV International Forum (GIF) voted unanimously to extend offers of membership to China and Russia.[30] GIF was chartered in 2001 to coordinate research activities required to develop advanced nuclear reactor designs and to lay the groundwork for licensing, constructing, and operating those designs. Russia has much to offer an international forum, as it has been operating the world's only commercial fast breeder reactor. Fast breeder reactors can use naturally occurring U-238 rather than enriched U-235. China is developing fast breeder technologies in cooperation with Russia and hopes to implement a fast breeder reactor commercially before 2030.

In January 2007, the United States released its Global Nuclear Energy Partnership (GNEP) strategic plan. GNEP seeks to promote the widescale use of nuclear energy, while taking actions that will limit its potential to contribute to the risk of nuclear weapons proliferation and effectively address the challenge of nuclear waste disposal.[31] One goal of GNEP is the development of proliferation-resistant technologies, including advanced "burner" reactors that would utilize spent nuclear fuel from traditional reactors while generating tremendous amounts of electricity in the process. This would reduce the amount of plutonium remaining in spent reactor fuel and, it is hoped, would not only reduce proliferation risks but also help dispose of the radioactive waste that is stockpiled around the world today, currently needing long-term management. Russia and the United States both have substantial research experience with these reactors.

GNEP provides a framework for China, Russia, and the United States to cooperate in the development of peaceful uses for nuclear energy technologies. In December 2006, the chair of the Chinese Atomic Energy Authority, Mr. Sun Qin, met with the U.S. secretary of energy to exchange views in the area of Chinese-U.S. nuclear energy cooperation and GNEP. The Chinese position on GNEP was open, constructive, and strongly supportive in the area of resisting any form of terrorism, including nuclear terrorism. Also in December 2006, U.S. President Bush and Russian President Putin formalized a nuclear energy cooperative plan that started as part of the agreement at the G8 Summit in St. Petersburg. In May 2007, China, Russia, the United States, and other nations agreed upon and issued a joint statement that addressed the peaceful use of nuclear energy in the framework of GNEP.[32] U.S. Energy Secretary Samuel Bodman said that international support for the GNEP framework offers "enormous potential to satisfy the world's increasing demand for energy in a clean, safe and proliferation-resistant manner."[33]

ENERGY EFFICIENCY—THE POTENTIAL TO CHANGE ENERGY CONSUMPTION PATTERNS

Many countries, including China, Russia, and the United States, have pursued energy security with an emphasis on increasing supply over moderating demand. This supply-side bias is explained in part by factors that include an institutional structure that facilitates supply expansion over demand moderation, the influence of powerful state-owned or privately owned energy companies, the lack of financial resources devoted to demand-side management, and the fact that measures to slow demand growth tend to be politically more difficult to implement than measures to expand supply.

In market economies, where consumer prices are deregulated, commodity prices can reflect fairly accurately the supply costs and thus contribute to macroeconomic optimization. However, energy prices often reflect only a part of the overall cost of delivering energy. For example, current energy prices do not include the military or government costs to protect energy infrastructure from terrorism or to support stability in supplier nations, as well as many of the long-run costs of environmental remediation.

The oil price shocks of the 1970s fostered higher efficiency, technological change and diversification of supply in consumer nations. The lessons learned from those events stand as a road map of how tight energy supplies can change global energy consumption habits. Will energy security concerns in the twenty-first century lead to similar improvements? Recognizing that energy security can be enhanced by improved efficiency, a second action plan that the G8 summit supported is renewed cooperation in the area of developing energy efficiency.

Energy gains from improved efficiency is equivalent to produced power, and it is often cheaper. Perhaps most important to the issue of energy security, it is not vulnerable to terrorist attack or disruption. Energy-efficiency improvements can be gained from all changes that result in decreasing the amount of energy used to produce one unit of economic activity. This is often measured by a unit called "energy intensity," which is defined as the ratio between total primary energy consumption measured in energy units and indicators of gross domestic product (GDP) measured in monetary units. To make these energy intensities more comparable across different countries, they are converted to purchasing power parity, a method that attempts to equalize the purchasing power of different countries' currencies. The use of purchasing power parities in measuring energy intensities greatly improves the comparability between nations with different levels of economic development.

Figure 3.4 is a plot of energy intensity for China, Russia, and the United States. Energy intensity is an economy-wide indicator of a very general relationship of energy consumption to economic development. While it is not an ideal indicator of energy efficiency, it is commonly used and provides a rough basis for projecting energy consumption and economic growth. Energy intensity calculations show that Russia uses about twice the amount of energy per unit of GDP as the United States and China. This situation can be explained by various factors, including lower energy efficiency, a more pronounced role in the national economy by energy-intensive industries, and lower price levels that are not fully corrected by the use of purchasing power parities. Since 1980, China has experienced the greatest improvement in energy intensity. Between 1980 and 2000, China quadrupled its gross domestic product while only doubling its energy demand. China's extensive efforts to promote energy efficiency are reflected in the calculated energy intensities in Figure 3.4. Unfortunately, this trend is beginning to reverse, and energy consumption has surpassed economic growth in China between 2002 and 2005. This has resulted in an increase in the energy intensity indicators during this time.

A wide range of production and consumption activities and geographic factors complicates measurements of real energy efficiency. Policy comparisons on energy efficiency are better made for sector-specific examples. Figure 3.5, which shows the amount of energy used relative to the amount of steel produced, indicates that steel production in China and Russia currently requires more energy than that in the United States. In this energy-intensive industrial sector, the consumption of energy per ton of output of steel reflects the waste, overproduction, and inefficient industrial

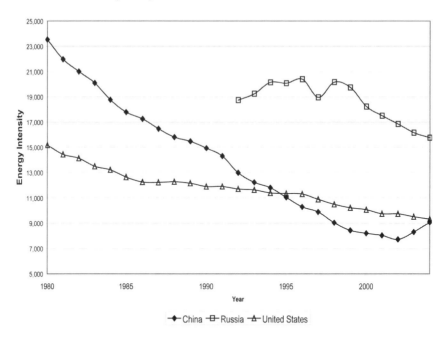

Figure 3.4   Energy intensity—total primary energy consumption per dollar of gross domestic product using purchasing power parities (Btu per 2000 US$). Data from Energy Information Administration, International Energy Annual 2004, Table E.lp, reposted August 23, 2006, available from http://www.eia.doe.gov/pub/international/-iealf/tableelp.xls.

practices that plague both China and Russia. While energy efficiency in steel production and other industrial sectors has certainly improved since the 1980s, neither country has yet been able to transform its industrial methods to the modern standards of production observed in the United States. If energy-efficient nations increasingly shared efficiency-promoting technologies with developing nations, this could have dramatic impacts on global energy consumption as China continues its rapid industrialization and urbanization.

In the six years following the 1979 oil shock, the United States cut oil use by 15 percent and Persian Gulf imports by 87 percent—while the economy grew by 16 percent. In the early and mid-1980s, gas mileage in new domestic cars improved by seven miles per gallon (mpg). Although technology has advanced in the last two decades, efforts to improve efficiency are not as intense as those in the years following the 1979 oil shock. The Russian automobile industry produces vehicles with fuel consumption that is 30 percent higher than Japanese passenger cars and 50 percent higher than commercial-size (10–12 liter) American tractor engines. Experts project that the inefficient Russian car industry results in 7–8 metric tons of motor fuel consumption annually, accounting for about 20 percent of total demand.[34] Much of the public is averse to increased gasoline taxes to curb consumption, and in the

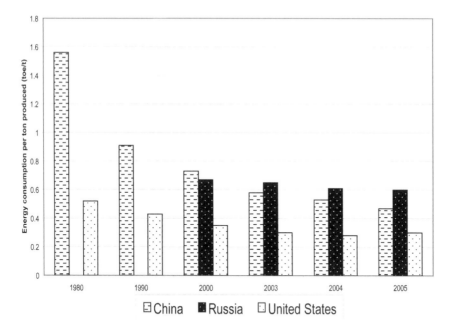

Figure 3.5   Energy consumed per ton of steel produced (tons of oil equivalent/ton). Data from World Energy Council, Energy-Efficiency Policies and Indicators: WEC Report 2001, Annex II, http://www.worldenergy.org/wecgeis/publications/reports/eepi/policies_indicators/policies_indicators.asp. Data for Russia in 1980 and 1990 is not available.

United States, demand for oil use in automobiles has not diminished with high prices. A marked preference for large cars, trucks, and utility vehicles is undiminished (Figure 3.6). Implementing efficiency standards that encourage the widespread use of hybrid gas/electric vehicles and adopting other fuel-efficiency improvements can conserve gasoline.

Estimates of the gains that could be derived from implementing government regulations and investing in energy-efficient technologies vary dramatically. The United States Energy Policy released in May 2001 strongly supports energy efficiency, but the policy also estimates that energy-efficiency improvements would only supply 60,000 to 66,000 megawatts (MW) of a total required addition of 393,000 MW of electricity generation.[35] In addition, the policy did little to require improvements in the fuel efficiency of vehicles, which represents the greatest share of oil consumption. The stated goal to cut consumption by one million barrels per day was removed from the final version. In contrast, the United Kingdom (UK) White Paper on Energy, published in 2003, argued that up to 25–40 percent of future UK energy needs could be met by improvements in energy efficiency.[36] The World Energy Council's 2006 report on energy efficiency estimates that investment in research and development followed by demonstrations of new end-use technologies can

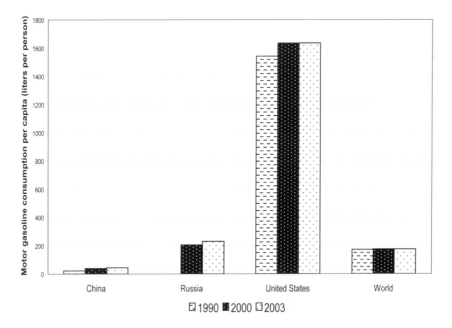

Figure 3.6   Motor gasoline consumption per capita (liters per person). Data from 2006 World Resources Institute EarthTrends: The Environmental Information Portal, available from http://earthtrends.wri.org/text/energy-resourees/variables.html.   Data for Russia in 1990 is not available.

potentially save at least 110 EJ (10^{18} joules) per year by 2020 and over 300 EJ annually by 2050. The success of such work would depend on investments of about US$4 billion per year.[37]

Global economic competition and global economic cooperation will intensify in the future. New partnerships between governments will be needed to improve policy and regulatory harmonization regarding international energy standards, thus reducing the risks associated with enforcing energy-efficiency standards at the cost of reduced competitiveness and slower growth. The world's most technologically advanced nations ought to be prepared to share energy-saving technologies, such as cleaner power stations, to improve global energy security and counter terrorist threats to the energy infrastructure.

CONCLUSION—SOLUTIONS

Energy systems are global networks that physically and economically cross national borders. In an increasingly global energy market that operates with little reserve capacity, supply and demand shocks triggered by a terrorist attack will be transmitted more rapidly from nation to nation through the global marketplace.

All nations have a shared interest in making the energy infrastructure more resilient to disruptions.

As the world's leading consumers and producers of energy, China, Russia, and the United States ought to take the lead in an international multilateral effort to establish acceptable rules and mechanisms to govern the exchange of energy and energy technologies between nations in the twenty-first century. These efforts could foster the development of a constructive global energy strategy based on internationally coordinated energy policies and rule-based markets. A coordinated global energy policy could stabilize price volatility in energy markets, establish mechanisms to limit the impact of terrorist strikes, coordinate capital investment in energy development, and support investment in science and technology to bring new technologies to fruition. Through cooperation, international support, and investment, science and technology developments will accelerate and transcend national borders to bring the next generation of energy technologies to serve humanity.

Without cooperation, energy competition among nations will exacerbate political tensions between rivals and hinder resolution of nonenergy-related political disputes. Global energy markets will be even more volatile and vulnerable to disruption by terrorists or natural disasters. Failure to achieve energy security could leave millions of people in poverty for lack of access to energy.

NOTES

1. Dr. Barton and Dr. Margelov wish to acknowledge NATO support for this research received under the Collaborative Linkage Grant Program (Grant NRCLG 982434). Dr. Sharyl Cross notes that the views expressed in this article are those of the authors and do not reflect the official policy or position of the George C. Marshall European Center for Security Studies, the U.S. European Command, the Department of Defense, or the U.S. government. We thank Jeanne Sirota for her valuable efforts in compiling relevant research material in support of this project.

2. Alex P. Schmid, *Terrorism and Energy Security: Targeting Oil & Other Energy Sources and Infrastructure*, Memorial Institute for the Prevention of Terrorism Web site, 2007, http://www.terrorisminfo.mipt.org/pdf/Terrorism-Energy-Security-032007.pdf (accessed March 27, 2007), 3.

3. Al Jazeera Web site, http://english.aljazeera.net/NR/exeres/6FBAC513-985B-426D-BDE8-DF877123F178.htm (accessed March 20, 2007).

4. Ibid.

5. Schmid, *Terrorism and Energy Security*, 3.

6. Ibid.

7. MIPT Terrorism Knowledge Base, *Terrorist Incident Reports: Incidents by Target*, Memorial Institute for the Prevention of Terrorism Web site, 2007, http://www.tkb.org/IncidentTargetModule.jsp (accessed March 20, 2007).

8. MIPT Terrorism Knowledge Base, *Terrorist Incident Reports: Incidents by Target*, http://www.tkb.org/Incident.jsp?incID=28482 (accessed March 28, 2007).

9. Schmid, *Terrorism & Energy Security*, 5.

10. G8 Summit 2006/St. Petersburg, *Global Energy Security,* Official Web site of the G8 Presidency of the Russian Federation in 2006, http://en.g8russia.ru/docs/11-print.html (accessed March 16, 2007).

11. Fatih Birol, "World Energy Prospects and Challenges," *Australian Economic Review* 39, no. 2 (June 2006): 190–95, http://ssrn.com/abstract=909829.

12. Gaukhar Mukhatzhanova, *U.S.-Russian Civilian Nuclear Cooperation Agreement,* Center for Nonproliferation Studies, July 2006, http://www.nti.org/e_research/e3_78.html (accessed April 4, 2007).

13. G8 Summit 2006/St. Petersburg, *Global Energy Security.*

14. Mikhail V. Margelov, *Rossiya na Global'nom Rynke Yglevodorodov Osnovnye Tendentsii Protivorechiya i Perspektivy [Russia in the Global Hydrocarbon Market: Basic Tendencies, Contradictions and Prospects]* (St. Petersburg: St. Petersburg State University Press, 2005).

15. Erica Downs, *Grappling with Rapid Energy Demand Growth,* Brookings Foreign Policy Studies, Energy Security Series, China, December 2006, 1.

16. Ibid., 25.

17. Jiang Lin, *Trends in Energy Efficiency Investments in China and the U.S.,* Ernest Orlando Lawrence Berkeley National Laboratory, June 2005, LBNL-57691, http://china.lbl.gov/publications/china-ee-57691.pdf (accessed May 9, 2007).

18. Energy Update, "Dutch Disease, a 'Curse' of Resource-Rich Nations," *USAID Energy Update Report,* issue 3 (June–July 2005): 4,http://www.usaid.gov/our_work/economic_growth_and_trade/energy/publications/newsletters/2005-3_eu_jun-jul.pdf (accessed April 4, 2007).

19. Artem Kobzev, "There's No Such Thing as an Energy Superpower," interview with Alexei Arbatov, *Gudok* 117 (July 2007).

20. Garegin Aslanyan, *Russia's Energy Efficiency and Indicators,* Centre for Energy Policy, Introduction to Energy Indicators Workshop, International Energy Agency, April 2006, 12, http://www.iea.org/Textbase/work/2006/indicators_apr26/Aslanyan_Russia.pdf (accessed May 9, 2007).

21. Ibid.

22. Baker Institute Policy Report, *The Changing Role of National Oil Companies in International Energy Markets—Executive Summary,* James A. Baker III Institute for Public Policy, Rice University, March 2007, Number 35.

23. Ibid., 18.

24. Ibid.

25. U.S. Congress, Senate, Staff Report, Permanent Subcommittee on Investigations of the Committee on Homeland Security and Governmental Affairs, "The Role of Market Speculation in Rising Oil and Gas Prices: A Need to Put the Cop Back on the Beat," 109th Cong., 2nd sess., S. Prt. 109-65, July 27, 2006, available from http://hsgac.senate.gov/_files/SenatePrint10965MarketSpecReportFINAL.pdf (accessed June 7, 2007).

26. Energy Information Administration, China's Nuclear Industry, http://www.eia.doe.gov/cneaf/nuclear/page/nuc_reactors/china/china.html (accessed August 7, 2007).

27. Polina Lion and Dmitri Vysotski, "A Nuclear Renaissance in Russia," *Turbomachinery International* (November–December 2006): 20–22.

28. Energy Information Administration, U.S. Nuclear Reactors, http://www.eia.doe.gov/cneaf/nuclear/page/nuc_reactors/reactsum.html (accessed May 28, 2007).

29. Ibid.

30. U.S. Department of Energy, press release, July 13, 2006, http://www.energy.gov/news/3841.htm (accessed May 9, 2007).

31. U.S. Department of Energy, *Global Nuclear Energy Partnership Strategic Plan,* U.S. Department of Energy, Office of Nuclear Energy, GNEP-167312, January 2007.

32. U.S. Department of Energy, press release, May 21, 2007, http://www.gnep.energy.gov/gnepPRs/gnepPR052107.htm (accessed August 16, 2007).

33. Ibid.

34. Aslanyan, *Russia's Energy Efficiency,* 6.

35. U.S. National Energy Policy Report of the National Energy Policy Group, May 2001.

36. United Kingdom, Secretary of State for Trade and Industry, *Energy White Paper: Our Energy Future—Creating a Low Carbon Economy* (Stationary Office, London, February 2003).

37. World Energy Council, *Energy Efficiencies: Pipe Dream or Reality?* (World Energy Council, London, February 2006), http://www.worldenergy.org/wec-geis/global/downloads/statements/stat2006.pdf (accessed May 9, 2007).

China's Growing Ecological Footprint: Global Threat or Opportunity for Collaboration?

Elizabeth C. Economy, Jennifer L. Turner, and Fengshi Wu

Over the past 25 years, the Chinese economic miracle has brought millions out of poverty, but at a major cost to China's environment. The statistics on China's environmental problems highlight a potentially grim outlook for the country. In terms of air pollution, 16 of the world's 20 most polluted cities are in China. China already consumes more energy (most of it low-grade coal) and emits more greenhouse gases than any country except the United States. (It has already surpassed the United States as the largest emitter of the greenhouse gas carbon dioxide.) Acid rain from coal burning affects two-thirds of the country (as well as Korea and Japan). Natural resource degradation and biodiversity loss trends are equally sobering. Twenty percent of the country's plant and animal species are endangered. Deforestation, along with the overgrazing of grasslands and overcultivation of cropland, has contributed to biodiversity loss, soil erosion, and local climate change. Overall, approximately 40 percent of China's land is affected by soil erosion and 10 percent is contaminated by heavy metals.[1] Water scarcity in the northern region has created eco-refugees fleeing farmland turned desert, and severe water pollution has degraded more than 75 percent of the rivers flowing through Chinese cities to a level where they are unsuitable for drinking or fishing.[2]

This chapter will explore China's growing environmental problem from two perspectives—threats to domestic economic, environmental, and social stability, and the impact on the global environment. China is not alone in either its growing domestic environmental troubles or its contribution to global environmental problems. Russia and the United States also face air and water quality challenges, particularly arising from the nature of their energy production. Moreover, they are both significant contributors to global environmental challenges, such as the trade in illegal timber and climate change. The case of China demands special attention because of the country's skyrocketing growth and consequent dramatically rising environmental pollution and degradation. Yet, the shared nature of these environmental challenges highlights the opportunity for Russia, China, and the United States to learn from each other and to develop cooperative approaches to these common environmental threats.

China's air and water pollution, damming of transboundary rivers, and timber and oil imports have all elicited increasing criticism from the international community. China's air pollution has become a growing irritant to its neighbors. While most pollution in the U.S. West Coast is still from local sources, scientists suspect that Asian pollution—such as mercury from power plants and the growing fleets of cars in China and smoke from forests burning in Siberia—are all reaching U.S. shores on the spring winds across the Pacific.[3] China's rapidly expanding hunger for natural resources—particularly oil, timber, and hydropower—is raising considerable concerns internationally. Chinese growth in oil demand has averaged over 7 percent annually since 2000. Many in the U.S. Congress have condemned China's expanding search for oil in unstable countries and cited its impact on global oil markets as a threat to U.S. energy security. China's demand for timber and timber products has led imports to more than triple between 1993 and 2005. Forests in the Russian Far East (RFE) are making up a growing share of China's timber imports—many of which are illegal.

While the pollution and natural resource challenges facing China are formidable, the openness of the Chinese government for internal reforms of environmental management and interest in outside models to mitigate problems of pollution and resource shortages highlight an important opportunity for Russia, the United States, and other countries to assist China. Such collaboration could not only be good for the environment, but could help build more goodwill in both Sino-U.S. and Sino-Russia relations. Strengthening relationships with China is increasingly crucial as Russia and the United States pursue some important global security agendas, such as the war on terrorism and negotiations with North Korea.

CHINA'S AIR POLLUTION

Domestic Catastrophe Sparking Global Concerns

In great part, China's economic success has been built on a foundation of ecological destruction, with air quality as the most obvious sign of the country's poor enforcement of pollution control. China is home to some of the most air-polluted cities in the world, which has led some researchers to consider it "the air pollution capital of the world."[4] Degrading air quality is causing severe domestic environmental and human health problems. For example, both the World Bank and the Chinese Academy of Environmental Planning estimated that over 400,000 premature deaths in China and 75 million asthma attacks annually can be blamed on air pollution.[5] China's acid rain affects one-quarter of the country and one-third of its agricultural land, diminishing agricultural output, eroding buildings, and contributing to respiratory problems. According to one report, 75 percent of the people in China's 340 monitored cities breathe unclean air.[6]

The main drivers of China's poor air quality include heavy reliance on coal for its energy needs, poor energy efficiency and conservation practices, and growth in automobile use.[7] Pollution stemming from coal burning and cars in China poses major health and environmental threats domestically and internationally. Besides high CO_2 emissions, China emits 25 percent of global mercury and is responsible for nearly 50 percent of the acid rain impacting Japan. American and Russian policymakers are growing increasingly concerned about China's air pollution, particularly greenhouse gas emissions and sandstorms. Intimately linked to China's air problems is the country's search for more energy overseas. China's air degradation is increasingly a global problem, and Russia and the United States are well placed to improve communication and cooperation with China to help strengthen pollution control and increase energy efficiency.

Greenhouse Gas Emissions

In the summer of 2007, international energy experts declared that China had surpassed the United States in greenhouse gas (GHG) emissions—although cumulatively, U.S. emissions will remain greater for at least a decade due to the long life of CO_2 emissions in the atmosphere. The lack of widespread coal-washing infrastructure and scrubbers at Chinese industrial facilities and power plants highlight the potential negative domestic and global air impacts of China's plans to build 562 new coal-fired power stations by 2012. The expansion of China's power plants alone could nullify the cuts required under the Kyoto Protocol from industrialized countries.

It is unlikely China will be able to reduce its greenhouse gas emissions in the foreseeable future. Although over the past few years, the Chinese government has pushed energy efficiency and diversified its energy portfolio to expand nuclear and renewable energy development, due to exploding energy demand, the dependence on coal will remain high.[8] To produce one unit of GDP, China uses eight times more energy than Japan and four times more energy than the United States. According to prominent Chinese researchers, even under the best scenario, by 2020 coal will still account for 59.4 percent of China's total energy consumption, and oil 25.9 percent, which means nuclear and renewable energy would be less than 14 percent.[9] Thus, China's carbon and other greenhouse gas emissions probably will not decline much from the current baseline.

The Russian and U.S. governments ought to be concerned about China's rapid increase in greenhouse gas emissions for at least two reasons. First is the impact on global climate change in general. Second, China's greenhouse gas emissions have caused various short-term yet tangible environmental problems in the region—for example, acid rain. Research data show that China's sulfur and nitrogen dioxide emissions have contributed to acid rain in its neighboring countries and regions including the RFE.[10] The effects of acid rain in RFE is undoubtedly worrisome, since the region has some of the most pristine forests on earth and is home to many endangered wildlife.[11] In this case, Russia, due to its geographic proximity, is currently more affected by China's greenhouse gas emissions than the United States.

The Ocean of Sand

Besides CO_2 and SO_2 emissions, sand dust is another major component of China's air pollution.[12] Every spring season, northern China suffers fierce sandstorms. On April 8, 2006, a strong sandstorm swept northwest China, stranding thousands of air passengers, halting hundreds of vehicles, and burying miles of railways.

Since 1998, American news media have repeatedly reported various amounts of dust clouds in the West Coast and Midwest states that were plausibly caused by trans-Pacific air pollution—mostly from China.[13] Many researchers, including Robert Talbot, director of the University of New Hampshire's Climate Change Research Center, have found that sand dust and other pollutants from Asia travel across the Pacific Ocean and reach the western U.S. coast.[14] Eastern Russia also feels the impact of some of China's sandstorms. The RFE Hydrometeorology and Environment Monitoring Administration tested the atmosphere in Kamchatskaya Oblast, Amurskaya Oblast, and other areas of the RFE during a sandstorm in late March 2002, and found sulfate concentrations four to six times the normal rate; nitrates were twice as high; and dust pollution greater by five times or more.[15]

Over the past 10 years, the Chinese government has made a considerable effort to slow desertification by banning illegal logging in national forests and undertaking major reforestation and grassland protection work in western and northern areas. However, because China's desertification stems from long-term overgrazing and cultivation and high population growth dating back to the 1950s, it is not clear whether China can forestall desertification in its northern provinces in the next decade.[16]

China's Energy Hunger and Opportunities for International Cooperation

With China's sustained GDP growth (57 percent since 2000), energy consumption has increased almost 100 percent, and Chinese oil demand growth has averaged over 7 percent annually, since 2000. Besides investments in new infrastructure and a renewed focus on nuclear, renewables, and natural gas, the government has increased oil imports and encouraged its national oil companies to expand exploration around the globe.

This growing overseas exploration has sparked a kind of "energy nationalism" in the United States, due to concerns over China's impact on the global oil markets.[17] However, both the U.S. and Chinese economies are intertwined to such an extent that their respective dependence on oil—the two countries account for one-third of global oil consumption—requires collaboration on the part of both governments to assuage each country's concerns over energy security. Since the United States still consumes three times as much as China, the United States should take the first step to demonstrate its commitment to lessen its dependence on oil. There exist many opportunities in the United States and other industrialized countries for diffusing tensions over China's energy demands, both through assistance in energy efficiency and involving China in multilateral institutions, such as the International Energy Agency.

China's continued dependence on coal highlights the need for even more international collaboration with China on energy-efficiency initiatives, clean coal technologies, and policies to help improve the capacity of China's environmental watchdogs to better monitor power plants and enforce emissions control and trading policies. Although China's air problems are becoming a major international concern, there is a noted lack of effective trilateral-cooperation frameworks between Russia, the United States, and China. There exist more collaborative mechanisms, both governmental and nongovernmental, between China and the United States than between China and Russia in solving air pollution problems. For example, American nongovernmental organizations (NGOs) and private foundations, such as Environmental Defense, the Natural Resources Defense Council, and the Energy Foundation, have all introduced important policy innovations to promote clean, efficient energy technologies and measures in China.[18] The U.S. government could do more: In stark contrast to Japan and the European Union, U.S. government agencies do not provide loans or grants to the Chinese government for environmental projects.

China's cooperation with Russia on air quality issues is even more limited than that with the U.S. government, remaining limited to the framework of the Northeast Asian Subregional Program of Environmental Cooperation (NEASPEC), which so far has only implemented one short-term collaborative air quality monitoring project since 2002.[19] Sino-Russian energy cooperation is predominantly focused on resource exploration but not energy efficiency or clean energy development.[20]

CHINA-RUSSIA-U.S. TIMBER TRADE

The Timber Trade

While international attention has been focused on the bargaining between China and Russia over natural gas and oil, the rapidly increasing cross-border trade in timber is becoming almost as high-stakes and essential to continued Chinese economic growth as its energy quest. At first glance, the rapidly increasing timber trade might appear to be simply a fortuitous fit between high supply and high demand. Russia, which is home to about 20 percent of the world's forests, now provides China with about 50 percent of its raw timber needs—more than the next 12 suppliers combined.[21] China, for its part, is the largest consumer of timber in the world. Its plywood production now exceeds U.S. production, making China the largest plywood-producing country in the world, and it also has contributed more than

50 percent of the global production growth in paper in the last decade, becoming the second-largest producer in the world.[22] As a result, all along the 3,000-km border that China and Russia share, dozens of border crossings have sprung up over the past several years to facilitate this burgeoning timber trade.[23]

Much of this timber trade, however, is rooted in illegal logging practices. Weak governance in many forest-rich countries—Russia included—contributes to a situation in which the ability to log without a license, log in protected areas outside of concession boundaries, and cut protected tree species is widespread. Forestry management is also highly decentralized and fundamentally weak in China. Over the past decade, China has become the largest importer of illegally logged timber in the world, and Chinese logging companies doing business abroad have gained a reputation for their willingness to ignore local logging laws and regulations. The results are devastating for both the local and global environment. What happens to the world's forests is important not only for domestic issues such as soil erosion and flooding, but also for issues that cross international boundaries such as biodiversity and climate change. Economically, the host government almost always fails to benefit from the tax revenues of a booming logging business.

Increasingly, however, the world is becoming aware of the importance of protecting its forest resources. A number of efforts are underway to reverse negative trends in Russia, as in other countries. Russian and international NGOs have become quite active in monitoring and proposing solutions to the challenge of illegal logging. Greater engagement, however, is needed by both the Chinese and Russian governments, as well as Chinese NGOs. In addition, the United States, Japan, and other countries that are recipients of final-processed timber products need to ensure that the supply chain reflects best practices.

Chinese Demand

Chinese demand for timber and timber products is growing exponentially. During 1993–2005, imports more than tripled; and, according to the international environmental NGO World Wildlife Fund (WWF), China's demand for timber, paper, and pulp will likely increase by 33 percent again during 2005–2010.[24]

Greenpeace (citing figures from the International Tropical Timber Organization) has reported that five out of every 10 tropical hardwood logs shipped from the world's threatened rainforests are now heading for China—more than to any other destination. China is now the world's largest plywood producer and exporter. Its export market has grown from less than one million cubic meters annually in 1998 to nearly 11 million cubic meters in 2004. In one area of China that Greenpeace visited, there were an estimated 9,000 plywood mills consuming vast numbers of ancient hardwood trees from rainforests in countries such as Papua New Guinea.[25] There have also been sharp increases in pulp imports. By 2003, China imported almost three times as much pulp as paper in RWE (round wood equivalent).

This extraordinary demand is not surprising, given that China has become the manufacturing center of the world. From children's toys to chopsticks, China is the locus of an increasing number of goods produced more cheaply than anywhere else, and wood products are no exception. China is rapidly becoming the number one producer of furniture, floorboards, and various paper products. The United States, Japan, the European Union, and China itself provide a large and growing market for these products. At the same time, China is in the midst of a vast experiment in urbanization, with plans to create cities for 400 million people during 2000–2030. Housing and infrastructure to support these cities are an additional source of Chinese demand for the world's timber resources.

Finally, over the past decade, Chinese leaders have become increasingly concerned about their own forest resources, putting human and financial capital behind efforts to protect their much-diminished forests and to undertake reforestation campaigns. These efforts became especially urgent in the aftermath of the flooding of the Yangtze River in 1998, in which at least 3,000 people were killed, 52 million acres of land were inundated, and $20 billion in economic damages was incurred. Rampant logging, along with the destruction of wetlands, was blamed, and China's leaders banned logging throughout much of western China. The result has been an ever-growing outward quest for China to fill its timber needs, as well as those of the international community, from the forests of the rest of the world.[26]

The Challenge: China Abroad

With such rapid and dramatic growth in Chinese demand, little has been done in the majority of timber-rich countries to think strategically about how to manage their remaining forest resources and to protect against rampant illegal logging. Already, an estimated 50 percent of China's total timber imports are reported to be illegal.[27]

Some of the trade in illegal timber can be traced directly back to Chinese logging companies and their intermediaries. According to Global Witness, for example, Chinese companies are carrying out large-scale, unregulated logging and mining operations in Burma: "Large parts of forest along the China-Myanmar border have been destroyed, forcing [Chinese] logging companies to move even deeper into Myanmar's forests in their search for timber."[28] Moreover, 95 percent of the timber that China imports from Myanmar is cut in violation of Burmese laws for the protection of forests. Not only is the environmental cost severe, but the economic cost to Myanmar is also significant—an estimated US$250 million.

Exploitation of Southeast Asia's forests, however, cannot meet China's timber needs. The Center for International Trade in Forest Products at the University of Washington projects that by 2025, China could face a deficit of 200 million cubic meters of wood per year. To satisfy that demand, China is increasingly looking to Russia, where about 42 percent of China's total log imports are now derived. Russia's forest resources far exceed those of other Asia Pacific countries, such as Indonesia and Burma, that also supply China. How China and Russia manage this growing trade is particularly important because Russia's forests are of great ecological significance. David Gordon notes:

[Siberian and Russian Far East] forests are host to one-fifth of the world's forests, the value of biodiversity in the region is immeasurable. Besides some of the wildest most pristine places on the planet, Russia's forests are home to a number of endangered species. These forests are also crucial to the livelihood of indigenous people who depend on them for their traditional ways of life. As well, they play an important role as carbon sinks to mitigate climate change, second only in effectiveness to Brazil's dense Amazon forest. Once these forests are irresponsibly cut for short-term gain, these values are gone forever.[29]

Already the task looms large. China is the top export destination for Russia's timber and, given that 80 percent of the timber production from Russia's Far East is exported, China is a major force in the RFE timber market overall;[30] WWF estimates that as much as 20–50 percent of this Russian timber is illegally logged.[31]

The Challenge of Forest Management in Russia and China

One of the most striking features about the Russia-China timber trade is that authority for forestry management and trade in both countries is highly decentralized, making central government oversight quite difficult at every stage of the process. In Russia, the 1997 Forest Code decentralized authority for significant forest management responsibilities without providing adequate implementing regulations, management capability, or funds. Local authorities became dependent on income from forestry charges and fees and fines from timber companies. Moreover, inadequate funding of local forest services has produced poor law enforcement, illegal logging, and excessive cutting.

Russia's forest industry is also highly fragmented. A 2006 report noted that: "There are over 20,000 operating enterprises, the majority of which are small, low-capacity enterprises unable to meet obligations of long-term leases, develop infrastructure, process wood, and have no forest management knowledge at all." An estimated 52 percent of logging enterprises work at a loss. Many of them have poor equipment and no harvesting infrastructure.[32] Although at one point Russia was a major processing center, its domestic market has shrunk and cannot compete internationally. The share of processed wood in overall forest production in the RFE consequently has dropped from 56 percent in 1990 to 10 percent today.[33]

Chinese interest in Russian timber increased significantly after the 1998 logging ban and transformed northeast China into a major timber-trading center. The major centers are Suifenhe in Heilongjiang and Manzhouli in Inner Mongolia.[34] A study conducted on the China-Russian Far East log commodity chain reveals that there are over 400 individual traders who act as middlemen at these major ports of entry.[35]

In addition, Chinese logging companies are moving into Russia, as they have in Burma and Papua New Guinea.[36] Numerous small Chinese firms have established ventures in border areas of Russia. Reports from Primorskiy Krai indicate that these Chinese processing enterprises are small (typically from 7 to 15 employees), fully staffed with Chinese labor and purchase timber mainly from illegal loggers. There are also much larger efforts underway. Three Chinese companies, Star Paper, Zhuhai Zhenrong, and Huacheng International, for example, have signed a memorandum of understanding to invest US$278 million in a wood processing project in Chitinskaya Oblast to process 1.5 million m^3 of logs annually and produce 300,000 m^3 of timber products and 400,000 tons of pulp.[37]

Within China, the timber importing and distribution process is highly decentralized. There are hundreds of timber markets in Shanghai, Guangzhou, and neighboring provinces. Imports may go either through a provincial distribution network or directly through import/export companies to wood processing firms and for export.[38] According to one study, "During the 1980s, regulation of the import trade was gradually loosened so that trading moved from a few state-authorized trading companies to the abolishment of any import permit requirements for wood products. Currently any company that has legally registered for international trade is allowed to import wood products."[39]

With little government oversight in either country, the illegal timber trade between China and Russia is flourishing. There are few controls placed within Russia on loggers, and virtually none at the points of cross-border trade and once the logs enter China. Illegal practices such as logging without a license, logging in protected areas, taking protected tree species, and logging outside of concession boundaries are widespread.

Even when not illegal, many practices in the Russian logging industry are problematic: according to one study, 40–60 percent of the timber is lost during logging and transport; the extraction of the best timber and best species degrades the overall quality of the forests; permits to conduct intermediate thinnings are commonly abused and officially sanctioned; and poor forest harvesting and slash-treatment practices have exacerbated fire conditions.[40]

Moreover, reports detailing the nature of the challenge may actually underestimate the problem. Chinese State Forestry Administration official statistics essentially represent the planned production according to the logging quota, and do not account for a large portion of undeclared production: "Industry sources have indicated that real timber production is almost double the official level due to a large-scale over-quota logging." WWF estimates that in 2003, 35.7 million cubic meters were undeclared. That is about the same level as the officially declared number.[41] The Chinese Academy of Forestry estimates that the real production of sawnwood—much of which is derived from Russian timber—was five times higher than officially stated.[42]

The Policy Response

Responsibility for better management of Russia's forests remains overwhelmingly a job for the Russian government, but given the global security implications, both China and secondary markets such as the United States and Japan should become far more deeply engaged.

Russia has struggled to develop a new Forestry Code that would attract foreign investment, develop the country's physical infrastructure, promote transparency, change the tariff policy, and develop mechanisms for fighting timber poaching and illegal trade. A draft law was put forth in 2004 but, 1,500 amendments later, has still not been passed by the Russian Duma as of April 2006.[43] There is widespread disagreement among policymakers, producers, and environmental NGO representatives concerning how best to grow Russia's timber industry while at the same time protecting its valuable forest assets.[44]

Responses from the Chinese side essentially take two forms: the first is a denial of any Chinese complicity in the illegal timber trade. For example, Cao Qingyao, the spokesperson for China's State Forestry Administration, stated in February 2006, "It's a common responsibility of the world's countries to protect and develop forest resources but not the responsibility of a single country or region. The Chinese government has consistently performed its internationally-shared responsibilities, opposed and firmly cracked down on illegal deforestation and illegal imports. China enforces rigid control over imports."[45] Or, as Lei Jiafu, vice head of the Chinese State Forestry Administration, stated in January 2005, "It is out of the question that the country would satisfy its domestic demands by increasing tree felling from neighboring countries."[46] In other instances, under fierce pressure, China has pledged to improve its practices, promising, for example, to work with the Indonesian government to stem the import of illegal timber. This was followed more recently by a pledge to "only allow in timber [from Burma] which has been lawfully licensed."[47]

China has also signed on to a number of regional and global agreements to combat the illegal trade in timber, including the Santiago Declaration, the International Tropical Timber Agreement, an East Asian Forest Law Enforcement and Governance Agreement,[48] and a memorandum of understanding with Indonesia concerning cooperation in combating illegal trade of forest products. However, China does not have any implementing regulations or mechanisms in place to monitor effectively whether logs are imported legally or illegally.

There is also an important role to be played by third parties. Most of China's timber exports are destined for G8 markets,[49] and the import value of the wood-based products, which the United States alone is likely to import from China during 2006, is likely to exceed $3 billion. Within the G8 countries, however, there is only weak consensus about how to combat the illegal timber trade. At the G8 Summit in 2005, British Prime Minister Tony Blair pushed for strong legislative action by consumer countries. However, the United States argued behind the scenes that demand-side actions that involved new import or procurement regulations could not move forward, and lobbied Canada, Japan, and Russia to block the UK proposal. In the end, the governments agreed only to take measures to ensure that no illegally logged timber would be used in government procurement; any additional steps would be voluntary.[50]

While governments attempt to balance competing interests and dicker over priorities, the NGO community has stepped up to the plate. Russian and Chinese scientists have agreed to coordinate the establishment of an "Amur Green Belt," conducting joint surveys of the forest bordering the two countries and developing steps to manage Chinese log purchasing in Russia.[51] World Wildlife Fund (Vladivostok) has worked to expand commercial plantations in order to replace at least some of the timber exported to China. In addition, the Nature Conservancy is spearheading a project with Chinese officials to monitor and track the cross-border timber trade with Russia through a bar code system.[52] Many NGOs also support efforts to increase domestic Chinese timber production through policy reforms, such as fees, regulations, and tax reforms for legal and sustainable wood sourcing.[53]

Much of the NGO work relies on using the media to pressure China and Russia to improve their practices. Forest Trends, for example, advocates writing articles in the press, enhancing the involvement of NGOs such as Greenpeace and Global Witness that do investigative work, and developing a major campaign in advance of China's Green Olympics in 2008 to highlight illegal wood products from Russia. Friends of Siberian Forests and Forests Monitor also lobby customs officials, brief journalists, and meet with Chinese NGOs. One NGO, after identifying specific companies known to engage in the illegal timber trade with China, then encouraged China to promote an initiative that would facilitate purchases of only legal timber imports from Russia, and pushed Russian companies to process more timber.[54]

NGOs have also reached out to the G8 countries, pressing them to support monitoring to help detect forest crimes and to audit government performance by developing timber tracking systems, chain-of-custody certification, and timber trade.[55] Fundamentally, however, reversing the negative trend in the illegal timber trade between China and Russia will require both strong domestic oversight measures to be adopted as well as pressure from consumers such as the United States and Japan. To date, there is little progress on any of these fronts.

CHINA'S WATER WOES

Multiple Water Crises

In light of the growing regional and global tensions surrounding China's timber and oil consumption and air pollution, it is no surprise these issues have received much more attention in the international community—in terms of press and assistance—than China's water woes. China's severe water degradation and scarcity contribute to population movements, health risks, food security problems, and rising income disparities. Domestically, these problems raise humanitarian concerns and also have the potential to affect China's social, economic, and political stability. Insufficient water—due to both shortages and pollution—is already limiting industrial and agricultural output in some areas and represents a major threat to China's high economic growth rate and food production unless solutions are quickly found. River ecosystems are being threatened by both pollution and major infrastructure projects. Most notably, China's hunger for energy has fueled a new wave of dam building in southwestern China—in the Mekong, Salaween (Nu), and Yangtze rivers—and in the north along the Heilongjiang/Amur River that runs along the China-Russia border.

Severe pollution is affecting all major rivers in China, threatening human health and disrupting industrial production, as well as destroying river ecosystems. Weakly regulated industries and insufficiently coordinated management of water resources are two of the main institutional failures that are driving this severe water pollution problem in China.

China has the highest total emission of organic water pollutants in the world—equal to those of the United States, Japan, and India combined.[56] Since 2002, approximately 63 billion tons of wastewater flow into China's rivers each year, of which 62 percent consists of pollutants from industrial sources and 38 percent consists of poorly treated or raw sewage from municipalities.[57] Although wastewater treatment was a major priority in the Tenth Five-Year Plan (FYP, 2001–2005), a 2004 inspection by the State Environmental Protection Administration (SEPA) of sewage treatment plants built since 2001 found that only half of them were actually working, and the other half were closed down because local authorities considered them too expensive to operate.[58]

Water pollution is causing growing agricultural losses, as well as increasing protests against industries by farmers who have lost use of land and water and cannot sell their "toxic" harvests. Along China's major rivers, especially the Huai, Hai, and Yellow, communities report higher-than-normal rates of cancer, tumors, spontaneous abortion, and diminished IQs due to the high level of contaminants in the soil and water.[59]

While pollution and overextraction are the major causes of degraded watersheds, many rivers—particularly the Yangtze—are equally threatened by deforestation, conversion of wetlands for agriculture, and unsuitable construction and infrastructure projects in the flood plain, all of which have led to bigger and more damaging floods. Moreover, ill-planned hydrological projects on the Yangtze have disrupted the river's natural flow, damaging the basin's ecosystems and leading to considerable loss in biodiversity and the productivity of the river.[60]

Water Conflicts

In addition to the environmental and economic costs of water degradation, polluted water and shortages have contributed to social unrest in China. Besides citizen disputes over major dams, such as the Three Gorges Dam, conflicts between and within provinces over water pollution and the construction of smaller dams are growing in number and even becoming violent. Unless the government addresses severe water problems, these conflicts, in combination with other protest movements in China (e.g., over land grabs, excessive fees, and joblessness), could play a major destabilizing role in the country.

Since the mid-1990s, when a report from the Central Committee of the Chinese Communist Party acknowledged that environmental degradation and pollution represented one of the four leading causes of social unrest in China,[61] the Chinese government has become more transparent in revealing numbers on protests surrounding water and other environmental disputes. For example, in 2007, China's

State Environmental Protection Administration announced that in 2006, 51,000 environmental-related protests had taken place in China.

Regional and Global Impacts of China's Water Woes

The growing instability and conflict generated by China's severe water pollution and shortages should be a concern to the international community, for an unstable China could play a destabilizing role in Asia. The regional impact of China's water pollution was illustrated quite suddenly when on November 13, 2005, an explosion at a PetroChina chemical plant in Jilin province released over 100 tons of benzene into the Songhua River. The Songhua flows into Heilongjiang province, where it supplies drinking water for the provincial capital of Harbin, and another 600 kilometers downstream is the main water supply for the Russian city of Khabarovsk. For several days, provincial and local officials in Jilin hesitated to inform downstream governments or SEPA about the spill. Once informed, Harbin officials also tried to cover up the crisis, first by telling its city residents 10 days after the spill that the water supply system would be cut off for "routine maintenance." However, in the face of growing rumors of a major chemical spill, municipal officials quickly revised their announcement, stating that the water system would be shut down for four days to prevent citizen exposure to benzene.[62] Following the spill, many downstream Russian governors became more vocal about the long-standing water pollution problem in the Amur. Some bilateral water monitoring agreements have emerged since the Songhua spill, but whether such monitoring will lead to significant improvements in local water management remains questionable.

Besides water pollution flowing into rivers in neighboring countries, another growing concern has been the increase in marine water pollution from China. Perhaps the largest transboundary water issue attracting international criticism has been China's dam building in southwest China that threatens the flow of the Mekong and planned dams on the Amur River.

Transboundary Rivers

China is a riparian country of 19 international lake and river systems. China's management of transboundary waters has become a sensitive issue only in a handful of these basins, most notably the Mekong. However, there is the potential for conflict to increase in some of these basins as the Chinese government pushes economic growth, particularly in western China.[63]

China's development of the upper reaches of the Mekong River causes much concern in the region. As only an observer rather than a full member of the Mekong River Commission (MRC), China is not obligated to clear its planned eight-dam construction projects with downstream countries. The first dam (Manwan) was completed in 1996 and caused unusually low water levels in the Mekong in northern Thailand. In December 2001, China completed the Dachaoshan dam on the Mekong, which is feared to have disastrous effects on fisheries and farms in Vietnam,

Thailand, Laos, Cambodia, and Myanmar. The Xiaowan, the third in the cascade of eight dams, began construction in 2001 and International Rivers Network reports that this dam will markedly lengthen dry-season flows and block 35 percent of the silt that nourishes the floodplains downstream.[64]

While China's lack of formal participation in the MRC is often lamented as a major obstacle in protecting the Mekong, some researchers have pointed out that China is being pulled into engagement around the basin through other regional economic development mechanisms, such as the Greater Mekong Subregion framework that the Asian Development Bank has launched to promote socioeconomic development in the Mekong's six riparian countries. Another initiative is the Quadripartite Economic Cooperation initiative launched in 1993 by China and Thailand to promote economic cooperation among the upstream riparian countries.[65]

Marine Pollution

In light of the low rate of wastewater treatment and growing industrial emissions in Chinese rivers, it is not surprising that estuaries and coastal areas near estuaries are plagued with heavy pollution problems. The most heavily polluted coastal areas include Bohai Bay and the mouth of the Yangtze. Exacerbating China's coastal and marine pollution is the fact that many coastal cities pump at least half of their wastewater directly into the ocean. In 2004, 169,000 km^2 of marine waters were categorized as polluted, an increase of 27,000 km^2 in 2003. Of this polluted water, 63,000 km^2 were moderately or heavily polluted.[66]

China's coastal pollution is beginning to worry its closest neighbors, Korea and Japan. However, a more burning marine environmental issue is China's growing consumption of fishery products from the ocean, which is strongly linked to the country's growing freshwater pollution. Per capita consumption of fishery products in China doubled from 2.5 kilograms (kg) in 1988 to 5.2 kg in 2002. While aquaculture accounted for 2 percent of the total agricultural output in 1980, by 2000 it jumped to 11 percent. Since 2002, China has become the biggest exporter of fishery produce in the world. Chinese fishers and fishery companies have had to expand their fishing in the coastal zones of other countries or the high seas to meet this growing domestic and international demand, since few of China's rivers and coastal waters are clean enough to support robust aquaculture production. To keep fish alive, farmers apply excessive amounts of antibiotics and fungicides, many of which are illegal in industrialized countries.[67] Unhealthy drug residues on China's fish are becoming both a domestic and international concern.[68] International bans of China's fish products have increased over the past five years. Such bans have a major impact on importing countries, which depend quite heavily on China's aquaculture products.

The Chinese government has encouraged deep-sea fishing through preferential policies. Currently, over 1,800 oceangoing fishing vessels under Chinese registry are fishing the waters near some 40 countries in three oceans, which has produced considerable tension and even high-seas and diplomatic clashes with other countries.[69] Competition for the shared fish stocks of the China seas (Yellow Sea, East China

Sea, and South China Sea) has intensified considerably over the past 20 years as fish catch rates have declined due to pollution and overfishing. Many species in the China seas have declined so precipitously that they now face total extinction.[70] Although China has negotiated a network of bilateral fishery management agreements with Japan, South Korea, and Vietnam, clashes among Chinese and other fishers flare up regularly. While none of these countries would ever go to war over such incidents, they do represent yet another irritant in bilateral relations with China.

Future Steps to Mitigate Risks from Water Problems

The Chinese government has welcomed considerable international assistance to help the country address water problems, which has helped policy development, river basin management reforms, standard setting, and technology adoption. However, serious institutional changes must take place for new water policies and technologies to be successful in the long run—specifically the clash between bureaucracies to control water and the contentious issue of unclear water rights.

The international community, particularly the United States and Russia (which, among other countries, are the least engaged in water projects in China), could do more to help reduce the risks growing water problems pose to China. It will be crucial for the international community to work with progressive trends in China across all sectors (e.g., government, NGOs, private law firms, and business). Similar to the energy sector, the U.S. NGO community has been increasingly active in working on water issues in China, particularly in catalyzing multi-stakeholder projects to promote stronger governance.

CONCLUSION

The economic reforms in China that have brought rapid industrialization, raised standards of living, and freed many rural people from agricultural work have also produced declining environmental conditions that directly impact the health of the Chinese people and their economy. The choices the Chinese government makes today in terms of environmental protection and energy conservation will have a global impact well into the future. Although China's pollution challenges are severe and its natural resource needs are great, they do hold many opportunities for international assistance.

International NGOs are already active players working to resolve the critical environmental issues that have arisen in part as a result of China's dramatic economic growth and resulting environmental challenges. These challenges very clearly engage not only China but also Russia, the United States, and the rest of the world. In many respects, however, the governments of each of these countries have fallen short in their response to such challenges as transboundary air and water pollution and the illegal trade in timber. While cross-border or globalized environmental degradation further complicates the relationships among China, Russia, and the United States, it is critical for each of these countries to recognize the opportunity that exists for the environment to exert a positive impact on the trilateral relationship by 1) reshaping the overall context of trilateral interactions; 2) modifying each country's calculation and perception of future collaboration; and 3) introducing new grounds for negotiation and the potential for the construction of new trilateral institutions.

NOTES

1. "China Launches Unprecedented Forestry Programs," http://www.china.org.cn/baodao/english/newsandreport/2002july1/13-2.htm.

2. Elizabeth C. Economy, *The River Runs Black: The Environmental Challenge to China's Future* (New York: Cornell University Press, 2004); and Pamela Baldinger and Jennifer Turner, *Crouching Suspicions Hidden Potential: U.S. Environmental and Energy Cooperation with China* (Washington, DC: Wilson Center, 2002).

3. Warren Cornwall, "An Import from Asia: Bad Air," *Macon Telegraph,* April 26, 2006.

4. Jonathan Watts, "China: The Air Pollution Capital of the World," *Lancet* 366, no. 9499 (2005): 1761.

5. Ibid.

6. Clifford Coonan, "Seeds of a Clean, Green City," *South China Morning Post,* September 1, 2004, 18.

7. Elizabeth C. Economy, "China's Environmental Challenge," paper prepared for the Eurasia Group China Task Force, New York, October 20, 2005.

8. For general information on China's energy consumption patterns, see Linden Ellis, "Energy in China Fact Sheet," *China Environment Forum,* http://www.wilsoncenter.org; and Erica S. Downs, "The Chinese Energy Security Debate," *China Quarterly* 177 (2004): 21.

9. Feng Fei, Feng Qi Zhou, and Qing Yi Wang, "Guojia nengyuan zhanlüe de jiben gouxiang (zong baogao)" ["Basic Concept for the Country's Energy Strategy (General Report)"], *Beijingshi kewei [Beijing Science Committee],* March 1, 2006.

10. Thorjorn Larssen et al., "Acid Rain in China," *Environmental Science & Technology* 40, no. 2 (2006): 418–25; Vladimir Bashkin and Miroslav Radojevic, "Acid Rain and Its Mitigation in Asia," *International Journal of Environmental Studies* 60, no. 3 (2003): 205–15; and S. P., "More Acid Rain in East Asia's Future," *Science News* 159, no. 24 (2001): 381.

11. Due to economic reform and growth after the 1990s, coal consumption in the Russian Far East has already increased and caused air pollution and other environmental problems. The acid rain effects caused by Chinese greenhouse gas emissions can be seen as an exacerbating factor in this case. See Michael J. Bradshaw and Peter Kirkow, "The Energy Crisis in the Russian Far East: Origins and Possible Solutions," *Europe-Asia Studies* 50, no. 6 (1998): 1043–63.

12. Sandstorms not only directly transfer dust, but also blow over gaseous pollutants as well.

13. Examples of such reports include Carl T. Hall, "Air Pollution Crossing Pacific: Studies Find Contaminants from China, Japan Blowing to West Coast," *San Francisco Chronicle,* December 7, 1998, A4; "Haze from Asia Spread over U.S," *San Diego Union-Tribune,* April 18, 2001, A6; "U.S. Landfall of Big Asian Dust Storm a Washout," *Associated Press,* March 29, 2002; and "Central Asia Dusts Up Denver Skyline," *Denver Post,* April 14, 2005, B1.

14. Julie Chao, "Coal Fuels China's Economy, and Pollution Worldwide," *Cox News Service,* October 6, 2004.

15. Vladimir Kucheryavenko, "Current Trends in Russian-Chinese Cooperation in the Far East," Guest Research Fellow Paper, Center for East Asian Studies, Monterey Institute of International Studies, Monterey, CA, 2005, 25.

16. Ben Harder, "China's Deserts Expand with Population Growth," *Science News* 169, no. 9 (2006): 142.

17. David Zweig and Bi Jianhai, "China's Global Hunt for Energy," *Foreign Affairs* 84, no. 5 (2005): 25.

18. For example, the San Francisco–based Energy Foundation's China Sustainable Energy Program has been working with Chinese government agencies, research centers, and NGOs for nearly eight years promoting energy-efficiency policies and projects in the transportation, buildings and appliances, industry, electric utilities, renewable energy, and low carbon development sectors. In the early 1990s, Environmental Defense partnered with a Chinese NGO to set up SO_2 emission trading projects in the two medium-sized cities of Benxi and Nantong. These projects led China's State Environmental Protection Administration to choose Environmental Defense as its partner in 2002 to create a national cap and trade program aimed at reducing SO_2 emissions by 20 percent.

19. Kim Myungjin, "Environmental Cooperation in Northeast Asia," *Impact Assessment & Project Appraisal* 22, no. 3 (2004): 191.

20. Kent Calder, "The Geopolitics of Energy in Northeast Asia," guest presentation, Korean Institute for Energy Economics, Seoul, Korea, 2004, http://www.iea.org/Textbase/work/2004/seoul/Kent_Calder.pdf. Also see note 13.

21. Dennis Chong, "Russia: Industry Plunders Forests," *Standard,* March 27, 2005.

22. D. He and C. Barr, "China's Pulp and Paper Sector: An Analysis of Supply-Demand and Medium Term Projections," *International Forestry Review* 6 (3–4) (2004); and Xiufang Sun, Liqun Wang, and Zhenbin Gu, "China and Forest Trade in the Asia-Pacific Region: Implications for Forests and Livelihoods," *Forest Trends,* January 2005.

23. David Gordon, "Bribes, Corruption and Logs: How Lawlessness is Destroying Russian Forests," *Pacific Environment,* July 15, 2001, http://pacificenvironment.org/article.php?id=154.

24. Chong, "Russia: Industry Plunders Forests."

25. Michael McCarth, "China Crisis: Threat to the Global Environment," *Independent,* October 19, 2005.

26. Serious questions have been raised about the efficacy of the logging ban. "In a forest study of over 28 provinces in China, a gloomy picture emerges. Growth rates are being reduced due to short term unsustainable (excessive logging) or under-reforestation of the industrial or natural forest. Due to the logging ban, the harvest volume beyond the year 2000 was expected to continue dropping. However, there has been a long period of over-cutting in the timber forest, and in 2003 the illegal logging volume was 116 million m3 (Xu et al 2003). This both brings into question the value of the logging ban and recognizes that most, if not all, of the illegal logging must be occurring in the small percentage area of the nearly mature or mature forest, or they are already harvesting the best of the slow growing plantation wood to meet demand.

27. "A Choice for China: Ending the Destruction of Burma's Northern Frontier Forests," *Global Witness,* October 2005, 24.

28. Ibid.

29. Gordon, "Bribes, Corruption and Logs."

30. E. Katsigris, G. Q. Bull, A. White, C. Barr, K. Barney, Y. Bun, F. Kahrl, T. King, A. Lankin, A. Elbedev, P. Shearman, A. Sheingauz, Yufang Su, and H. Weyerhaeuser, "The China Forest Products Trade: Overview of Asia-Pacific Supplying Countries, Impacts and Implications," *International Forestry Review* 6 (3–4) (2004): 243.

31. Chong, "Russia: Industry Plunders Forests."

32. "Russian Federation Solid Wood Products Annual 2006," *USDA Foreign Agricultural Service GAIN Report* no. RS6007 (February 15, 2006).

33. Katsigris et al., "China Forest Products Trade," 241.

34. "Xiufang Sun, E. Katsigris, and A. White, "Meeting China's Demand for Forest Products: An Overview of Import Trends, Ports of Entry, and Supplying Countries, with Emphasis on the Asia-Pacific Region," *International Forestry Review* 6 (3–4) (2004): 234.

35. Song et al., 2005 in Sun, Wang and Gu, "China and Forest Trade," 6.

36. Katsigris et al., "China Forest Products Trade," 241.

37. Ibid., 243.

38. Sun, Wang, and Gu, "China and Forest Trade," 2.

39. Ibid., 9.

40. Katsigris et al, "China Forest Products Trade," 238–39.

41. Sun, Wang, and Gu, "China and Forest Trade," 3.

42. Ibid., 7.

43. "Duma Not to Send Back Draft Forest Code—Moscow Court," *Russia and CIS Business Law Weekly,* April 11, 2006.

44. Erik Hansen and Marina Muran, "Russian Federation Solid Wood Products Forestry Sector Continues to Struggle 2005," *USDA Foreign Agricultural Service GAIN Report* no. RS5075 (November 2, 2005).

45. "China Able to Handle its Timber Demand," *People's Daily Online,* February 28, 2006, http://www.illegal-logging.info/news.php?newsId=1290.

46. "A Choice for China," 24.

47. "China Must Act on Pledge to End Illegal Burmese Timber Imports," press release by *Global Witness,* March 8, 2006.

48. One of the central points of this agreement was for governments to crack down on illegal logging in Asia and to stop the illegal timber trade and initiate forest management programs. The document declared that the countries would "take immediate action to intensify national efforts, and to strengthen bilateral, regional and multilateral collaboration to address violations of forest law and forest crime, in particular illegal logging, associated illegal trade and corruption, and their negative effects on the rule of law" and "involve stakeholders, including local communities, in decision-making in the forestry sector, thereby promoting transparency, reducing the potential for corruption, ensuring greater equity and minimizing the undue influence of privileged groups." Global Witness.

49. "A Choice for China," 24.

50. "G8 Ministers Pledge to Curb Illegal Logging, Climate Change," *Environment News Service,* March 21, 2005, http://www.ens-newswire.com/ens/mar2005/2005-03-21-05.asp.

51. "Russia, China Join Efforts to Preserve Forest," June 23, 2004, http://www.vnagency.com.vn.

52. "Zhongguo senlin ziyuan zhuangkuang," Publication of Greenpeace International (Luse Heping), March 23, 2006, http://www.worldwatch.org/features/chinawatch/stories/20060323-1.

53. Kerstin Canby, "Questions About the Legality of China's Wood Product Imports," *Forest Trends Vancouver,* January 2006.

54. "Major Timber Trade Issues Between Eastern Siberia and Northern China," part of the project Building Capacity in NGOs in the Russian Far East and Siberia to Monitor Illegal Logging Operations and the Timber Trade, published by Friends of the Siberian Forests (FSF), Bureau for Regional Forests Monitor (FM) with the assistance of the European Union, June 2004.

55. "G8 Ministers Pledge to Curb Illegal Logging, Climate Change," *Environment News Service,* March 21, 2005, http://www.ens-newswire.com/ens/mar2005/2005-03-21-05.asp.

56. "China's Water Problems," *New Agriculturist,* 2005, http://www.new-agri.co.uk/04–5/focuson/focuson4.html.

57. U.S. Department of Commerce, International Trade Administration, *Water Supply and Wastewater Treatment Market in China,* January 2005.

58. "China Politics: Green-tinted Glasses," *Economist Intelligence Unit,* July 6, 2004. Drawn from Economy, "China's Environmental Challenge."

59. Economy, *River Runs Black*; Jean-François Tremblay, "Chinese Riot Over Pollution," *Chemical & Engineering News* 83, no. 16 (April 18, 2005).

60. For example, because the water surface of Honghu Lake along the Yangtze River has been reduced from 80,000 hectares to 27,000 hectares, the number of species it contains has dropped from 3,000 in the 1950s to 1,500 today, which limits livelihood options for local fishers. See China Council on International Cooperation in Environment and Development, *Promoting Integrated River Basin Management and Restoring China's Living Rivers,* CCICED Task Force on Integrated River Basin Management Report, Beijing, 2004.

61. Shi Ting, "Academics Warn that Social Unrest Could Post Threat to Economy; Corruption is Singled out as a 'Highly Possible' Trigger," *South China Morning Post,* September 9, 2004.

62. Luis Ramirez, "Residents Flee Chinese City as Taps Go Dry Over Water Poisoning Scare," *Voice of America,* November 23, 2005, http://www.voanews.com/english/2005-11-23-voa23.cfm.

63. Mikiyasu Nakayama, "China as a Basin Country of International Rivers," in *Promoting Sustainable River Basin Governance: Crafting Japan-U.S. Water Partnerships in China,* ed. Jennifer L. Turner and Kenji Otsuka (Chiba, Japan: Institute of Developing Economies, 2005), 63–71.

64. International Rivers Network (IRN), "China's Upper Mekong Dams Endanger Millions Downstream," *Briefing Paper 3,* October 2002.

65. Nakayama, "China as a Basin Country."

66. *2004 Report on China's Marine Environment Quality,* Chinese State Oceanic Administration (SOA), Beijing, 2005.

67. Linden Ellis and Jennifer Turner, "Aquaculture and Environmental Health in China," research brief by the Woodrow Wilson Center's China Environment Forum, 2007, http://www.wilsoncenter.org/index.cfm?topic_id=1421&fuseaction=topics.item&news_id=2360,31.

68. Li Yong Yan, "China Goes Fishing," *Asia Times,* March 17, 2005, http://www.atimes.com/atimes/China/GC17Ad01.html.

69. Ibid.

70. David Rosenberg, "Managing the Resources of the China Seas: China's Bilateral Fisheries Agreements with Japan, South Korea, and Vietnam," *Japan Focus,* June 30, 2005, http://www.japanfocus.org/article.asp?id=319.

Perspectives from the United States, Russia, and China on Countering Ideological Support for Terrorism

Graeme P. Herd, Rouben Azizian, and Yu Yixuan

INTRODUCTION

Countering ideological support for terrorism (CIST) is perhaps the most underdeveloped and understudied aspect of countering terrorists. After 9/11, reports and governmental strategies from states around the world have appreciated and acknowledged the importance of the ideological and hearts and minds dimensions of counterterrorism, but there appears a general failure to define its nature, scope, and contours, and it is thus hardly surprising that CIST efforts are, with few exceptions (Singapore, South Africa), weak and unfocused.[1] To be effective in the twenty-first century, states that take a lead in countering terrorists and violent extremists need a CIST strategy that is global, self-supporting, and sustainable rather than fragmented, implemented piecemeal, and contradictory. Before examining U.S., Russian, and Chinese approaches to CIST, let us first define ideology and examine its role in supporting violent extremism and terrorism.

Ideologies are patterned forms of thinking about politics that are intended to be disseminated and consumed by large groups of people. They are characterized by clusters of ideas, beliefs, opinions, values, and attitudes that provide shared understandings of directives and plans of action to uphold, justify, change, or criticize the social and political arrangements of a state or other political community and are always the product of groups.[2] Ideologies compete to control political language in order to wield the necessary power to fulfill a program of political action.[3]

Ideologies are intertwined with politics. They identify problems and issues around which to mobilize support. They provide an explanation of the causes of our problems, which may be a scapegoat (i.e., individuals, groups, or states and their policies), or equally, a wholly legitimate and accurate explanation for the problem. Ideology suggests a program of action to address and overcome the problem—and how individuals in isolation can contribute to that solution. For terrorist groups, it is the story that matters, as it is the center of gravity for terrorists, and the message shapes the attitudes of the target audience to violence. In short, ideologies can form the interpretative framework that gives legitimacy to actions of extreme violence.

How do the United States, Russia, and China understand the issue of countering ideologies that support terrorist action and sustain terrorist groups, and how do they approach this challenge? This chapter will first address U.S. approaches to CIST, before exploring Russian and then Chinese perspectives. In each study, it notes the assumptions that underpin the various strategies and how these assumptions frame perspectives on terrorism as an international security challenge. The chapter concludes by assessing how this issue is likely to shape U.S., Russian, and Chinese relations: it argues that although all three states stress the need for international cooperation to counter terrorism, the ideological component undercuts efforts at cooperation and partnership and reinforces trends towards competition and rivalry.

U.S. CIST STRATEGY

U.S. foreign and security policy, from the "Global War on Terror" to "rogue state" and "regime change," can be fully understood only through the prism of 9/11. According to this post-9/11 outlook, elaborated in the American National Security Strategy (NSS) of September 2002, the nexus of terrorists, tyrants, "terrible weapons," and failed states was deemed to pose imminent threats to the United States; and preemptive strikes against these foes could be justified. The NSS served as the basis of the Iraq war (Operation Iraqi Freedom) in 2003, and Operation Enduring Freedom of October 7, 2001, laid the framework by attacking Taliban–al Qaeda links in Afghanistan. In response to the shocking impact of 9/11, the Bush administration determined that it would use force abroad in regions of critical strategic interest and seek to dominate the international system so that no strategic challenge would ever again be posed. It is within the context of the wider U.S. Grand Strategy as defined by the global war on terror (GWOT) that we can turn to U.S. CIST efforts.

In February 2006, the Department of Defense (DoD) published a *National Military Strategic Plan for the War on Terrorism* (NMSP-WOT).[4] It was developed by the chairman of the Joint Chiefs of Staff and supports the national government strategy for the war on terrorism by outlining strategic guidance for military activities and operations. The plan emphasizes that violent extremism, in its various forms, is the primary threat to the United States and its allies and interests, and that the global war on terror is a war to preserve ordinary people's ability to live as they choose in free and open societies. The plan defines the conflict as a struggle of moderate and extremist ideas within Islam rather than a religious or cultural war, with the United States prepared to ally itself with those who are moderate in their belief to achieve its aims. "Moderates" and "mainstream" are terms used to describe those who do not support these extremists. However, this does not mean that they are necessarily unobservant, secular, or Westernizing. The main criterion for designating a person, group, or institution as moderate and mainstream is opposition to the killing of ordinary people.

The U.S. military has also defined its role as "establishing conditions that counter ideological support for terrorism." DoD has five elements in its CIST role: security, military operations, humanitarian support, military-to-military contacts, and conduct of operations. It suggests that it is committed to understanding the culture, customs, language, and philosophy of the enemy in order to more effectively counter extremist ideology and defeat it. It wants to deny extremist terrorist networks what they require to operate and survive. In more concrete terms, this includes reducing the role of religious figures and leaders who promote extremism, breaking ties and critical nodes between them and their supporters, developing and creating opponents (moderates), and isolating audiences from the message. To kill or capture extremist messengers and deter the audience from listening—through humanitarian support to alleviate suffering, for example, or conducting military operations so as to reduce alienation—appear to be the direct and indirect DoD means, respectively, to a CIST end. A decisive point is reached when societies lead the fight against the extremists at the tipping point of moderates against hard-liners.

According to the NMSP-WOT, ideology is "the component most critical to extremist networks and movements and sustains all other capabilities. The critical resource is the enemy's strategic center of gravity, and removing it is the key to creating a global anti-terror movement."[5] Ideology, as an abstract set of values, beliefs, and ideals, infuses and organizes the functions and processes and resources of all other critical but more concrete components listed: "leadership, safe havens, finance, communications, movement, intelligence, weapons and personnel."[6] The NMSP-WOT notes that the United States should contribute "to the establishment and maintenance of a global environment inhospitable to violent extremists and all who support them."[7] Integral to NMSP-WOT is the concept of "supporting mainstream efforts to reject violent extremism."[8] There is an implicit assumption that the mainstream in any given society or state is moderate and thus opposed to ideologies that support violent extremist means. The reality may be that the majority of the population supports violent extremism, the moderate minority isolated in its opposition. The NMSP-WOT offers little guidance or approach to such a reality, particularly with respect to the application and utility of military force in such circumstances.

The need for a balance between CIST activities and the wider U.S. counterterrorism effort is identified but not resolved: "The way in which we conduct operations—choosing whether, when, where and how—can affect ideological support for terrorism. . . . The conduct of military operations should avoid undercutting the credibility and legitimacy of moderate authorities opposed to the extremists, while limiting the extremists' ability to spread their ideology."[9] Moreover, President Bush dismisses the relationship between U.S. actions in the name of GWOT and the ability of extremist ideologies to gain resonance and attract sympathizers from the general public, and supporters from sympathizers, and thus sustain terrorist power and resilience. Bush states, "Some have also argued that extremism has been strengthened by the actions of our Coalition in Iraq—claiming that our presence in that country has somehow caused or triggered the rage of radicals. I would remind them that we were not in Iraq on September the 11th, 2001—and al Qaeda attacked us anyway."[10] Such thinking suggests that, at least publicly, there is little realization of the relationship between the U.S. application of coercive force and the ways in which terrorist groups can utilize this to bolster their confidence and image, increase recruitment, and establish credibility amongst a target audience and legitimacy of terrorist messages and ideology.

The role of U.S. military force to "defeat terrorists and their organizations" will help determine the nature of coordination between DoD and other U.S. government agencies and partner nations. In turn, the nature of this coordination will impact heavily on the extent to which the U.S. armed forces contribute "to the establishment of conditions that counter ideological support for terrorism."[11] The way in which the United States kills and captures terrorists impacts on partner cooperation, and these two elements impact on CIST. This pathway and interrelationship is not acknowledged. CIST efforts appear to be a byproduct of military-led counterterrorist operations. There is no organizing principle that privileges CIST efforts in the "Long War" against all others. The NMSP-WOT itself is not CIST-led.

Direct/indirect CIST activities lack clarity: "Targeting ideology includes: amplifying the voices of those who promote alternative ideas that emphasize tolerance and moderation; promoting freedom and democracy; de-legitimizing extremist ideological leaders; and providing alternatives to extremist education systems (e.g., some madrassas), among others."[12] This is a useful list of CIST activities, but the direct and indirect methods the U.S. armed forces will undertake with respect to this agenda are unclear. Which part of this agenda is best addressed by other agencies and departments in the U.S. government, particularly the Department of State (DoS)—"the lead Federal agency for this effort?"[13]

Karen Hughes, the under secretary of state for public diplomacy and public affairs at the DoS, is charged with devising a CIST strategy for the U.S. government. In 2005, an Advisory Committee on Cultural Diplomacy, a congressionally mandated panel, stated that "America's image and reputation abroad could hardly be worse" and that "there is deep and abiding anger toward U.S. policies and actions." It cited polling that found that large majorities in Egypt, Morocco, and Saudi Arabia "view George W Bush as a greater threat to the world order than Osama bin Laden."[14] By 2007, the global image of America slipped further, even among publics in countries closely allied with the United States. Asked by the Pew Global Attitudes Survey in 2007 whether they liked or disliked American ideas about democracy, respondents in many countries replied in the negative and suggested that people are superimposing the concept of democracy and democratic values on U.S. foreign policy (in particular the invasion of Iraq).[15]

A number of weaknesses and limitations in the DoS approach can also be noted. An underlying assumption is apparent—U.S. values and ideals are innately superior and appealing to all terrorists (indeed, it assumes that given the chance, everyone would live like Americans), if only they get a fair hearing. This assumption is false; fundamentalist ideas and ideals are resilient and continue to be persuasive, particularly when the underlying causes and basic conditions that support and buttress extremist ideologies are not addressed. A terrorist group provides a rationale for its pursuit of political power that justifies the choice to use violence in order to recruit followers (both true believers in the cause and opportunists who like action and the feeling of belonging). These motives develop a sense of camaraderie that ensures group loyalty, solidarity, and self-protection.

At best, DoS CIST strategy aims to "offer a positive vision of hope and opportunity that is rooted in our values" and "isolate and marginalize violent extremists" by targeting three strategic audiences: key influencers (agents of social change and opinion leaders), vulnerable populations, and mass audiences.[16] Although U.S. public diplomacy aims to promote the "diplomacy of deeds," it fails to address the nature of U.S. policies and the perception of them in the types of terrorist groups upon whom the United States has declared war. This repeats past policy mistakes—in Afghanistan, the United States brought radical Arabs to fight the Soviets, helped train them, and reinforced and radicalized their ideals. A short-term gain (defeat of the Soviets) brought together and helped fuse fundamentalists into a transnational source of strategic threat. It is widely argued that Iraq has the same function today, as does support for corrupt authoritarian strategic partners in the region. The public diplomacy efforts undertaken by DoS do not appear to address global, regional, and national perceptions of U.S. policies undertaken in the name of the GWOT.

RUSSIA: COUNTERING THE IDEOLOGICAL APPEAL OF TERROR

Russia has been directly and seriously affected by terrorism. Like the United States, it is wary of radicalization in the Islamic world, such as the Talibanization of Afghanistan, and has been contributing to international efforts toward fighting al Qaeda and other international terrorist groups. Like China, it experiences ethnoseparatist challenges involving the use of terrorist methods and therefore closely associates terrorism with ethnic separatism, a prism the United States does not automatically adopt. Finally, Moscow suggests that the primary source of its domestic terrorism, i.e., Chechnya, is the external support provided to Chechen militants.

Interestingly, and quite importantly for the prospects of joint counterterrorist strategy, it is not only the international terrorist groups who are perceived by Moscow as hostile, but also the Western democracies with their consistent pressure on human rights issues and insistence on negotiations with Chechen militants. President Putin and other senior Russian officials have criticized the United States and European countries for refusing to extradite Chechen rebels and "applying double standards" in the global struggle against terrorism.[17] Foreign Minister Sergey Lavrov laid down a clear requirement for counterterrorist cooperation between Russia and the West by noting that: "it is time to once and for all abandon double standards with regard to terror, whatever slogans it may use as a cover. Those who killed children in Beslan and seized planes for the attack on America are creatures of the same breed."[18]

Given prevailing trends in Russia's domestic political evolution, the divide between Moscow and America lies even deeper than that. It represents the values gap and not just the issue of how best to deal with ethnic separatists. Expressing the prevalent mood of Russia's political establishment, the still very influential Yevgeny Primakov, former foreign and prime minister of Russia, stated that Washington's "thoughtless plan" to export its own model of democracy is the cause of the current crisis in the dialogue between the West and the Islamic world and contributes to the strength of al Qaeda.[19]

If Washington can be "accused" of a value-based approach to terrorism, the same can be said of Russia's perspective too. Moscow's "value card" seems to be growing anti-Americanism. The Russian government, for example, demonstratively dialogues with Hamas and Hezbollah while refusing to talk directly to Chechen rebels. Moscow's interaction with these extremist groups clearly has geopolitical intent: Russia pursues the goal of leveraging these ties against the United States as a way of retaliation for the West's contacts with Chechen rebels.

For the reasons listed above, Russia's counterterrorist strategy is complex and multifaceted. It is influenced by direct security threats, domestic political dynamics, and uneven relations with the West. For the purpose of analysis, Russia's concrete counterterrorist steps can be divided into international efforts and domestic policies, which in reality are closely intertwined, as our brief introduction implies.

Russia's international efforts in countering terrorism include diplomatic initiatives in the United Nations and bilateral cooperation with like-minded and terrorist-affected nations, as well as multilateral cooperation with members of the Commonwealth of Independent States, Collective Security Treaty Organization, and the Shanghai Cooperation Organization. In the most elaborate and comprehensive way, Moscow's international strategy was pronounced by Foreign Minister Lavrov in his article "In the Face of a Common Threat," published in the Russian Diplomatic Academy's Yearbook.

With regards to countering the ideological appeal of terrorism, the document argues that the elimination of poverty and illiteracy as a breeding ground for extremism is a priority. In addition, the promotion of a dialogue with the Islamic world is a priority. Moscow has gained observer status with the Organization of the Islamic Conference. In March 2006, Russia invited representatives of 20 Islamic states to the first-ever meeting of the Russia-Islamic World Strategic Vision Group. Moscow's close interactions with Islamic countries and groups, particularly with Hamas, have upset Chechen militant groups. The Hamas delegation's declaration in Moscow that Chechnya was a domestic affair of Russia, and that Hamas did not interfere in the domestic affairs of other countries, must have been particularly painful.[20]

By playing the geopolitical card, the Russian government has thus achieved an important international success in weakening ties between Chechen separatists and their international Islamist supporters. This accomplishment complements and aug-ments Moscow's undeniable progress in stabilizing in the last two years the situation in Chechnya, as well as reducing the number of Chechen extremist actions in Russia proper.

The three pillars of Russia's policy of pacifying Chechnya include tougher military operations in the region and increased economic investments, as well as a policy of "Chechenization." In all three areas, the progress has been notable but not necessarily sustainable. According to influential Russian security expert Alexei Arbatov, the best strategy for political settlement in Chechnya includes three major steps. It is, first, a process of depriving the terrorists of support from the local population. As long as a significant proportion of the population supports the terrorists, it is futile to com-bat them. Second, it means creating a split in the ranks of the armed opposition. Part of the opposition consists of terrorists; the others are conducting guerrilla warfare. And if a split could be created in their ranks, it would be possible to reach a peace agreement with certain groupings. Third, international isolation of the terrorists is necessary. These three policy avenues, supported by the successful use of military force and based on clear legal norms, can produce success.[21]

The implementation of this strategy is, however, constrained by rampant corrup-tion in both Chechnya and Russia proper, lack of human rights supervision, and sub-ordination of the Russian justice system to arbitrary executive will. According to independent Russian media reports and international human rights groups, in the past seven years, Russian troops in Chechnya have indiscriminately targeted not only members of the Chechen resistance, but tens of thousands of innocent civilians who have been either summarily shot, or abducted, tortured, and then ransomed to their families. The Council of Europe's Anti-Torture Committee released a public state-ment on March 13, 2007, deploring the continued "resort to torture and other forms of ill-treatment" and "unlawful detentions" of civilians by the law enforcement agen-cies operating in Chechnya. The statement contained an expression of regret at the failure to improve the situation in Chechnya since the committee's two previous such public statements of concern, in July 2001 and July 2003.[22]

As part of the policy of "Chechenization," President Putin has installed a succes-sion of loyal Chechen politicians to head a pro-Moscow administration. In addition, Moscow is scaling back the Russian troop presence in Chechnya and has transferred part of the responsibility for eradicating the resistance to the Chechen presidential guard and the Chechen police force—which is composed to a large extent of former resistance fighters who took advantage of successive amnesties to surrender. Another element of "Chechenization" is the attempt of the current Chechen administration to promote "traditional" Islam in Chechnya and counter foreign-inspired, radical Islamic propaganda. The Chechen authorities have, for example, started an ambi-tious project of building "Europe's largest mosque," capable of accommodating 10,000 worshippers.[23]

Meanwhile in Moscow, the Russian government has adopted a series of blueprints for the reconstruction of essential infrastructure in Chechnya and earmarked billions of rubles to finance such work. For years, however, the lion's share of such funds has been embezzled, frequently with the connivance of the pro-Moscow Chechen administration.

The effectiveness of Russia's effort in Chechnya depends on the success of its Chechenization policy, that is, in handing authority over to loyalist Chechen leaders willing and capable of cooperating with Moscow in the reconstruction of Chechnya as a republic of the Russian Federation. Key to the success of that approach is Moscow's ability to help loyalist Chechens unite for peaceful reconstruction (rather than impose its own choices on them), to provide resources toward that reconstruction, and to see to it that those resources are properly used and not stolen. According to Dmitri Trenin from Moscow's Carnegie Foundation, that is a tall order.[24] To provide security for the reconstruction effort, Russia needs disciplined, well-trained, and well-equipped military, police, and security forces. It needs to root out unprofessional practices and corruption in those services, and bring to justice those abusing their power and living off the war. This will mean ending the semi-paralytic condition of the law enforcement agencies and vastly improving the quality of the police and security services. Institutional reformation in Chechnya must still overcome at least 700 opponents within the remnants of a Chechen resistance and a combat situation that is deteriorating, according to the commander of the Group of Federal Forces in the North Caucasus, Colonel General Yevgeny Baryayev.[25]

Given the general rise of Russian ethnonationalist feelings in the last few years and direct attacks against people from the Caucasus, the reconciliation in Russian-Chechen relations seems to be problematic. While Russia's improved economic situation allows Moscow to invest more in Chechnya, a successful campaign should also include a significant level of decentralization. This seems unlikely in the current political climate in Moscow. The continued imposition of Chechen leaders from Moscow does not guarantee a buy-in from the Chechen population and therefore will continue to feed separatist, including violent, aspirations.

CHINA: COUNTERING POVERTY RATHER THAN IDEOLOGY

When we turn to China's approach to countering terrorism, it is necessary to first answer a critical question: does China have a "strategy" or "policy" to counter ideological support for terrorism? If this question is understood in the strict sense of its key words, unlike the United States, China does NOT have a definite CIST "strategy" or "policy," and so does not use this formulation. In remarks, statements, and speeches related to the issue of terrorism, Chinese leaders and officials have seldom mentioned the concept of "ideology" and have never generally linked terrorism with a certain ideology except in terms of a specific case—China once officially rebutted ideological support for "East Turkistan" terrorist forces,[26] which suggests that the Chinese government approaches the issue cautiously.

China's attitude to CIST should be studied in the whole context of its principles and stances about terrorism. The Chinese view about "what is terrorism" determines all aspects of the country's efforts to oppose it. Although an official definition of terrorism remains to be achieved, there are relatively broad criteria to distinguish terrorist activities: in an official document named "China's Position Paper on Counter-Terrorism," terrorism refers to activity that "endangers innocent lives, causes losses of social wealth and jeopardizes security of states, constitutes a serious challenge to human civilization and a serious threat to international peace and security."[27] Clearly, the Chinese definition is an operational one. It emphasizes the specific consequences of terrorist activities, and avoids addressing more complicated and subtle aspects. This focus on symptoms rather than causes does not reflect deliberate oversight or intentional evasion; rather, it accurately reflects the Chinese view of terrorism. From the perspective of the Chinese government, terrorism "emerges because of profound and complex political, economic, social, ethnic, regional and historical factors. It is necessary to adopt a combination of political, diplomatic, economic and social and other measures and resort to all possible means" to eradicate it.[28] This statement suggests that the causes of terrorism cannot be generally reduced to any single factor, and the element of ideology is certainly not an exception.

Moreover, China's official expressions strictly distinguish terrorism from religious and ethnic conflicts. The conflicts between religions, ethnic groups, and nations are in the list of "traditional security issues," while terrorist activity is the distinct form of "non-traditional security issues."[29] Such a differentiation implies not only that these two categories of security issues should be managed with different means, but also implies terrorism is a relatively new phenomenon. China's view might be expressed in the following way: terrorism, which definitely cannot be lumped together with any religion, ethnic group, nation, or ideology, constitutes a "big public hazard" to all humans. The fight against terrorism is "the combat between peace and violence, not the conflict between ethnic groups, religions or civilizations."[30] Since terrorist groups are "the extreme evil forces," their religious and ethnic statements certainly cannot represent the mainstream of those religious and ethnic groups; on the contrary, the religious and ethnic statements to some extent are regarded as "a pretense" in order to cloak their evil ends.

The case of East Turkistan terrorist forces, which are the only direct terrorist threat to China through the separation of the Xinjiang Uygur Autonomous Region from China, perfectly captures China's approach to terrorism. In an effort to oppose separatist ideologies, in its official statements the Chinese government traces back the continuity of central governance to ancient times—the Han Dynasty (206 BC–220 AD)—to reaffirm Xinjiang as "an inseparable part of the unitary multi-ethnic Chinese nation." It also enumerates the new development of all ethnic groups after the PRC was founded, and emphasizes that the separatists have neither historical evidence nor practical reasons to justify their actions.[31] In particular, government documents carefully inform the readers that the extreme beliefs of terrorists can only lead to abuses by emphasizing the multiethnic and multireligious victims of terrorist attacks, including the Uygur and Islamic people. Moreover, government sources argue that the ideology of "independent East Turkistan" itself is a fabrication—the very concept of "Turkistan" is only a vague geographic term; it has never referred to a political entity.[32]

Given that China rebuts the separatist statements rather than the religious extremism of East Turkistan terrorist forces, the government believes it can sidestep unnecessary religious or civilization disputes that would only complicate a resolution to the real problem. While such a tactical approach implies a high degree of political prudence, it also reflects the relative weakness of Chinese counterterrorism efforts, as extremist religious or other ideological beliefs have actually played an important role in the terrorist activities.

Chinese official policy is to stress the patriotic nature of religious affiliation. It stresses that for all religious groups—Muslims, Catholics, Protestants, and Buddhists—patriotism is of greater importance than religious affiliation. The phrase "Ai Guo Ai Jiao" that is integral to Chinese religious policy expressions means "love our country and be faithful to your religion." Although this policy was made long before the emergence of contemporary counterterrorism policies, it now plays a role in managing religious ideologies.

But the weakness of Chinese CIST efforts can also be understood when we review the importance of counterterrorism within the context of the broader national security agenda. Compared with its significant role in the national security strategy of the United States, counterterrorism strategy is not a first-tier issue in China's national security policy. The top threat to China's security is the Taiwan issue, and the People's Liberation Army's compelling responsibility is to safeguard national unity. The terrorist threat is at the bottom of the list of all the threats China encounters.[33] Following recent attacks against Chinese workers in Africa and Asia, Chinese officials were careful to avoid use of the word "terrorism" when they condemned the attacks, preferring to see these attacks as geographically disparate, generated by different causes and so unconnected.

China only needs to counter particular East Turkistan terrorist forces; in general, participating in counterterrorism operations globally is an opportunity for China to ameliorate relations with the United States, as well as to take on the international responsibilities of a center of global power and have a voice on issues of global importance. For example, in international relations China always upholds multilateralism and the key role of the United Nations in the resolution of international security issues. China emphasizes the authority of the United Nations and its "dominant role" in international counterterrorism, calls for international cooperation, and criticizes unilateralism, thus supporting China's broader approach to managing international order.

However, the question still exists: given the understanding that terrorism emerges from "complicated root causes" and that a comprehensive and network security approach is needed to tackle it, what is the best way to operationalize such thinking? In addressing the root causes of terrorism, China stresses an economic element— poverty. Poverty is a main cause of social injustice, as well as religious and other kinds of extremism. Working for development in order to narrow the gap between the developed countries and the developing countries is a significant part in the process of fighting against terrorism.[34] Such a statement may well appear rather abstract and rhetorical to the United States and other countries that directly face terrorist attacks. Nonetheless, given its current status and domestic conditions, China's stress on poverty as a root cause of terrorism is consistent with its basic foreign policy principles. China is undergoing a great transformation to a modern state that began in the middle of the nineteenth century and has not yet ended. At present, the majority of Chinese people's main demand is for improved living conditions and quality of life, and so foreign policy should identify and create opportunities to serve this domestic aim. Moreover, from China's perspective, development is one of the main trends (another main trend is peace) of the world today, which has not been changed by counterterrorism efforts, so the economic and social concerns, rather than ideological ones, should be underlined in the course of the fight against terrorism.

China's "Develop the West" policy emerges mainly from the domestic concerns to narrow the gap between eastern and western China. But from the perspective of policy expectations rather than policy intentions, it can be logically incorporated in the efforts of countering terrorism, as it has the effect of ameliorating local grievances that could become mobilizing factors for terrorist groups. Given the context of "Develop the West," China's view of one main root cause of terrorism—poverty— might be further understood. "Develop the West" is a strategy related not only to peripheral provinces such as Xinjiang and Tibet, but also to some central Chinese provinces because "western part of China" means "under-developed" in contemporary China. The relationship between the specific ways of implementing this policy in Xinjiang and its effectiveness with the efforts to counter terrorism is a subject of future field work.

A final focus should be on the implications of China's approaches toward countering ideological or other causes of terrorism. China has no CIST strategy or clearly expressed policy, which is determined by the present security circumstances China encounters and by the important responsibilities the Chinese government has. Terrorism is actually a secondary concern. China's priority concern is how to cope with the Taiwan issue, and that is understood as defending the integrity of the country and related to the military-defense understanding in the context of defense policy. The Taiwan issue is regarded as an effort for a state to maintain territorial integrity, while China's "new security concept" pays attention to maintaining international security. Thus, compared with the great transformation and some overwhelming immediate security issues China must address, terrorist threats are not among the top items on the agenda. The "complicated root causes" of terrorism implies that countering some single ideological, ethnic, or religious element supporting terrorism might aggravate tensions between certain belief or ethnic groups, and might even damage the relationships between some important countries, such as China and the United States, which will make the work of countering terrorism more difficult.

ASSESSING PROSPECTS FOR GREAT POWER COOPERATION, COMPETITION, OR RIVALRY

An effective way to increase international CIST cooperation is to stress that cooperation between governments is based on shared interests. This has an important ideological aspect—the basis for cooperation is rooted in shared threat assessment rather than a predilection to uphold authoritarian regimes that happen to be strategic partners or promote particular alternative ideologies that are understood to cloak wider neo-imperial geopolitical agendas. This entails being clear about policy priorities and their rationality in order to safeguard against the accusation that cooperation is instrumental and a hidden agenda is in play—accusations that only served to weaken counterterrorism and CIST efforts and strengthen ideological support for terrorists. Otherwise, resentments and latent grievances are fed, undercutting the effectiveness of such cooperation.

The cornerstone of George W. Bush's second-term administration has been the promotion of the freedom and democracy agenda. Condoleezza Rice has stated that the "organizing principle of the twenty-first century" is the expansion of freedom all over the world. The U.S. National Security Strategy in 2006 explicitly sets "the genius of democracy" in opposition to the "terrorist tyranny" and directly compares this post-9/11 "battle of ideas" with the Cold War ideological contest between democracy and communism. This post-9/11 bipolar world order appears to be the conceptual comfort zone of Bush administration key actors rather than reflect a reality. In the Cold War, for example, the United States supported democratic ideals and practices (as well as authoritarian but Western-leaning states—"our bastards" in the words of U.S. UN Ambassador Jeane Kirkpatrick) against another secular ideology, communism. As part of this effort, the United States helped delegitimize Communist Party elites and claimed to support the aspirations of freedom-loving peoples and societies in Soviet space. In the post-9/11 world, however, the United States supports military elites in Pakistan and theocratic but West-leaning elites in Saudi Arabia against religious ideologies embraced by the majority of populations, not in post-Soviet space but in the Greater Middle East.

Given that the latest U.S. NSS also argues that the fundamental character of regimes matter *as much as* the distribution of power among them, then it is clear that domestic governance is a key determinant in international relations and stability of the international system. U.S. CIST efforts, and their stress on democratization as a panacea, are likely therefore to bleed over into U.S. relations with Russia and China, recreating the conceptual and ideological framework of the Cold War—in other words, helping to frame interstate relations along more competitive than cooperative lines. The U.S. NSS states "Political, religious, and economic liberty advance together and reinforce each other."[35] Although Russia and China are hardly likely to oppose this principle and "support" tyranny, they would certainly disagree that freedom can be imposed from without, particularly through exported revolution or as a consequence of military intervention. Democracy cannot be spread by force of arms; it needs to be negotiated and gradual in order to be sustainable. Moreover, they will also argue that vital strategic interests trump the ideological color of a regime.

Indeed, by 2006 these hitherto latent tensions had come to the fore. Vice President Cheney accused Moscow of using its control over energy supplies as tools of "intimidation or blackmail" against its neighbors, "undermin(ing) (their) territorial integrity," and "interfer(ing) with democratic movements" at the

NATO-EU conference in Vilnius, Lithuania, in May 2006. This has lead to a war of words, with President Putin accusing the United States of hypocrisy, of behaving like a "wolf," and utilizing the freedom and democracy agenda instrumentally to better achieve its strategic interests.[36] These interests center on the perception that the United States has a strategic goal to control petroleum resources globally, to ensure that it remains strategically dominant—*primus inter pares*—into the twenty-first century. Within this additional context, hardliners in Moscow and Beijing are strengthened by such rhetoric and are less likely to cooperate in GWOT efforts. Robert Kagan, a leading neoconservative strategist, has argued that Washington now faces as much of an ideological struggle against the two great powers—the democratic West and authoritarian capitalism—as a contest for control over resources: "Until now the liberal West's strategy has been to try to integrate these two powers into the international liberal order, to tame them and make them safe for liberalism. If, instead, China and Russia are going to be sturdy pillars of autocracy over the coming decades, enduring and perhaps even prospering, then they cannot be expected to embrace the West's vision of humanity's inexorable evolution toward democracy and the end of autocratic rule."[37] Azar Gat posits a new bipolarity based around an enlarged democratic West (with the incorporation of "New Europe") and a "new second world" led by authoritarian-capitalist Russia and China, replacing the defeated totalitarian capitalist states of Germany and Japan.[38]

The way in which the United States has formulated its CIST strategy, creating a paradigm that views the world as divided into two—freedom and democracy as a moral good and antidote to the other, which by definition is characterized by terrorism, failed and rogue states, and supporters—impacts U.S. strategic relations with semiauthoritarian Russia and authoritarian China. The United States, China, and Russia have obvious interests in cooperating to counter terrorism, all three states declare the necessity and their willingness to undertake such cooperation, and real cooperation at the practical level does take place. However, this chapter argues that the U.S. stress on the CIST and the democracy promotion nexus is a potential impediment to effective cooperation: strategic framing can undercut operational success. For this reason, there is a strong potential that interstate relations will continue to be characterized more by rivalry and competition rather than cooperation.

NOTES

1. Anne Aldis and Graeme P. Herd, *The Ideological War on Terror: Worldwide Strategies for Counter-Terrorism* (London: Routledge, 2007).

2. David Miller, ed., *The Blackwell Encyclopaedia of Political Thought* (Oxford: Oxford University Press, 1997), 235–37.

3. Roger Scruton, *A Dictionary of Political Thought* (New York: Harper Collins, 1983), 213.

4. Chairman of the Joint Chiefs of Staff, "National Military Strategic Plan for the War on Terrorism," Washington, D.C., February 1, 2006 (hereafter NMSP-WOT 2006), http://www.strategicstudiesinstitute.army.mil/pdffiles/gwot.pdf (accessed July 17, 2007).

5. Ibid., 18.

6. Ibid., 5.

7. Ibid., 6.

8. Ibid., 8.

9. Ibid., 7, 18.

10. "President Discusses War on Terror," Chrysler Hall, Norfolk, VA, October 28, 2005, http://www.whitehouse.gov/news/releases/2005/10/20051028-1.html (accessed July 17, 2007).

11. NMSP-WOT, 2006, 24.

12. Ibid., 19.

13. Ibid., 24.

14. Barry Schweid, "Report Finds Negative Image of U.S. Abroad," Associated Press, September 28, 2005.

15. Pew Research Center for the People and the Press, "Global Unease with Major World Powers and Leaders: 47-Nation Pew Global Attitudes Survey Finds Rising Environmental Concerns," June 27, 2007, http://pewresearch.org/pubs/524/global-unease-with-major-world-powers-and-leaders (accessed July 17, 2007).

16. Strategic Communication and Public Diplomacy Coordinating Committee, "U.S. National Strategy for Public Diplomacy and Strategic Communication," June 2007, 1–34, http://uscpublicdiplomacy.org/pdfs/stratcommo_plan_070531.pdf (accessed July 17, 2007). See also Robert J. Art and Louise Richardson, "Conclusion," in *Democracy and Counterterrorism: Lessons from the Past,* ed. Robert J. Art and Louise Richardson (Washington, DC: U.S. Institute of World Peace, 2007), 591–96.

17. Simon Saradzhyan, "Putin Warns FSB on Terrorists and NGOs," *Moscow Times,* February 8, 2006, http://www.themoscowtimes.com/stories/2006/02/08/11.html.

18. Sergey Lavrov, "In the Face of a Common Threat," *Diplomatic Yearbook–2004,* Russian MFA Diplomatic Academy, http://www.russianembassy.org.za/statements/mar05.html.

19. Interfax, March 27, 2006.

20. "HAMAS Leader: Chechen Problem is a Domestic Russian Affair," Regnum News Agency, April 3, 2006, http://www.regnum.ru/english/600413.html (accessed July 26, 2007).

21. Alexei Arbatov, "Luboe primenenie sozdoet problemy" ["Any Application Will Create Problems"], *Nezavasimaya Gazeta,* September 27, 2004, http://www.ng.ru/courier/2004-09-27/13_arbatov.html (accessed July 17, 2007).

22. Council of Europe, European Committee for the Prevention of Torture and Inhuman or Degrading Treatment or Punishment, "Public Statement Concerning the Chechen Republic of the Russian Federation," March 13, 2007, http://cpt.coe.int/documents/rus/2007-17-inf-eng.pdf (accessed July 17, 2007).

23. "Samaya bol'shaya mechet' v Evrope budet postroenna v Groznom" ["Largest Mosque in Europe to Be Built in Grozny"], *Novaya Politika,* July 13, 2006, http://www.novopol.ru/news10176.html (accessed July 26, 2007).

24. Dmitri Trenin, "Russia and Anti-Terrorism," in "What Russia Sees," *Chaillot Paper,* no. 74, ed. Dov Lynch (January 2005), 99–114, http://www.iss-eu.org/chaillot/chai74.pdf (accessed July 17, 2007).

25. Interfax, October 13, 2006.

26. See "East Turkistan Terrorist Forces Cannot Get Away With Impunity," issued by the Information Office of the State Council of China, January 21, 2002, http://www.china-un.org/eng/zt/fk/t28938.htm (accessed July 17, 2007); also see White Paper, "History and

Development of Xinjiang," issued by the Information Office of the State Council of China, May 26, 2003, http://news.xinhuanet.com/zhengfu/2003-06/12/content_916306.htm (accessed July 17, 2007).

27. "China's Position Paper on Counter-Terrorism," issued by the Information Office of the State Council of China, http://www.china-un.org/eng/zt/fk/t28929.htm (accessed July 17, 2007).

28. Statement by Foreign Minister Tang Jiaxuan at the UN Security Council Ministerial Meeting on Counter-Terrorism, October 14, 2003, http://www.china-un.org/eng/zt/fk/t28934.htm (accessed July 17, 2007).

29. Statement by Deputy Foreign Minister Shen Goufang at the Opening Ceremony of the Workshop on Counter-Terrorism, Asia-Europe Conference, September 22, 2003, http://www.fmprc.gov/cn/chn/ziliao/wzzt/2297/2298/t26276.htm (accessed July 17, 2007).

30. Statement by Vice Foreign Minister Wang Yi at the Conference for International Security Policy in Munich, February 2, 2002, http://www.fmprc.gov.cn/chn/ziliao/wzzt/2297/2301/t4658.htm (accessed July 17, 2007).

31. White Paper, "History and Development of Xinjiang."

32. In a Chinese scholar's view, some Russians, Germans, and other European scholars have a one-sided viewpoint of Turkish studies. They do not know Chinese and cannot read Chinese historical records about Turks, and can rely only on Persian and Arabic materials. See Wang Shumei, "Fantujuezhuyi de lishi kaocha" ["A Historical Review on Pan-Turkism"], *Shijie minzu [World Ethnics]* 2 (2000): 31–33; see also "'East Turkistan' Terrorist Forces Cannot Get Away With Impunity," Permanent Mission of the People's Republic of China to the UN, http://www.china-un.org/eng/zt/fk/t28938.htm (accessed July 29, 2007).

33. See the White Paper, "China's National Defense," (2006, 2004, 2002), http://www.china.org.cn/english/features/book/194486.htm (accessed July 17, 2007).

34. Statement by Vice Premier Qian Qichen at the Summit of the "Madrid Club," March 11, 2004, http://www.fmprc.gov.cn/chn/ziliao/wzzt/2297/t186833.htm; also see http://www.china-un.org/chn/zt/fk/t40104.htm (accessed July 17, 2007); and statement by Vice Foreign Minister Wang Yi at the Conference for International Security Policy in Munich, February 2, 2002, http://www.fmprc.gov.cn/chn/ziliao/wzzt/2297/2301/t4658.htm (accessed July 17, 2007).

35. "The National Security Strategy of the United States," March 2006, 4, http://www.whitehouse.gov/nsc/nss/2006/ (accessed July 17, 2007). In addition, the NSS notes that Chinese military expansion in a nontransparent way increases tension (41) and China is criticized for "supporting resource-rich countries without regard to the misrule at home" (42).

36. Judith Ingram, "Putin Chastises US on Democratic Ideals," Associated Press, May 10, 2006.

37. Jim Lobe, "Hawks Looking for New and Bigger Enemies?" Inter-Press Service, May 9, 2006, http://www.ipsnews.net/news.asp?idnews=33143 (accessed July 17, 2007); Robert Kagan, "End of Dreams, Return of History," *Policy Review,* 143 (June–July 2007), http://www.hoover.org/publications/policyreview/8552512.html (accessed July 26, 2007).

38. Azar Gat, "The Return of Authoritarian Great Powers," *Foreign Affairs* (July–August 2007): 59–69.

Responses to Border/Internal Security Threats: "The Terror of Disease and the Disease of Terror"[1]

Liu Jianjun and Deron R. Jackson

This chapter will consider how internal security threats present challenges for states and the international system as a whole in the twenty-first century. Given the dramatic increase in communication and trade across state boundaries since the end of the Cold War, many issues that may once have been seen primarily as local concerns are becoming problems that raise global alarm. Two threats in particular have darkened the first decade of the new century and serve to illustrate the dilemma facing both societies and policymakers. The first case involves a resurgence of infectious diseases and the potential for the increased mobility inherent in the modern world to turn a regional outbreak into a worldwide pandemic. The second challenge, made starkly clear by the September 11 attacks on America and subsequent violence in Europe and elsewhere, is the use of terrorism by extremists who are driven by a radical ideology that finds adherents on virtually every continent.

Although disease and terrorism may seem to be unrelated phenomena, arising from distinct political or biological processes, this chapter will argue that both do, in fact, have much in common when considered from the perspectives of their effects on society and how governments or the international community respond. First, a comparison of the challenges posed by pandemic disease and terrorism can serve to illustrate the interdependence of states in an increasingly connected world and the roles played by states and international organizations in shaping internal security affairs. In effect, all states face a similar dilemma of achieving prosperity in a modern, globalized world economy that thrives on openness and a freer flow of goods and people around the world than ever before in human history—factors that also serve to increase opportunities for terrorists in one region of the world to strike out against a country on the other side of the planet or permit the transmission of disease. A state could theoretically seek to maximize its security by isolating itself from the movement of people, goods, and ideas and thus insulate its population from perceived carriers of danger and disease. However, such an approach is extremely unlikely, if not impossible. A state cannot now, if it ever could in history, maximize its security through isolation without considerable cost to the prosperity and freedom of its citizens.

Second, and coupled with this prosperity dilemma, is the challenge of deciding how best to allocate finite resources to combat internal security threats, whether from terrorism or pandemic disease. As with the pursuit of traditional military security, no country is wealthy enough to afford defense against all possible dangers. As the classic strategist Sun Tzu is cited as cautioning, if you try to be strong and make your preparations everywhere, you will be weak everywhere.[2] Governments and their citizens must nevertheless make some reasonable preparations for their own safety. Once again, taking a page from Sun Tzu's most famous quotation "know the enemy and know yourself; in a hundred battles you will never be in peril," the first step to considering a successful strategy comes with a thoughtful self-analysis of the meaning of security in the domestic context.[3] Is the current era, freed from the looming devastation of the Cold War, more secure or less secure in relative or absolute terms? Is domestic security measured simply in the safety of individual lives or property? Can a country provide safety for its citizens only by constructing its own domestic security system, or must it reach out to establish a more comprehensive approach?

Security is not purely an individual requirement that can be achieved independently. Instead, the security of the individual citizen depends on the stability of society as a whole. The breakdown of order in New Orleans after Hurricane Katrina demonstrated not only the immediate threat to individual lives in the wake of a stunning natural disaster, but also the loss of security for all residents that was compounded by the dissolution of local authorities' ability to maintain the rule of law and provide resources to relieve the suffering of those trapped in the city. Only through the infusion of assistance from outside the affected area was some semblance of control restored. Even then, significant effort and assistance from allies and friendly states such as Mexico was needed to cope with the scale of destruction and disruption.

In a broader global context, the special significance of security in the modern world likewise can be properly understood only as having a dual nature, based upon the interrelationship of individuals to each other and the connection of one nation or society to another. The loss of security in one country arising from a breakdown of confidence at the individual level could lead directly to the loss of security for many states around the globe. If, for example, Pakistan were to descend into chaos and become an ungovernable collection of provinces, leaders in Washington, London, Moscow, and Beijing would certainly be seized with concern about the loss of positive control over Pakistan's nuclear arsenal and weapons-making technology.

At the same time, despite the renewed threat of terrorism and a resurgence of infectious disease, an opportunity exists to rebuild relations between people within society and at the same time improve relations between countries. In the current era of increasing globalization, a comprehensive approach to security can be seen as a kind of public resource of vital importance to nations, organizations, and individuals alike. Although traditional approaches to the study of security in international relations have always paid special attention to military aspects of threats to safety, which typically address the external national interests of states, growing concerns about ecological degradation, disease, and terrorism make issues of human security a common primary concern among many countries of the world.

In the era of globalization, public security cannot be simply viewed as a distinct phenomenon or a purely national phenomenon. Rather, it has become a global phenomenon. Nuclear pollution and other forms of environmental contamination cause equal effects in the whole world. In this sense, threats to security from ecological sources are effectively democratic, because the amount of nitrate in groundwater remains no less important for a senior government minister than for the common citizen.

Similarly, as terrorist groups have become more violent in the past decade, the scope of their victims has broadened to include all members of society, often without regard for national origin. Unlike terrorist movements in the past, which sought to be very discriminate in their attacks, such as the kidnapping and assassination plots of Germany's Red Army Faction (RAF) or other self-styled leftist movements, the suicide bombers of today have, by comparison, become comparatively egalitarian, willing to kill rich and poor alike. Here again, modern terrorism resembles a biological pathogen that strikes without regard for social status or national identity. In the face of such threats, whether from terrorism, disease, or the environment, public security no longer refers to the risks confined to a particular group. For the first time in human history, security issues originating at the local level can quickly become matters of global concern.

As an example, the outbreak of Severe Acute Respiratory Syndrome (SARS) in Asia began as a local event of epidemic disease. However, it soon aroused fear all over the world and quickly became an immediate challenge for public safety in virtually every industrialized country. In China, the SARS outbreak demonstrated the dilemma that as a country becomes more engaged in global affairs, it not only opens itself up to new opportunities to promote its interests and increase its prosperity, but it also exposes itself and other states to new risks. Furthermore, given the reciprocal risk to the rest of the world by the opening of new areas to global commerce and regularized contact, incidents that formerly may have been local dangers are quickly elevated to international crises, bringing with them calls for a state to take action not only for the safety of its own citizens, but to ensure the safety of people on the other sides of oceans.

As the process of globalization increases the interdependence and interconnectedness of countries, situations like the outbreak of SARS or avian influenza will only increase as well. Therefore, the greater the degree of international exposure a country has, the greater the possibility that a country's domestic public crisis will be converted into an international public crisis, multiplied by the growing number of states and regions participating in the global economy on a regular basis. With the development of globalization, the dividing line between domestic and foreign affairs is becoming blurred. However, neither international institutions nor individual national policies have managed to adequately keep pace with the breakneck tempo of this transforming process. Is it possible, therefore, that terrorists or other violent groups may be able to exploit this period of history for their own advantage and exercise a disproportionate degree of influence by their local actions over the flow of global events? If that were the case, it would not be the first time the world confronted such a prospect. Thus, having given initial consideration to the peril presented by our own vulnerabilities, we must take into consideration the other half of Sun Tzu's axiom, to know the enemy as well.

LESSONS FROM HISTORY

Neither terrorism nor pandemic disease is a threat unique to the present day. In the case of terrorism, a reader who picked up a newspaper or journal 100 years ago could have found written accounts of a sinister international network whose declared aim was to wage war against the Western world and its dominant socioeconomic order. To its bloody list of victims, this ruthless movement claimed the lives of an American president, several other heads of government, and leaders of global industry. Further confounding efforts by Western governments to combat this threat, the terrorists cleverly organized themselves in a broad, distributed global network that segregated the militants, who would carry out actual attacks, from the movement's senior leadership, which sought to remain at large—spreading the message and inspiring future acts. This was the age of the suicide bomber, who clutched explosives to his chest and embraced death in pursuit of a greater cause. This was the age of the Anarchists, 100 years before the rise of Islamist terror and al Qaeda.[4]

Similarly, 90 years ago, as the threat of Anarchist terror had passed its peak and the Great War was winding down, pandemic influenza swept across the globe, killing more people in 10 months than were claimed in the preceding four years of combat in World War I.[5] In America alone, the death toll from the "Spanish flu" of 1918 has been conservatively estimated at 550,000 lives in 10 months. Losses of that scale are equivalent to over 180 terrorist attacks of the magnitude of September 11, or one such attack roughly every two days.[6] Unlike terror attacks against New York City, Washington, London, Madrid, or Moscow, the effects of the 1918 flu were not localized events confined to a handful of locations in one single country. From 1918 through 1919, the lethal influenza struck every corner of the planet, and its victims were numbered in the tens of millions.

Despite the devastation inflicted by the Spanish flu, it was basically repressed from modern memory, not to return to prominence in the public mind until the resurgence of disease in the form of SARS or bird flu. Although Alfred Crosby titled his classic work on the 1918 flu *America's Forgotten Pandemic,* it was not only America, but most of the world, that forgot the visit by "the Spanish lady." The effects of the flu in China may well be lost to history, as the available literature appears to disagree on the extent of Chinese losses. Focused as it was on the United States, Crosby's work makes no mention of China and says little about Asia, focusing instead on outbreaks in Europe, Africa, and of course, America itself.[7] Barry's more recent book offers no accurate statistics, only speculating that the losses were "huge but unknown."[8] A more recent study by two Hong Kong–based doctors examines the limited records available in a few cities such as Shanghai, which suggest an equivalent rate of infection in China, but a notably lower rate of mortality.[9]

In either case, once the threat of terror or plague subsides, the tendency has been in many societies to forget about it and move on to new, more pressing challenges. In the case of the Anarchists, that particular threat faded with the coming of World War I, and the subsequent danger of revolution took a new form as the Bolsheviks seized power in Russia. Over time, both the Anarchists and the Spanish flu came to be generally viewed as historical exceptions, thankfully consigned to the past, never to return. In the United States, for example, although the 1920s saw a rebirth of the Ku Klux Klan and also witnessed the selected use of terror to a certain degree in labor disputes of that era, there was little impulse for change until the rise of left-wing extremists such as the Weather Underground and others in the 1960s.[10] Government agencies' pursuit of these violent radicals as well as other opposition groups led ultimately not to expanded counterterrorism powers, but to the passage of legislation placing clearer limits on domestic surveillance and intelligence collection. Neither the radical left-wing groups of the 1960s and 1970s nor the brief concern with antigovernment violence prompted by the Oklahoma City bombing of 1995 represented a serious, widespread threat to the safety of U.S. citizens, and as a result, there was little pressure from those citizens to change the way America confronted terrorism to any great degree. Terrorism remained largely an internalized security issue addressed with the tools of law enforcement, which, due to the nature of the American federal system, placed much of the actual responsibility out of the primary control of policymakers in Washington. As the twentieth century drew to a close, a generally comfortable consensus on the distinctions between internal security and international security would continue to hold sway in most capitals of the world.

The September 11 attacks, followed by strikes in other countries by groups drawing inspiration or direct support from al Qaeda, changed the perception of terrorism's challenge to most countries in the world. Whereas terrorists from the 1970s onward often sought to gain international attention for what were essentially localized struggles within or against a single state, such as terror campaigns by various Palestinian groups, the strategy of al Qaeda reflects the opposite objective—to use localized attacks to achieve much broader effects on the international scene. China's experience with domestic terrorism in the late twentieth century paralleled that of the United States, being focused on threats generally confined within China's own borders, such as the sporadic attacks by Uighur separatists in its western provinces. Now, however, China is collaborating with Russia in recent war games that focus on combined efforts to fight terrorism.[11] Similarly, the SARS outbreak and the appearance of avian influenza have forced a reevaluation of an individual state's ability to shield itself from a lethal peril that can arrive the next time a commercial airliner touches down after a long flight from some distant corner of the planet.

A central difficulty for policymakers is to find a way to establish priorities in dealing with these threats. Although responses may appear materially different, in terms of politics, the problems associated with a pandemic are essentially the same as dealing with terrorism—balancing security and liberty while at the same time making decisions about the vulnerability posed by open borders and markets and the overall costs associated with security measures. In terms of spending, therefore, competition for resources between agencies charged with countering terrorism and those preparing for a potential pandemic are likely to be based on zero-sum thinking. Neither a rich developed country such as the United States nor an emerging power like China can afford to spend billions of its currency at home and abroad fighting terrorism while at the same time spend billions more on preparations to fight a pandemic. Then again, what country can afford *not* to make reasonable preparations for a pandemic given the potential devastation it can bring, as the experience of 1918 shows? The prospect that terrorists might acquire and employ nuclear weapons is sufficiently grave to compel states to do whatever is necessary to avoid such an outcome.

However, in terms of assessing the threat posed by terrorism and pandemic disease, the point is not to make a direct quantitative comparison in terms of their respective death tolls. If that were done, it would be obvious the potential devastation of a pandemic dwarfs that of even the fiercest terrorist movements. On the other hand, absent a sudden mutation of bird flu into a more virulent strain capable of enhanced human-to-human infection, it is far more likely that terrorists will draw more attention by killing people in the coming year. How should governments and societies, individually and working together, prioritize their response to either of these threats, with terrorism being the most immediate danger but pandemic disease potentially more deadly?

KILLING IS INCIDENTAL. PROPAGATION IS FUNDAMENTAL. LETHALITY IS COUNTERPRODUCTIVE.

Herein lies the real challenge in "knowing the enemy" and evaluating the nature of the threat posed to citizens, governments, and the world as a whole. In this regard, it is essential not to lose focus on the fact that killing is not the object of either a virus or a terrorist. On the contrary, the purpose of terrorism is not to kill, but to achieve some political objective. Although the use of force may serve many purposes for a terrorist group, excessive brutality can be a hindrance in achieving the ultimate political objective. Similarly, for an influenza virus, even a deadly pandemic variant such as that of 1918, killing the human hosts too ferociously can be counterproductive to the fundamental imperative of reproducing and spreading. A virus that is too lethal, such as Ebola, can burn itself out and cease to spread if it kills its victims too efficiently.

This analogy holds, however, only for terrorist groups who have an identifiable political agenda, which appear to be the majority. It does not describe the behavior of the far more limited number of apocalyptic movements whose objective is to inflict mass damage for the sole purpose of bringing on the end of the world or provoking the collapse of the prevailing social order. The Japanese cult Aum Shinrikyo would likely fall in this latter category. Al Qaeda and other Islamist groups, however, should be considered to fit in the first category for whom terrorism is like unto war as defined by Carl von Clausewitz, "a true political instrument, a continuation of politics, carrying out the same with other means."[12]

Increasing lethality, however, is one of the clearly identified shifts observed in terrorism over the last 10 years. The trend toward a reduction in the number of attacks, yet a rise in the rate of fatalities, was documented several years before the September 11 attacks, which serve to date as a high-water mark of international terrorism.[13] Within the United States, a perceived pressure to escalate the level of violence was attributed to Timothy McVeigh's planning for the 1995 bombing of the Murrah Federal Building in Oklahoma City, the deadliest terrorist attack in U.S. history up to that time.[14] Why should this escalatory trend change?

One reason is the basic difficulty of increasing lethality beyond that achieved in the September 11 attacks. The 1993 bombing of the World Trade Center certainly had greater ambitions—to topple one tower into another—but the conventional explosives used were insufficient to the task. The use of a nuclear explosive or other weapon of mass destruction might generate a higher loss of life. However, such weapons thankfully remain difficult to acquire, despite the alleged interest expressed in them by certain groups. In addition, even when terrorists do lay hands on such weapons, they may be difficult to employ effectively, as the Aum Shinrikyo attack on the Tokyo subway using Sarin gas suggests. In the absence of more devastating weapons, terrorists appear to have developed an alternative approach, emphasizing the synchronization of attacks over a broader area that generate a higher composite death toll from a set of smaller attacks.

Ultimately, however, a more compelling reason for certain terrorist groups to reverse these trends and reduce the level of fatalities generated by their actions is that excessive levels of violence may be counterproductive in achieving their long-term political goals. The more violent and dangerous a terrorist group appears, the more willing a society may be to approve governmental intervention to prevent future attacks or more willing to use force externally to punish the attacker or its supporters. For violent domestic extremists, excessive violence exercised within a society is also unlikely to engender sympathy for the group's cause. In the case of the IRA in the United Kingdom and ETA in Spain, public shock at the loss of life after a given attack was followed by the respective groups' departure from the absolute path of armed struggle.[15] However, for those groups who do feel compelled to continue their campaign through the use of some form of coercive force, there may be an appeal to adapt modern theories of warfare derived from high-tech combat to the comparatively crude methods of terrorists.

EFFECTS-BASED WARFARE CONCEPTS AND FUTURE TERRORIST STRATEGY

Credit for the first public recognition that new technology would soon provide weapons with a greater degree of precision that would revolutionize military operations is generally given to the former Soviet Marshal Nikolai Ogarkov, who developed the term "reconnaissance-strike complex" to describe the impact of such technology on warfare. It was not until after the 1991 Gulf War, known as Operation Desert Storm, that the military establishments of many countries, China chief among them, sought to draw lessons from the rapid American victory over an enemy that was numerically superior, at least on paper.[16] Most analysts considered the result of that conflict to have been heavily influenced by the use of precision-guided weapons by American and allied forces, as Ogarkov had predicted. Although new weapons were indeed vital in achieving a quick military defeat of Saddam Hussein's forces, an equal if not greater contribution to the coalition's success was due to the strategy for using precision weapons in a campaign based on a concept of "parallel attack." As described by Colonel John Warden in his 1995 essay "The Enemy as a System," this view uses a description of an adversary based on five concentric rings.[17] These include a central leadership core, outward to the military forces on the battlefield, illustrated by Figure 6.1. Connecting the leadership and the military are such things

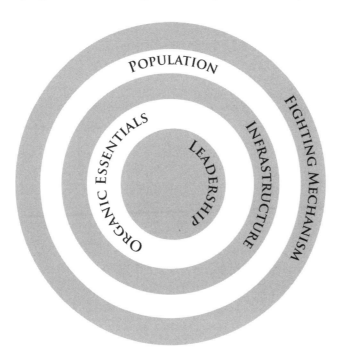

Figure 6.1   Warden's "Enemy as a System" concept for targeting.

as the civilian population of the target country, critical infrastructure, and other essentials.

The advantage of parallel attack is that it allows for the bypassing of certain rings or engaging them simultaneously. Under this model, an attacker does not need to engage an enemy in a "serial" fashion, defeating the enemy's fielded forces before moving on to attack or otherwise subdue his population. On the contrary, it may be more useful to bypass the fielded military forces and attack infrastructure and support networks to such a degree that the military forces become isolated and ineffective for combat.

Terrorists have been able to follow this ring-based approach without the benefit of technology, however. Al Qaeda has demonstrated an ability and willingness to attack American forces directly, as evidenced by the attack on the USS *Cole* in a Yemeni port in 2000. The September 11 attacks clearly illustrate the ability to attack a civilian population, bypassing any fielded military forces. The 2001 anthrax attacks, perpetrated by a still-unknown actor, disrupted mail delivery and processing in the United States, a key element of the nation's infrastructure, which caused considerable economic strain. The cash flow of many businesses in the eastern United States was cut when customers' bill payments were locked up with other contaminated mail shipments. Recent terrorist attacks in Saudi Arabia have begun to target the oil industry, particularly facilities in the Gulf region, which are essential to the economies of the United States and most other industrial countries. With respect to the final, leadership ring, the ability of terrorists to bypass all other levels and reach the leadership core is evident from history in the assassination of President McKinley by an Anarchist, as well as the alleged target designated for United Airlines Flight 93, the U.S. Capitol building.

Like a terrorist, a virus can effectively conduct a parallel attack even without a coherent will to do so. Working in reverse order from the center outward, we can see that in 1918, the influenza struck world leaders such as President Woodrow Wilson, who became ill with it while in France for the peace negotiations. Although the Spanish flu didn't kill Wilson or any other world leader of similar stature, it did strike a young future president, Franklin Delano Roosevelt, who, at age 36, caught the flu and developed double pneumonia.[18] Current strains of avian influenza clearly have had an impact on food production, an essential element of supply, as the common method of protecting against transmission to humans has generally been to slaughter whole flocks of chickens and other birds raised for meat. The public health infrastructure would begin to quickly shudder under the strain of a pandemic since virtually all hospitals lack surge capacity and staff to respond to such an event.[19] That a virus attacks a population directly is clear, as is it evident that a military force is not spared assault, given the experience of the American military in World War I in camps such as those established at Fort Devens, one of the worst-hit sites in America in 1918.[20]

While terrorists may have already demonstrated an ability to strike across the spectrum of society in a manner similar to concepts in modern military strategy, albeit without the use of high technology, a greater concern for the future lies in their adaptation of another view of modern warfare known as "effects-based operations."[21] This concept is another outgrowth of precision targeting and refers to an ability to achieve control over an adversary without inflicting large amounts of physical destruction. Instead, discrete targeting coupled with attacks in parallel across an enemy system can have the same crippling effect on an adversary as a far greater level of material devastation. Disruption of a sophisticated system, therefore, may be more important and easier to achieve with the right strategy and tactics than directly engaging superior military forces in a manner most terrorist groups cannot hope to do. Strategies of indirect attack such as this, which have gained greater attention in light of precision-weapons development, are not new, but are ancient recommendations in Chinese strategy, as espoused by Sun Tzu and often cited as part of Mao Zedong's concepts of revolutionary warfare.[22]

An indirect, effects-based attack on a society viewed as a system is therefore not simply applicable to modern warfare, but can be evident both in terrorist attack situations and under conditions of an infectious pandemic. A terrorist attack is, by its very nature, intended to be part of an effects-based approach rather than one intended at having a truly crippling material impact on a society. As Bruce Hoffman includes in his list of characteristics defining terrorism, one of the most distinctive is that terrorism is "designed to have far-reaching psychological repercussions beyond the immediate victim or target."[23] An example of one such effect can be found in the Washington, DC, area sniper shootings. After a series of long-range shootings that targeted individual shoppers at gas stations and a home improvement store, residents quickly changed their behavior and minimized their exposure at such locations, even though the actual number of deaths was quite low. Following the shooting of a teenaged student, worried parents began keeping their children at home, which had the related effect of drawing many parents out of the workforce temporarily so that one of them could stay to care for the children. As for infectious disease, once the outbreak of SARS became evident, there was a prompt effect on air travel to and from Asia, as well as related economic activity in other affected areas.

By identifying critical elements of a modern social, political, or economic structure, future terrorists may be able to maximize the effect on society with a minimal use of force matched by limited or no actual loss of life. Avoidance of large-scale casualties need not be a moral decision, but merely a practical one, calculated to increase the pressure on a government and drive a wedge between the population and authorities. Citizens who suffer the negative effects of a disruptive attack but who need not fear for their individual safety may be inclined to place some of the blame for the disruption on the government's inability to maintain order rather than on the terrorist group for initiating it, perhaps in a limited manner similar to sympathy induced by striking labor unions. However, the increasing points of vulnerability and interdependence in a modern society will present more targets of opportunity for future terrorist groups, as well as a pandemic event.

INCREASING VULNERABILITY OF GLOBALIZED SOCIETIES

While it might seem reasonable to believe modern societies, possessing technology and medical knowledge far advanced from that of 100 years ago, should now have considerable advantages over the old, twin scourges of terrorism and disease, a prudent analysis of the contemporary world must also admit that with advances have also come a certain degree of fragility and vulnerability. These can be exploited either consciously, as in the case of a terrorist group focusing on effects-based targeting, or unconsciously, as in the case of a virus that mimics similar effects in spreading as part of a global pandemic. Several modern trends or developments merit more detailed study in this context.

One such feature is the increasing degree of urbanization in the developing and developed world. According to the UN Population Division, over the next 25 years, the percentage of the world's population living in urban areas will increase to 60 percent, up from 47 percent in the year 2000.[24] This trend has significant implications for combating both terrorism and the potential for a pandemic. Urban areas can often provide greater cover for terrorists to hide among a civilian population. They also represent a target-rich environment for those groups who desire to inflict casualties in pursuit of their cause. With respect to disease, densely populated cities provide a similarly target-rich environment in which a virus can adapt and spread.

The linkage of cities to other regions also represents a twofold vulnerability for terrorists and disease to exploit. Air travel now makes it possible for both infected persons and violent extremists to travel from one corner of the world to another in a matter of hours. Such rapid global mobility was not present in earlier generations of terrorism, nor in the pandemic of 1918. It reflects, however, the aforementioned prosperity dilemma by which a country cannot seek to maximize its protection against either disease or terrorism by maximizing the control it exercises over its borders without a negative impact on its ability to trade with the rest of the world.

The other vulnerability associated with the interconnectedness of cities is their increasing dependence on one another or distant regions for resupply, particularly with respect to critical resources needed in a crisis such as energy, food, and medical supplies. In the case of that most basic need, food, in contrast to past generations wherein the majority of food sustaining a city was grown in a farm belt surrounding it in the immediate area, this is no longer true for many regions of the United States.[25] According to the Grocery Manufacturers Association, the typical resupply cycle for retail grocery stores has dropped from eight days in 1999 to less than four days.[26] This is driven by the practice of just-in-time inventory management from which many industries have gleaned considerable savings, and as a result, such approaches will be retained by businesses despite their acknowledged weakness in a crisis.[27] Furthermore, to be competitive in a global market, producers elsewhere will likely be compelled to follow just-in-time, on-demand production and delivery methods as companies find it necessary to minimize idle inventory to maximize profitability.

Of particular importance in a crisis is the maintenance of this supply network, which itself relies upon a smoothly functioning transportation system able to move goods internally within a country as well as across its borders. Transportation networks are potentially vulnerable to disruption or degradation either by compromising the fuel supply system or by a direct threat to the safety of truck drivers and other transport workers. A terrorist group could achieve this effect by either a bombing or sniper campaign across the many thousands of miles of indefensible highways in industrialized countries. A pandemic would cause a similar effect by targeting the workers in this industry as with every other. Not only could a sizeable percentage of truck drivers be expected to fall ill, for example, but the mere threat of exposure to a pandemic might persuade the remaining healthy population to stop traveling, as was the case in Asia with SARS, or to stop working temporarily. With a greater proportion of the population sheltering themselves in their homes, a prolonged disruption in the steady pulse of food delivery, or even the perception of a break in food supply, could quickly turn a city under stress into a city in chaos, such as witnessed in New Orleans after Hurricane Katrina.

ANALYSIS AND AREAS FOR RESPONSE AND FURTHER STUDY

How, then, should individuals, states, and the global community respond to the dual threats of terrorism and pandemic disease? In reflecting on the problems presented by political factions in a democratic system, James Madison wrote in *Federalist* 10 that there were two basic options: removing the causes of faction, or controlling the effects. Just as Madison argued it was impossible to remove the causes of faction, so too, it is unlikely the political causes that inspire terrorism or the biological processes that result in pandemics can be eliminated. What remains, therefore, is the option of controlling the effects of both. In essence, this requires that same degree of self-understanding and awareness advised by Sun Tzu. Having understood how the impact of terrorist attacks or pandemic disease may be magnified by the effects upon society, steps must be taken to identify those points of vulnerability and mitigate the effects. Regardless of whether or not future terrorist groups deliberately adopt an effects-based strategic approach, the results may be the same as if it were intentionally designed as such.

In the case of a virus, no political will is evident, but the sheer speed and magnitude of an outbreak would have comparable results as discussed above. Individuals and societies as a whole can be made more resilient by even modest amounts of advance planning and preparation, both materially and psychologically, in ways that are useful against both pandemics and terrorist strikes aimed at large-scale disruptions. Improved early surveillance of disease outbreak patterns can help governments detect and mitigate biological weapon attacks by terrorists.[28] Points of fragility in existing systems of security and supply must be identified in peacetime in order to prevent the propagation of effects and magnify the advantages for terrorist groups. Regardless of whether or not a deliberate strategy of this sort is applied by terrorists, adherence to Sun Tzu's dictum to "know yourself" and conducting a self-critique will yield benefits, whether the blow comes from a radical group of individuals or some new disease.

Tempering the effects of either terrorism or disease cannot be achieved entirely by an individual country. Eradication of the smallpox virus was achieved only by a collective effort of nations working together toward a common public health goal, despite the deep systemic and ideological divisions of the Cold War. In the modern day as well, the breeding ground for some future extremist group or pathogen will often be outside a state's own borders. To be proactive, nations will be obliged to work together both in terms of making preparations before a crisis and in collective response after one has struck. Improving that response involves a better appreciation and refinement of the functions served by existing international frameworks.

In terms of immediate response to a crisis, a broad range of intergovernmental and nongovernmental organizations exist covering almost all fields of public life around the world. Organizations such as the Red Cross, Doctors Without Borders, and the World Health Organization (WHO) can make prompt contributions in the event of an emergency. In some cases, particularly before the scope of a crisis is formally acknowledged, engagement between such organizations and the affected state or states can be a source of tension. For example, China felt great external pressure from international organizations because of SARS and avian influenza. Although the purpose of this pressure was not intended to infringe upon the country's sovereignty, bur rather to provide assistance, the initial reaction was defensive. Efforts to reduce this level of friction and suspicion must be made to ensure valuable time is not lost, particularly in the case of communicable disease or the discovery of a developing terrorist threat.

To reduce friction in times of crisis, collaborative structures can be used for planning and assessment of the basic requirements each country may have. In such venues, representatives can exchange views on how each country defines its own concepts of public security. These organizations act as brokers, socializers, and teachers, establishing in the process a broader framework for international public security.[29]

Another function served by such entities is that of a clearinghouse for information. Public security activities often require a substantial amount of accurate and high-quality information about threats to ensure effective precautions are taken to contain the danger. Due to the transnational features of many threats, it is virtually certain that one single country is not able to collect all the relevant information. The resources of developing countries, in particular, are often insufficient to the task, although they themselves are frequently on the front lines of the emerging threat. By making available a wide array of authoritative, yet unbiased, experts to assess the situation on the basis of established standards, local officials may be better prepared to make reasonable decisions to help cope with these events. Current efforts at the WHO are aimed at this challenge.[30]

However, the interrelationship of public security and private security introduced at the start of this chapter remains a key dilemma. Information sharing, as described above, is an essential link in achieving success. At the international level, where concern exists for global public security, the process of globalization continues to engender suspicion among nations. One such case had been Indonesia's initial reluctance to share the genomic data relating to new strains of avian influenza. This was due to worry that more developed states would use the information to develop vaccines that would be available only in limited quantities and thus first supplied to citizens of those more advanced countries, not to Indonesia or others.[31] On the individual level, suspicion and even panic can develop after an outbreak or terrorist attack, as citizens fearing for their own lives may react in dangerous or irrational ways that undermine public security. Unless reliable information is provided quickly by trusted government or international sources, behavior at the individual level may immediately complicate or otherwise impede the provision of relief aid or restoration of public safety. Here again, the problems confronting China during the SARS outbreak may be studied for useful lessons applicable not only there, but in other settings as well.

CONCLUSION

The ultimate test in formulating an effective defensive strategy is in the allocation of resources. In this last critical dimension, the consideration presented in this paper of how pandemic disease and terrorism present similar challenges in terms of their effects on society should be useful to policymakers forced to make difficult choices between meeting immediate demands and preparing for more distant dangers. Since September 11, 2001, many states have sought to improve their security by increasing spending on measures designed to defend against terrorist attacks. However, most soon discovered the truth behind Sun Tzu's warning that attempts to be strong at every point of weakness will only result in weakness at every point. Furthermore, just as countries began to study in earnest the problem of countering international, cross-border terrorist movements, flare-ups of infectious disease like SARS and bird flu pulled them in a new direction, with its own high price tag. Although the threat from terrorists in many countries is seen as very real and immediate, the threat from pandemic disease is more difficult to predict and, at present, may be seen as regionalized despite the potential for rapid spread. How then should policymakers balance the demands for the citizens for individual and public security protection against both near-term and long-term threats without sapping their budgets? No state today is rich enough to provide a seamless defense against either danger alone, and thus it stands to reason that complete safety from both disease and terrorism is impossible.

To maximize results while minimizing resources, therefore, effects-based strategies must be developed that bear fruit in preventing and responding to terrorist attacks as well as infectious outbreaks. These will take the form of self-analysis to identify and address fragile points within each country's systems to promote resilience and ensure that the effects of a terrorist attack, disease, or other natural disaster are not magnified by poor preparation and planning. Where individual or national efforts are insufficient, the characteristic of rapid mobility in a globalized world, which is often a source of potential vulnerability, must be exploited as an advantage to provide a swift but flexible response to emerging dangers. Such a response can only be customized to the danger at hand and deployed quickly enough to have an impact if a formalized practice of improved information sharing is present and functional in advance of the next crisis, whether it arise from extremists or from nature itself. Despite the confrontation of the Cold War, the nations of the world united in the pursuit of greater public health to eliminate smallpox.[32] Concerted efforts to improve public security at the global level might substantially reduce the threat of terrorism and significantly improve responses to infectious disease, despite the inevitable mutation of new pathogens. The confidence-building effects of cooperation on both these dangers, which have no respect for artificial state borders, may in time serve as a basis for countries in the twenty-first century to address other, more seemingly intractable security threats confronting them.

NOTES

1. The authors would like to express their appreciation to Liu Honsong and Fang Zheng for their assistance in the preparation of this paper. The opinions in this paper are those of the authors alone and do not represent the policies of any government or institution.

2. Sun Tzu, *The Art of War,* trans. Samuel B. Griffith (Oxford: Oxford University Press, 1963), 98.

3. Ibid., 84.

4. For a concise discussion of the Anarchists and their times, see Barbara Tuchman, *The Proud Tower* (New York: Random House, 1996).

5. Alfred W. Crosby, *America's Forgotten Pandemic* (Cambridge: Cambridge University Press, 1989), 207.

6. The estimate of 550,000 American deaths is taken from Crosby, *America's Forgotten Epidemic,* 206. Other projections claim a higher death toll. John Barry, for example, cites a modern government estimate of 675,000 deaths from a population roughly one third as large as the U.S. today. See Barry, *The Great Influenza* (New York: Penguin Group, 2005), 450.

7. Crosby, *America's Forgotten Pandemic,* 37.

8. Barry, *Great Influenza,* 364.

9. K. F. Cheng and P. C. Leung, "What Happened in China During the 1918 Influenza Pademic?" *International Journal of Infectious Diseases* (July 2007): 362. The reason for the difference between mortality rates in China and the rest of the world is unknown. One theory is that with many influenza viruses originating in Asia, the Chinese population may have obtained a baseline immunity due to exposure to a similar strain at some earlier point. The authors speculate that some traditional Chinese medical practices may have alleviated the suffering of patients. As fewer victims developed pneumonia in China (at least as reported in the limited available data), this effect may be at the heart of the discrepancy. Many fatalities in America and elsewhere resulted from complications such as severe pneumonia and other systemic immune system response issues brought on by exposure to the Spanish flu.

10. For examples of violence by the KKK and in labor unrest, see Paul M. Angle, *Bloody Williamson* (New York: Alfred A. Knopf, 1952). A notable exception to the relative absence of domestic terrorism in the middle of the twentieth century was the attempted assassination of President Harry Truman by Puerto Rican nationalists. For details on the motives and methods behind that attack, consult Stephen Hunter and John Bainbridge, *American Gunfight* (New York: Simon and Schuster, 2005).

11. "China's Objectives in Xinjiang," *Jane's Security News,* August 13, 2007, 1.

12. Carl von Clausewitz, *Vom Kriege [On War]* (Berlin: Ullstein, 1998), 44.

13. Ian O. Lesser, Bruce Hoffman, John Arquilla, David Ronfeldt, Michele Zanini, and Brian Michael Jenkins, *Countering the New Terrorism* (Santa Monica, CA: RAND Corporation, 1999), 10.

14. Bruce Hoffman, *Inside Terrorism* (New York: Columbia University Press, 1999), 177.

15. In the case of the Basque ETA, it should be noted the Madrid railway attacks were not of their own making, yet had a dramatic effect on Spanish society and politics.

16. Andrew N. D. Yang and Milton Wen-Chung Liao, "PLA Rapid Reaction Forces: Concept, Training, and Preliminary Assessment," in *The People's Liberation Army in the Information Age,* ed. James C. Mulvenon and Richard H. Yang (Santa Monica, CA: RAND Corporation, 1998), 49.

17. John Warden, "The Enemy as a System," *Airpower Journal* (Spring 1995): 4.

18. Crosby, *America's Forgotten Pandemic,* 322.

19. Donald F. Thompson, "Terrorism and Domestic Response: Can DOD Help Get it Right?" *Joint Force Quarterly* (1st Quarter 2006): 17.

20. Carol R. Byerly, *Fever of War* (New York: New York University Press, 2005), 75.

21. David Deptula, *Effects-based Operations: Change in the Nature of Warfare* (Arlington, VA: Aerospace Education Foundation, 2001), 11.

22. Sun Tzu, *Art of War,* 91.

23. Hoffman, *Inside Terrorism,* 43.

24. Jonas Siegel, "Bugs in the System," *Bulletin of the Atomic Scientists* (March–April 2006): 34.

25. Ralph E. Heimlich and William D. Anderson, *Development at the Urban Fringe and Beyond: Impacts on Agriculture and Rural Land* (Economic Research Service, United States Department of Agriculture, June 2001), 45.

26. Bernard Wysocki and Sarah Lueck, "Margin of Safety: Just-in-Time Inventories Make U.S. Vulnerable in Pandemic," *Wall Street Journal,* January 12, 2002, 2.

27. Fred Savaglio and Bob Freitag, *Just in Time Inventory: Effects on Earthquake Recovery* (Cascadia Region Earthquake Workgroup, 2005), 3.

28. Office of Transnational Issues, *SARS: Lessons from the First Pandemic of the 21st Century* (Langley, VA: Central Intelligence Agency Publications Office, 2003), 12.

29. Yu Zhengliang, *International Relations in the Era of Globalization* (Shanghai: Fudan University Publishing House, 2000).

30. "How Dr. Chan Intends to Defend the Planet from Pandemics," *Economist,* June 16, 2007, 67.

31. "A Shot of Transparency," *Economist,* August 12, 2007, 65.

32. Smallpox has been isolated and is no longer present among the human population of Earth. Samples of the *variola* virus do still exist in research laboratories in a limited number of countries, making its "elimination" practical, but not absolute. See Richard Preston, *The Demon in the Freezer* (New York: Random House, 2002).

Part III ————————————————————————

Regional Security Issues and Challenges

Europe–Russia–United States: Whither Are We Drifting?

Dmitri Katsy, David H. Sacko, and Konstantin Khudoley

RUSSIA AND EUROPE: SAME CONTINENT, SEPARATE ENTITITES

Russia and Europe are currently drifting apart, and evidences to the contrary are rather few. Certainly for the moment, the sides are inconsistent in how they conceptually expound upon their historical past and project their own experience into the future. In any case, each side's domestic need for both changes to and conservation of its existing social structures generates mostly clashing political agendas that impede practical policy implementation.

The problem seems to be twofold. On the one hand, a mutually accepted and potentially sustainable strategy of relationships between "European" and "Russian" parts of the Eurasian continent still has to be better defined. Such a strategy could create new momentum for the wider development of existing areas of cooperation. On the other hand, Cold War animosities remain deeply engraved in the collective memories of both sides. This aspect has a powerful social influence, so it is unlikely to be disregarded in Russian and European politics in the near future. Hence, the existing structural mismatch between the sides, where economic, political, social, and military activities have been differently organized, is likely to be exacerbated. Even a brief analysis of recent political practices convincingly shows that immediate political incentives predominate over any long-term strategic considerations in present Russia-Europe relations. The ultimate outcome of these relations remains uncertain, but at least three characteristic moments have already become visible.

First, it is clear that contemporary Russia has not constructed democratic institutions emulating Western models, thus demonstrating its reluctance to do so in practice and, arguably, even in principle.[1] In any case, Russia has moved in the opposite direction with its own understanding of the necessity to centralize management of available resources and use of its domestic power structures for strengthening the role of the state. Naturally, the rise of the state was not to the immediate benefit of the country's business community and civil society. Notably, such a state-above-all tendency contrasts with what is generally accepted by the majority of European countries, where the role of the nation-state is diminishing due to the increasing efficiency of integration processes. Thus, one of the fundamental problems for Russia-Europe relations is that the two entities are generating starkly differing institutional identities while mutually erecting boundaries between those "inside" and "outside." Under these circumstances, Russia could easily come to be seen as Europe's Other once again. One potential danger of this *folie à deux* is that it could materialize in the form of a chain of mutually counterproductive actions that would tend to solidify the existing boundaries, rather than gradually dissolve them.

Second, the recent dual enlargements of the western structures, the North Atlantic Treaty Organization (NATO) and the European Union (EU), have not yet had a direct positive influence either on the greater part of Russian political and military elites or on the general population so far. The numerous *indirect* benefits from mutual trade and some other current activities should not be underestimated or neglected; however, it is well known that trade relations can have not just positive but also negative outcomes. This is well illustrated by the fact that globally, the gap between most technically advanced nations and less advanced nations grows wider. While this process is widely believed to be inexorable, in the case of Russia and Europe, this regrettable aspect has particular importance. The reality is that European states are much closer to what are usually labeled as postindustrial and/or information societies, while Russia is, by contrast, a typical example of an industrial society at best. The current situation is that about 25–30 percent of Russia's processing industries are expected to be competitive in the international market environment, while others can compete in the country's internal market only.[2] Arguably, as a country in transition,[3] Russia has to achieve at least two goals at the same time. One is to frame a polity concept aimed at avoiding regional insecurity while creating conditions for the country's sustainable development. The second is to implement efficient decision-making mechanisms in its internal policy while making its international actions acceptable for other states in the international environment. Theoretically, these two goals are not incompatible. In practice, however, each often has had to be reached at the expense of the other and produced mixed results. In general terms, this means that Russia and Europe are most likely to meet different challenges from impending globalization, so their strategic interests, again, may have too little in common for the emergence of any strategic political culture.

Third, and most importantly, the Russian elite, especially its most conservative military circles, differs from European elites in that it has mainly Soviet origins. What it currently wants is modernization without westernization;[4] nevertheless, just the opposite occurred due to the country's comparative advantages as a worldwide supplier of primary resources and energy. Understandably, however profitable this orientation is at the current juncture, it is unlikely leading to a positive outcome in the long run. Characteristically, since 1991 representatives of the Russian military industry have systematically claimed to be suffering losses in relation to the activities of other worldwide producers and employees in high-tech military infrastructure. By the end of the 1990s, they were sure that their industry was the only thing that could preserve the country's status as an industrialized nation.[5] The general perception of this fact could not but resonate in Russian domestic politics, where, in practice, NATO enlargement has never been deemed a justifiable process at any social level. Traditionally, NATO was also regarded negatively by much of the Russian public, so anti-NATO, anti-Western, and anti-American sentiments became powerful instruments in Russian domestic political contests.[6] Thus, remembering broken political promises not to enlarge NATO, Russia had to meet the unpleasant reality of its potentially insecure position between the European segment of the Eurasian continent and its biggest southeastern part, where many real and potentially destabilizing tendencies originate. Together, instability in the East and lack of openness from the West have turned Russia into itself to concentrate on its "traditional" ways of solving domestic problems while preparing to enter into the global environment as a separate and "non-Western" cultural entity.

THE UNITED STATES AND EUROPE: DIFFERENT WAYS, SAME DESTINY

"The U.S. is from Mars and Europe is from Venus."[7] The differences between the United States and Europe would seem to be as profound as the divergences described in the first section between Russia and Europe. Ideology, as well as power, divides the United States and Europe. The Europeans, according to the perspective popularized by Kagan, have a higher tolerance for insecurity after decades of American protection, and now will not fight to preserve what Americans commonly regard as universal freedoms. Europe insists, rather, on their preference for achieving security through multilateral institutions and a Kantian vision of a "perpetual peace" achieved through intergovernmental cooperation, liberal regimes, and economic intercourse. Americans, on the other hand, have a higher military capability and a willingness to use it, particularly following the events of September 11, 2001. Growing differences in foreign policy actions would seem to underscore this thesis. Even before the current Bush administration and its invasion of Iraq, this divergence could be seen in the United States' failure to ratify the Comprehensive Test Ban Treaty limiting nuclear weapon tests or even to give serious consideration to the Ottawa Treaty banning land mines. Both initiatives have wide popular and political support in Europe. Under the Bush administration, the Kyoto Protocol limiting carbon-dioxide emissions was withdrawn from Senate ratification, and the treaty guaranteeing U.S. participation in the International Criminal Court failed ratification in the U.S. Senate altogether.

In addition, several lesser-trumpeted treaties prescribing social conduct proposed much earlier, notably the International Convention on Economic, Social and

Cultural Rights (ICESCR, 1976), are widely signed into law in Europe, but remain ignored by the United States. If ideology is not driving Europe and the United States apart, another perspective holds that the changing polarity of the international political system is.[8] Without the unified security theme of Soviet containment, the union of West European security will inevitably fragment and revert to a multipolar state system in which powerful incentives for individual foreign policies exist. The inevitable anarchic character of this state system will override any ideological force, be it cooperative or conflictual in nature.

In foreign policy, the United States has unilaterally used force when member countries of the European Union have often urged restraint in favor of a multilateral institutional response. In addition, a difference in perspective between the United States and Europe is apparent, with Europe favoring longer-term outlooks on problems such as the Middle East. Europe holds that the linchpin to Middle East peace depends on an equitable resolution to the Palestinian-Israeli crisis, whereas the United States has concentrated its efforts on its plan to institute democracy in Iraq.[9] These efforts have been firmly rebuffed by the United Nations Security Council. In many respects, the United States has attempted to capitalize on its unipolar moment and its domineering military capability to use deliberate force to achieve security. These broadly painted differences as they are typically portrayed, however, obscure the great ideological convergence and shared security interests between the United States and Europe.

Importantly, the United States and the states of Europe are not inextricably on divergent courses driven by the forces of ideology or *realpolitik*. Their methods of attempting to achieve security surely have diverged, but the basic interests that security policy should serve for both the United States and European states remain more convergent than contradictory. Simply, the differences in worldview between the United States and Europe are often overstated. Clearly, U.S. foreign policy diverged from that of many European states in the situations delineated; however, a more nuanced assessment finds differences less in the goals than in the execution of policy to achieve those goals.

Most European states preferred that Iraq not be invaded and occupied, but agreed that Saddam Hussein should be contained and not allowed to acquire weapons of mass destruction. Europe believes in brokering a peaceful resolution to conflict in the Middle East starting with Palestine, not Iraq. Many European states continue to have an integral part in military operations in Afghanistan in the International Security Assistance Force.

This discussion raises a second question: at what level of generality can we even assume a unified European ethic? The analysis above describes a unified European economic and domestic political philosophy—as contrasted with Russia's—a unified ethic that evolved particularly from Cold War divisions. Can an analogous assumption be applied such that a unified European security philosophy is rendered sensible? Indeed, not all European states have completely broken with U.S. policy, and many continue to participate in U.S. military operations.

Europe and the United States have many more ties that bind,[10] representing the economic and political development fancied so much by Fukuyama's "End of History" thesis.[11] Post–Cold War works theorizing new grand strategic perspectives predict similar basic political preferences for the United States and Europe: democracy and capitalism.[12] In addition, the United States and Europe constitute the largest number of consolidated democratic, economically interdependent, and intergovernmental organization member countries representative of complex liberalism.[13] The very nature of this political liberalism has led to European states' debating, objecting to, and obstructing U.S. unilateral intentions. On the whole, though, the project of liberalism has led to more cohesion than is generally recognized. Theoretically, more explanations hypothesize cooperation and peaceful coexistence than any reasonable account predicting belligerence. Even from a *realpolitik* perspective, explanations for European reticence to hard-balance (that is, balance with military force) and for the United States' support of "bandwagoning" or "bystanding" are emerging.[14]

In an attempt at irony, Fukuyama predicted the end of history to be boring[15]—to wit, if we have reached this moment, it is, in fact, a moment with plenty of challenges for the United States and Europe. The United States and Europe have much to agree on in terms of mutual national interests. Both have interests in the stability of the greater Middle East, including Iraq and Palestine, primarily to maintain the stability of the oil supply to the world economy upon which both depend. Both have a security interest in nuclear nonproliferation in Iran. Both need predictable and sustainable relations with China and Russia.

The 2006 U.S. National Security Strategy predominantly focuses on the Global War on Terror, the trend of democratization and world free-market expansion, world energy security, and the need to diffuse problematic regional conflicts. While European security is affected by terrorism, democratization, globalization, energy, and regional problems, the strategy was preoccupied with the aforementioned challenges as they apply *outside* Europe. Given the American proclivity for focus on short-term interests, we must not lose sight of the fact that Europe, more than any other region, remains an absolute necessity to long-term U.S. security interests. The National Security Strategy of the United States, as articulated in 2006 states:

> Europe is home to some of our oldest and closest allies. Our cooperative relations are built on a sure foundation of shared values and interests. This foundation is expanding and deepening with the ongoing spread of effective democracies in Europe, and must expand and deepen still further if we are to reach the goal of a Europe whole, free, and at peace.[16]

A stable and secure Europe is of paramount importance to U.S. security. The question is, from the perspective of the United States, what are the primary security threats to Europe? Due in large part to the clear lines drawn during the bipolar era, rivalry, competition, and partnership were much more easily discerned than in contemporary times. An answer to this question may be found within the framework of three issues, namely, the NATO Alliance, international cooperation in the war on terror, and European energy security. Without the constraints of bipolarity, today's political possibilities are in fact more fluid for both competition and cooperation.

North Atlantic Treaty Organization

In the course of the past 15 years, both the organization and security concept of the North Atlantic Treaty Organization evolved. NATO's membership changed, incorporating first East Germany; then Poland, the Czech Republic, and Hungary; and most recently Estonia, Latvia, Lithuania, Slovenia, Slovakia, Bulgaria, and Romania. The EU and other established NATO countries postulate that "broadening the membership of NATO is part of a much broader strategy to help create a peaceful, undivided and democratic Europe, an objective shared by NATO, the EU, WEU [Western European Union], OSCE [Organization for Security and Cooperation in Europe] and the Council of Europe."[17] Conditions for NATO membership include accountability and liberal institutions at home, although the primary expectation is that each country should be able to shoulder its share of the defense burden. NATO thus took on a socializing role to promote security within just as much as to provide security without. Just as NATO began to expand, though, its static defensive posture was also altered when it conducted forward operations in Bosnia in 1993–95, and then in Kosovo in 1999. In addition, it has commanded the International Security Assistance Force in Afghanistan since 2003. Both these evolving currents have served to demonstrate security cooperation and true partnership between the United States and Europe. The United States and its NATO allies disagreed substantially on the pace and direction of NATO expansion, yet the point of uniting Europe under one security umbrella prevailed in practice. There was even more vociferous disagreement on the nature and conduct of offensive operations in Bosnia and Kosovo,[18] yet despite tactical conflicts between member countries, NATO's strategic objectives were primarily achieved.

In any political organization, there will always be substantially more disagreement than accordance. NATO's primary successes were found in its ability to endure, expand, and conduct the operations discussed above. Lately, an area of contestation between NATO members has been ballistic missile defense. Over the past several years, NATO has been planning a ballistic missile defense ability,[19] ostensibly to protect the European continent from a small-scale launch from North Korea or Iran. In the last six months, the United States announced a series of bilateral agreements with the Czech Republic and Poland, prompting Russian questions about the ultimate strategic aims of such a system and the system's impact on its own security. To this end, not all NATO countries agree that such a "missile shield" is in the European interest.[20] Ultimately, the NATO alliance members will most likely broker an agreement to deploy ballistic missile defense, but as in many security disagreements between the United States and Europe, the question is not whether the system will be implemented, but how and when. Multilateral military cooperation between the United States and Europe, in the form of the NATO alliance, thus continues to represent an area of some rivalry in limited issues, but overall it represents a boon for partnership between the United States and Europe. While NATO facilitated cooperation between the militaries of its European members, the United States, and Canada, the alliance's expansion, its ability to forwardly operate and its attempts to acquire a continental ballistic missile defense system created sources of tension between the United States and Russia. These tensions present serious challenges for future security cooperation.

Global Salafist Jihadis

Violent attacks either perpetrated or avoided clearly indicate that the United States and Europe have been targeted by the Global Salafist Jihadist movement.[21] Since the end of World War II, the locus of organized political violence has been steadily shifting from *between* states to *within* states. Increasingly, organized political violence involves the rise of violent nonstate actors.[22] Today, the dominant active military threat faced by the United States and Europe is Global Salafist Jihadis who seek the ultimate defeat of such "far enemies." As outlined in al Qaeda's theology and grand strategy, Europe and the United States represent a political, social, and economic challenge to the *Dar-al-Islam* (the abode of God)—the reemergence of true Islam in lands occupied by the Zionists or apostates. In order for these "near enemies" to be defeated, the "far enemies" (the United States and Europe) must be confronted and militarily defeated.[23] As Fawad Gerges writes, "The road to Jerusalem no longer passed directly through Cairo, Algiers, Amman, or Riyadh but rather through a double-lane highway, including stops in Washington, New York, Madrid, London, and other Western capitals."[24]

After al Qaeda piloted hijacked planes into the World Trade Center and the Pentagon, European support for political and military efforts against al Qaeda quickly followed. The European Council declared unity of purpose with the United States, and the NATO Council agreed that this attack was an action addressed by Article 5 of the Washington Treaty, which stipulates that an attack on one member is an attack on all. Within one month, both NATO and the European Union improved intelligence sharing, increased the protection of military assets in Europe and of access to ports and airports, granted unlimited overflight permission, and helped shut down al Qaeda's European funding networks. Since the 9/11 attacks, both Spain and the United Kingdom have been attacked by cells motivated by the same jihadist ideology. Even after these attacks, however, Europe's perception of what the United States calls the "Global War on Terror" is quite different. The United States proposes to make this war the new priority for cooperation with Europe—a kind of ideological combat similar to the Cold War—since now the countries of the global North have to react to a threat coming from yet another totalitarian ideology. Still, many Europeans do not accept the idea of a "war" on terror.

One popular perception in Europe is that methods used to deal with other terrorist groups in Europe, such as intelligence operations, police tactics, and the justice system, will serve the current terrorism threat better than the "militarized" methods employed by the United States.[25] Is this more evidence of planetary difference? Not so. Even though disagreements with the United States over its Middle East policy persist, there remains a basic accord in grand strategic terms. European countries have a clear reminder in the form of a potential homegrown recruiting pool constituted by the disenchanted children of Muslim immigrants living in Europe. Such individuals, fascinated with the concept of global jihad, were at the center of the London and Madrid bombings; many similar attempts have been foiled before coming to fruition.[26] In any case, Europe's homegrown jihadis have proven to be highly mobile, interconnected, well financed, and popularly supported. European law enforcement's task has been complicated, in turn, by open borders, poor coordination, and deficient communication of interstate counterterrorism strategies.[27] Europe and the United States agree that a conflict exists with Global Salafist Jihadis; however, once again the parties diverge when it comes to methods rather than substance. Sadly, Russia too has had experience with Global Salafist Jihadis. Terrorism on Russian soil has been primarily rooted with the problems associated with the Chechen separatist movements. Bombings in and around Moscow and the Beslan and Moscow theater hostage incidents are the touchstone events in Russia's own war against terror. Paradoxically, Russia's struggle to contain and eliminate terrorism on its own soil represents a great opportunity for cooperation with both the United States and Europe.

Energy

The security of energy and raw materials is of paramount importance to any economy, but particularly to those that share many interdependent links to other states, such as the United States and Europe. Being fundamentally a domestic issue, energy policy varies widely from state to state; only recently have international relations begun to incorporate it explicitly in security discussions. Both the United States and Europe have energy dependencies that may create security vulnerabilities or place them in disadvantaged interstate bargaining positions vis-à-vis their energy providers. A consensus in the United States is only beginning to emerge that admits to a foreign oil "addiction"; we are perhaps seeing the glacially paced formation of an energy policy to reduce U.S. dependence on oil, particularly from potentially unstable regimes in the Middle East, Venezuela, and Nigeria. Europeans, too, have a dependence on fossil fuels. In particular, Europe depends upon other states for its natural gas and crude oil, notably Russia for natural gas. The controversy over Russia supplying Europe's demand for natural gas can be traced back to the 1970s. In the 1980s, President Reagan used both the carrot and the stick to persuade Western Europe to reject a natural gas pipeline from the Soviet Union. In the past decade, Russia has been consolidating its delivery systems to become the primary natural gas supplier for Europe, creating a state of affairs not unlike the relationship between Canada and the United States. The supply-demand relationship between Russia and Europe, however, has been viewed with a great deal more alarm. Security considerations rarely come up in the U.S.-Canadian energy "relationship," but Russia is now widely considered to hold the key to European energy security in its hands.[28] Russia's primary gas pipeline company Gazprom recently purchased distribution rights for Caspian Sea natural gas through Kazakhstan and Turkmenistan. This purchase thwarted a U.S. initiative to build a pipeline through Turkey to transport natural gas around Russia directly to Europe and prompted criticism from the United States and Europe.[29] Ascribing a clear security motive to a market dynamic, Vice President Dick Cheney called Gazprom's pipeline holdings "tools for intimidation and blackmail."[30] In 2006, in reaction to similar foreign criticism of its policies, Russia stated that "attempts to limit Gazprom's activities in the European market and to politicize questions of gas supply, which in fact are of an entirely economic nature, will not lead to good results."[31] While much was made of the latter phrase of this quote, the essence of the rest was overlooked. It should not be forgotten that Gazprom's acquisitions are primarily a market interaction to which the Europeans have acquiesced. Certainly, there is a political dimension to this economic interaction— Gazprom is a state-owned monopoly— yet the global energy industry has not historically been an economic sector characterized by fair competition, or one that has allowed easy entry. Europe simply has not pursued other energy options, preferring instead to purchase Gazprom-transported fuel.

What options might the Europeans explore? Ultimately, this is a problem of economics, one which the Europeans can address through changes in supply policy. One effort to challenge Russia's role has been to build a pipeline from Turkey to Austria, the so-called Nabucco Plan, but this has created sufficient friction within Europe that it seems doomed to failure. In order to facilitate a greater feeling of security in this arena, the European Union requires a more coherent energy policy on one hand, and less individual domestic market regulation on the other.[32] The theory goes that if European Union members deregulated their vertically integrated energy companies, more cross-border trade would ensue, leading to more competition and thereby reducing the fear of energy disruption. Europe simply has not chosen to devote the funds to coordinate and develop the infrastructure to ensure a diverse set of supply sources of natural gas. This is one security issue in which Europe has the most power to choose.

RUSSIA AND THE UNITED STATES: SEPARATE POLITICS, SAME WORLD

Characteristically, those factors that unite the United States and Europe also present particular challenges for contemporary U.S.-Russian relations. In this case, existing geographical, cultural, structural, and ideological discrepancies traditionally generate political controversies. The crucial point is that Russia and the United States are not economically interdependent, which gives Moscow little leverage over Washington; conversely, Washington exerts little influence over Moscow for the same reason.[33] Unlike Europe with its newly expanded borders (and gas pipelines) to Russia, the United States neither is directly dependent on Russian energy nor are their main populations close. As it has been rightly noted, there seem to be "no big U.S.

businesses with big interests in Russia" so far.[34] Importantly, Russian big business, in its turn, has a different nature from that of the United States, since Russia has traditionally exported mainly raw materials, not high-tech technologies. Even though some exports of technology or arms sales[35] can be easily traced, they certainly do not constitute the main share of Russia's exports.[36] Fortunately or not, the world-famous Russian oligarchs have not really competed in the open international environment yet; the same is true of their current successors, who also attained their political weight under the protection of the state. Big business in Russia has not yet been a global player; due to the secondary role of Russian big business, becoming a global player may be undesirable if Russian (or U.S.) political leaders opt for mutually divergent *time-is-not-right* strategies. Taken together, such strategies would render the current lack of big business connections between the United States and Russia even less malleable in the years immediately ahead. Regrettably, this seems to be the most likely scenario, especially in the context of the mutually problematic nature of U.S.-Russia trade relations[37] and in the wake of imminent presidential elections in both countries in 2008.

It would be misleading, however, to believe that contemporary Russia is a hollow shell for the United States, or the reverse. Neither Russia nor the United States has its own planet, so coming challenges from the global political, economic, and security environment will compel the two countries to take account of each other in one way or another. It is very hard to imagine, even in theory, how Russia-Europe relations could be further developed without the United States. Despite this, different visions do flourish across Russia's current political spectrum.[38] While some of them favor the above-mentioned thesis about the growing transatlantic gap, they usually suggest somewhat hazy alternatives that may not be viable in practice, either in the midterm or in the long term.

At the same time, as noted first in the U.S. press and later in the Russian press, the United States did have reasons to take Russia into consideration.[39] Furthermore, what may be called "reasons" for the United States constitute a rational prescription for Russia. In brief, Russia has a strategically important and geographically diverse location. It is able to act both as an international facilitator and a mediator. It shares intelligence and supports nonproliferation. It is a member of influential international organizations, and it is able to defend itself as well as its partners. Understandably, all of these basic parameters have remained in place. Moreover, other reasons for extending mutual cooperation may yet emerge in the future, despite the current, and understandable, political perception that the U.S.-Russia partnership has frayed.[40] Indeed, any possible new achievements of mutual benefits will depend on both Russia's and U.S.-Europe's joint capacities to address collectively common concerns and priorities. Naturally, mutual security guarantees will be needed if truly sustainable long-term relationships with the western partners are to be built. Neither side in this extremely complicated process wants to run the risk of losing either its international status or control over its interests.

That is why one of the key tests of the joined effectiveness of the Europe-Russia-U.S. capacity is the current issue of ballistic missile defense in Europe. This is where the most influential parts of Russian society and the country's leadership have for years seen both potential and direct threats to Russia's national security.[41] Unsurprisingly, Russia's reaction to this U.S.-led initiative was mainly negative. The announcement that the United States planned to deploy a ballistic missile defense system in Poland and the Czech Republic[42] revived the idea of a possible Russian withdrawal from the Conventional Armed Forces in Europe Treaty. The Russian military even suggested "asymmetrical response" to the United States by deploying special equipment for the warning stations at Russian embassies[43] and successfully tested both ballistic and tactical missile weapons by the end of May 2007.[44]

The emerging problems in this area remind us of a classical security dilemma to which there is no permanent and lasting solution within the frameworks of the realist paradigm, which is dominant in contemporary Russia.[45] However, sliding into a period of relationship comparable to the Cold War seems unlikely.[46] Despite political rhetoric on this topic, which is not unexpected before the coming elections, contemporary realities have progressed too far away from the former bipolar system. Meanwhile, the world certainly has not become more secure. Notably, on April 30, 2007, it was announced that Russia did not support the plan to deploy elements of the U.S. national defense within the territories of the European states, but it was prepared to construct a territorial antimissile system in Europe together with NATO and the United States instead.[47] Importantly, Russia had also demonstrated to both the United States and Europe its willingness to cooperate on security matters in years past, despite the fact that the current results of this cooperation are rather selective, often specific, and too narrow to be appreciated domestically. What is even more significant is that no sustainable Russia-Europe strategy is likely to emerge if Russia-U.S. cooperation on security matters can not be qualitatively extended in the years ahead.

Naturally, there may be unofficial political acceptance of the need to live with unresolved differences, especially in the short run. Still, it is also true that those salient tendencies most likely to have global impact should not be neglected today just because the means for their possible implementation seem insufficient. During talks in Novo-Ogaryovo, U.S. Secretary of State Rice and Russian President Putin agreed that the rhetoric in U.S.-Russian relations should be toned down.[48] Their talks also recognized that current Washington-Moscow dealings were nothing like the hostility between the United States and the USSR. Eight days later, the Russian Duma indirectly illustrated this point by ratifying the 1995 Status of Forces Agreement (SoFA) with NATO, thereby demonstrating Russia's increasing interest in international cooperation on security matters. Despite all of the anti-NATO and anti-Western sentiments that were certainly aired during the discussion, the agreement was accepted by a clear majority of votes.[49]

It is noteworthy that the issue of the SoFA ratification was presented to the deputies as a necessity to increase *international* cooperation on security matters, not cooperation with NATO countries per se. Russia has associated itself with a multilateral framework of agreements between NATO countries and with 41 other states currently participating in the Partnership for Peace program (PfP), including almost all European states as well as Armenia, Azerbaijan, Georgia, Kazakhstan, Kyrgyzstan, Moldova, Ukraine, and Uzbekistan.[50] Some of these countries, namely Kazakhstan, Kyrgyzstan, and Uzbekistan, were Russian allies under the provisions of the Treaty on Collective Defense; while others, like Azerbaijan and Ukraine, had a Russian military presence on their territories. It is expected that SoFA may help to consolidate interactions between NATO, the European Union, its member-states, and other countries in the areas where they have common interests—starting with the issues of antiterror, international crisis management, counternarcotics, nuclear proliferation, natural disasters, and technogenous catastrophes.[51] Clearly, all of these areas of cooperation are important for international actors with global interests, be it Europe, Russia, or the United States.

At the same time, it must be admitted that a certain period of Europe-Russia-U.S. relations has ended, while a new one has yet to begin. Perhaps this is why the current situation is, in fact, balanced between divergent short-term incentives, thus complicating the means for elaborating any long-term strategic perspectives and shifting the currently irresolvable issues to an uncertain future. On such terms, no qualitative breakthrough can be expected soon, let alone a sustainable joint strategy. Still, it is also clear that all the sides will have to work together wherever possible.

The increasing ease of communication and travel, coupled with the interdependence of finance and trade and the increase of liberal domestic governance, has connected the global community in ways not seen before. Globalization is a dynamic process and has changed the static calculation of power and interest within the entire European-Russian-U.S. security nexus generally, but most particularly as those interests relate to China—the world's most dynamic economy. Ultimately, globalization is a force that rewards "the functioning core" with economic growth and stability and punishes the "nonintegrated gap" with stagnation and volatility.[52] Russia and China's policy choices guiding their interconnections will affect their security environment.

The United States and Europe integrated their social processes first. Cordell Hull's supposition that militarized war was preceded by economic war was made into policy by globalizing institutions like the International Bank for Reconstruction and Development, the International Monetary Fund, and the forerunner to the World Trade Organization, the General Agreement on Tariffs and Trade. Following the dissolution of the Soviet Union, Russia moved away from a command economy and has carefully chosen the terms of its economic intercourse with Europe and the United States. Clearly it is more open since 1991, but the level of interconnection between it and the world is outpaced by the rest of Europe. The upcoming Olympic Winter Games in Sochi will most assuredly serve Russian economic and social globalization. In the past 25 years, China has transformed into a committed believer in global economic institutions while being more skeptical of liberal governance and free communication.

Security has the propensity to change more rapidly in a globalized world system. The promise of globalization is peace and prosperity. Globalization's narrative tells us that security between Europe, Russia, the United States, and China will be more stable the more their economies are interdependent, the more their societies are connected, and the more their governments are liberal. States classically consider security in static terms, in terms of the current balance of power. Information exchange and economic integration, the first fruits of globalization, have made balance-of-power calculations much more difficult at the state level, but have increased cross-border societal and economic connectivity. Successful economic, social and political interconnections between Europe, Russia, the United States, and China will decrease the relevance of maintaining balances of power and create more positive sum outcomes. Given the systemic change promised by globalization, Russia will not have to explicitly choose between U.S./Europe and China. In the absence of the "zero-sum constraint," constructive relations on both its fronts are possible.

NOTES

1. In Western countries, this fact is perfectly understandable, too. For instance, Joseph Nye, in his interview with the Danish newspaper *Politiken* (February 18, 2007) diplomatically mentioned that neither the United States nor Europe has illusions about democracy in Russia anymore. From an academic point of view, however, we might be permitted to add that having no illusions could be just another illusion. Lo notes "As developments in Russia have shown—not only under Putin but also for much of the Yeltsin era—it is absurd to pretend that Russian and Western interpretations of pluralist democracy, a transparent economy and a civil society have much in common. To attempt to construct a viable long-term relationship on such a fragile basis is not only delusionary but counter-productive." Bobo Lo, "Russia and the West: Problems and Opportunities," UNICI Discussion Papers, May 2005, 2.

2. Ekaterina Semykina, "Vpered, nastupiv sebe na nogu" ["Tread on Your Foot and Start Forward"], *Delo,* March 26, 2007.

3. Notably, some distinguished Russian foreign policy analysts already claim that the transition period for Russia has been completed. For many others, however, Russia certainly remains a country in transition from its communist past. See, for example, Daniel Fried, "Russia: In Transition or Intransigent?" Testimony before the Helsinki Commission, Washington, DC, May 24, 2007, http://www.state.gov/p/eur/rls/rm/85479.htm.

4. Whatever this label means, it does not have a dominantly positive connotation in current Russian politics.

5. See, for example, Tor Bukkvoll, "Arming the Ayatollahs: Economic Lobbies in Russia's Iran Policy," *Problems of Post-Communism* (November–December 2002): 37.

6. Lev Gudkov, *Negativnaya Identichnost' [Negative Identity]* (Moskva: 2004), 674.

7. Robert Kagan, "Power and Weakness," *Policy Review* (June–July 2002): 223–33.

8. An early work outlining such forces is John Mearsheimer, "Why We Will Soon Miss the Cold War," *Atlantic Monthly,* August 1990, 35–50.

9. The Commission's Official Statement on the Middle Eastern Peace Process is at http://ec.europa.eu/external_relations/mepp/index.htm.

10. For a more expansive treatment of this idea, see Thomas Mowle, *Allies At Odds? The United States and the European Union* (New York: Palgrave, 2004).

11. Francis Fukuyama, *The End of History and the Last Man* (New York: Free Press, 1992, 2006).

12. Samuel Huntington, *The Clash of Civilizations* (Cambridge, MA: Harvard University Press, 1994); Thomas P. M. Barnett, *The Pentagon's New Map* (Berkeley, CA: Berkeley Trade Press, 2002).

13. Michael Doyle, *Liberalism* (Princeton, NJ: Princeton University Press, 1988); Bruce Russett and John Oneal, *Triangulating the Democratic Peace* (New Haven, CT: Yale University Press, 2004).

14. Thomas Mowle and David Sacko, in *The Unipolar World: An Unbalanced Future* (New York: Palgrave, 2007), propose an extension of Waltz's neorealism that accords with unipolarity. States have three choices in the face of military activity by the dominant power in the international system: 1) counter it with equal military force (balance), 2) do nothing (bystand), or 3) side with the stronger power and hope to share in the gains of the foreign policy (bandwagon). This volume argues that balancing will not be automatic in a unipolar period, but that "bandwagoning" and "bystanding" are likely behaviors.

15. Francis Fukuyama, "The End of History?" *National Interest* 16 (Summer 1989): 50–60.

16. "The National Security Strategy of the United States, 2006," 38, http://www.whitehouse.gov/nsc/nss/2006/.

17. Gebhart Von Moltke, "Ascension of New Members to the Alliance, 1997," http://www.nato.int/docu/review/1997/9704-2.htm.

18. Tedd Galen Carpenter, *NATO Enters the Twenty-First Century* (New York: Routledge, 2002).

19. NATO Missile Defence, http://www.nato.int/issues/missile_defence/index.html.

20. John Inocur, "Trying to Legitimize Missile-Shield Hostility in Germany," *International Herald Tribune,* March 13, 2007, 3.

21. Marc Sageman, *Understanding Terror Networks* (Philadelphia: University of Pennsylvania Press, 2004). Literally translated, Salafism means predecessors or early generations. Salafis view the first five generations of Muslims as examples of how Islam should be practiced. Islam was perfect and complete during the days of Muhammad and his early followers, and any innovation is a fundamental perversion. Global Salafist Jihadism is the political effort to reconfigure the international system to allow this early observance of Islam by vanquishing both near and far enemies that fundamentally run counter to "true" Islam.

22. Samuel P. Huntington, "Patterns of Violence in World Politics," in *Changing Patterns of Military Politics,* ed. Samuel P. Huntington (Boston: Free Press of Glencoe, 1962), 105–38. Numerous contemporary analyses confirm Huntington's classic work; see, for example, Louise Richardson, *The Roots of Terrorism* (New York: Routledge, 2007).

23. For a systematic overview of al Qaeda's grand strategy, see Sayyid Qutb, *Milestones* (Boulder, CO: Kazi Publications, 2003). For Qutb and al Qaeda, jihad is a permanent revolution against internal and external enemies whom they believe have perverted and appropriated Islam's fundamental nature. As Fawaz A. Gerges points out in *The Far Enemy: A New Definition of Jihad* (Cambridge: Cambridge University Press, 2005), this is not only a minority view, but a true perversion of Islam from the point of view of the majority of Islamic scholars.

24. Fawad Gerges, http://www.buzzle.com/editorials/10-17-2005-79122.asp.

25. Thérèse Delpech, "International Terrorism and Europe," *Chaillot Papers,* no. 56.

26. Andreas Ulrich, Holger Stark, Cordula Meyer, and Dominik Cziesche, "The Changing Threat of al Qaeda: How Widespread is Terrorism in Europe?" *Der Spiegel,* July 11, 2005, 1.

27. Ibid.

28. Ahto Lobjakas, "Brussels Mulls Over Its Energy Sources," Radio Free Europe, June 2, 2006.

29. Ilan Greenberg, "Russia to Get Central Asian Pipeline," *New York Times,* May 13, 2007, 15.

30. Ilan Greenberg and Andrew Kramer, "Cheney, Visiting Kazakhstan, Wades Into Energy Battle," *New York Times,* May 6, 2006, 20.

31. Roman Kupchinsky, "Gazprom Stares Down the West," Radio Free Europe, April 24, 2006.

32. A position recently articulated by the *Economist,* "A Bear at the Throat," April 17, 2007, 5.

33. Chrystia Freeland, "Criticism Stings, But It Beats Indifference," *Moscow Times,* July 7, 2006, 6–7.

34. Ibid.

35. According to Russian media, the country's arms exports were lagging behind the ones of the United States, France, and possibly Great Britain in recent years. See Igor Naumov, "Oruzhejnyj proryv" ["Arms Breakthrough"], *Nezavisimaya gazeta,* May 29, 2006, http://www.ng.ru/economics/2006-05-29/4_oruzhie.html.

36. "Eksport-import Rossii vaznejshih tovarov za yanvar'-mart 2007 goda" ["Export-Import of Most Important Russian Goods in January–March 2007"], http://www.customs.ru/ru/stats/ekspress/detail.php?id286=3660.

37. See "Ministr torgovli SSHA vyskazal nam vse za glaza" [The U.S. Trade Minister Told Us Everything Sight Unseen"], Izvestiya, April 5, 2007, http://www.izvestia.ru/economic/article3102839.

38. As it has been pointed out in recent Russian writings on inter-civilizational rivalry, it has become unsatisfactory to consider a traditional world "triangle of civilizational forces" (the West–Islamic World–China) as "we are present at the beginning of an even more dramatic act than the clash of the Western and Islamic civilizations—the act of civilizational, not just economic, division between the European Union and the U.S." Translated from Delyagin M. Rossiya, *Krizisy Globalisasii Politicheskij Klass,* no. 14 (2006).

39. See "Sem' prichin ne zabyvat' o Rossii" ["Seven Reasons Not to Forget about Russia"], Rosbalt Information Agency, http://www.rosbalt.ru/2004/01/26/140488.html.

40. Robert H. Donaldson and Joseph L. Nogee, *The Foreign Policy of Russia: Changing Systems, Enduring Interests* (Armonk, NY: M. E. Sharp, 2005), 368.

41. Understandably, Russia was seen as a threat for both Europe and the United States for a long period of time, too. That is why Russia's continuing partnership with the United States was often regarded as "paradoxical in that Putin maintained it even in the face of the U.S. policies that conflicted with important Russian interests, notably, antimissile defense, NATO expansion, the war in Iraq, and NATO intervention in the space of the former USSR. The likely explanation to this paradox is Putin pragmatism. He reconciled his administration to policies that were inevitable, those he could not prevent." Donaldson and Nogee, *Foreign Policy of Russia.* Two things, however, could be added here. First, any paradoxes seem to exist in human understanding of reality, rather than in reality as such. Second, any pragmatic deal, or pragmatic mode of behavior, must imply existence of mutually acceptable benefits; otherwise, any deal seems impossible to make in practice.

42. Understandably, a radar in the Czech Republic and 10 air-defense interceptors in Poland could not present an immediate threat for nuclear Russia. However, the very existence of a tendency that "new" European borders with Russia could solidify in the coming years

while Russia-China military cooperation may continue can not be regarded as a positive symptom.

43. Dmitri Litovkin, "Rossijskie posol'stva stanut chast'ju PRO" ["Russian Embassies will be Part of Antimissile System"], *Izvestiya,* March 20, 2007.

44. Madina Shavlokhova and Gennagy Savchenko, "'Iskander'—Schit, 'Satanenok'— Mech" ["'Iskander' is a Shield, 'Little Satan' is a Sword"], *Gazeta,* 96 (May 30, 2007): 2.

45. As it was noted, "Realists are rather skeptical as regards globalization and believe that its implications for international relations are overestimated. 'Power politics,' 'balance of power,' 'national interests' are still the most valuable theoretical categories for them. Realists view globalization mostly as the militarization of the international system and the emergence of the patterns of political control and domination which extend beyond borders (such as hegemonic control or spheres of influence), but they reject the idea of globalization is accompanied by a deepening sense of community." Alexander Sergounin, "The Russian Post-Communist Discourse on Globalization and Global Governance," *Post–Cold War Challenges to International Relations* (St. Petersburg: St. Petersburg State University Press, 2006), 237.

46. See, for example, Izabel Fransua, "Otkat k Holodnoj vojne vozmozhen lish' v umah ljudej, kotorum ne dostaet voobrazheniya" ["A Throw-Back to Cold War Is Only Possible in Minds of Those who Lack Imagination"], http://www.interfax.ru/r/B/exclusive/22.html? menu=1&id_issue=11755827.

47. Olga Semenova, "Possiya gotova sovmestno s NATO i SSHA sozdavat' evropejskuju PRO," ["Russia is Ready to Construct European Antimissile System Together with NATO and the U.S."], http://www.rian.ru/politics/20070430/64692840.html.

48. Arshad Mohammed, "Putin and Rice Agree Rhetoric Must be Toned Down," Reuters, May 15, 2007. Nonetheless, soon after announcing the informal agreement in Novo-Ogaryovo, public rhetoric in U.S.-Russian relations, in fact, substantively intensified, thus making current divergence in short-term political priorities even more evident.

49. Voting results were 328 ballots for (72.9 percent) and 90 ballots against (20 percent), while 32 deputies did not cast their votes (7.1 percent) and none abstained. See "Dnevnoe plenarnoe zasedanie Gosdumy 23 maja 2007 goda" ("Day-work Plenary Meeting of the State Duma from May 23, 2007"), Shorthand transcription No. 231 (945). (Shorthand transcription: "O ratifikatsii Soglasheniya mezhdy gosudarstvami-uchastnikami Severoatlanticheskogo dogovora i drugimi gosudarstvami, uchastvujuschimi v programme 'Partnerstvo radi mira', o statuse ih Sil ot 19 ijunya 1995 goda i Dopolnitel'nogo protokola k nemy"), http://www.duma.org.ru.

50. Ibid.

51. Ibid.

52. Barnett, *Pentagon's New Map,* 25–27.

8

Central Asian States and Policy Triangles: China, Russia, and the United States

Gregory Gleason and Zhang Jiadong

The contemporary international security situation in Central Asia has recent origins. When the USSR disintegrated in the early 1990s, the states of Kazakhstan, Kyrgyzstan, Uzbekistan, Tajikistan, and Turkmenistan were quickly and unexpectedly—as one observer expressed it—"catapulted" into existence as separate states.[1] While Central Asia was home to ancient societies, none of the five Central Asian countries had ever existed as an independent state within its present borders prior to the Soviet period. The political leaders in the Central Asian countries were not among the most ardent promoters of Soviet disintegration, but when the USSR came to its conclusion, the Soviet-era leaders of these new Central Asian states expressed relief that the "Bolshevik experiment" had come to an end. Kazakhstan's Nursultan Nazarbaev, who was then a leading Soviet communist party official, was among the most articulate in discarding communism. Nazarbaev announced to a surprised audience of Kazakh legislators in 1991 that the abandonment of the communist system was "only common sense."[2]

In the initial period after the Soviet collapse, some Western observers comprehended the postcommunist period as a linear transition from the communist model to Western-style institutions. Many Western policymakers, in the spirit of this "transitological" conception of the Soviet collapse, were apprehensive of the danger of postcommunist recidivism.[3] Consequently, a great deal of Western policy effort was specifically focused on preventing a return to communist rule. But these assumptions proved unfounded; there was only negligible and ineffectual effort in Russia to return to communist rule, and virtually no effort at all in the Central Asian countries.

The Central Asian former communist party leaders quickly and smoothly segued into new national political posts of the newly independent states. They proclaimed that their governments were, in form and function, returning to conventional and normal principles of secular, democratically oriented, and market-based independent countries.

It was in this context that Central Asian political leaders undertook to bring their governments and societies into conformance with internationally accepted standards of policy and practice of government, commerce, trade, and international diplomacy. But as the first decade of independence progressed, the Central Asian states found themselves in increasingly challenging economic circumstances. The broad economic structural adjustment required of the move from the command economy to a market economy was massive. The collapse of communism was followed by a severe economic depression throughout the region. Public infrastructure necessary for transportation, communication, education, and electric power, already suffering from long-postponed maintenance in the latter years of Soviet power, further deteriorated in the first years of post-Soviet independence. Many Soviet-era industrial enterprises, never designed to compete on world markets, were shuttered, liquidated, or simply abandoned. The newly independent governments struggled to define new roles and responsibilities as privatization shifted the countries' standing capital into a new private sector, for which the governments had not yet solidified reliable and legitimate systems for the protection of property rights and for the impartial adjudication of disputes. Ordinary commerce and cross-border trade became increasingly complicated, convoluted, and difficult, crowding out many entrepreneurs who sought to comply with formal legislation.

The increasing complexity of the security situation paralleled the trends in the economic situation. In the first days of independence, the Central Asian leaders saw themselves as entering a relatively stable security situation. The Soviet war in Afghanistan had already been brought to a close. The animosity toward the American superpower seemingly evaporated with the disintegration of the USSR. The nuclear arms race was brought under rein in July 1991 with the signing of the START I agreement, reversing decades of mounting tension. With the signing of the Lisbon Protocol in May 1992, Kazakhstan committed itself to the expeditious elimination of its nuclear weapons stockpile, receiving in return nuclear security assurances from the United States and Russia.[4] The initial relaxation of the security environment for the new Central Asia states, however, proved to be short-lived. Security conditions deteriorated for a number of reasons, but two factors stood out as particularly prominent—the nuclear security environment and the rise of threats from nonstate actors.

In signing the Lisbon Protocol, the Kazakh authorities had assumed the responsibilities of complying with the nonproliferation commitments of the Non-Proliferation Treaty (NPT). The Kazakh authorities were encouraged to assume that other countries in the Central and South Asian regions would do likewise in complying with the NPT. The Central Asian leaders were also given to understand that Russian post-Soviet strategic designs would remain respectful of the national sovereignty of the Central Asian countries. However, by the late 1990s it became clear that these assumptions were less than well founded.[5] The Indian nuclear weapons test in mid-May 1998 was soon followed later that month by a number of nuclear "devices" tests by Pakistan.[6] The tests demonstrated that Pakistan had overcome all the major hurdles on the nuclear path. The tests sent signals of alarm through the entire security environment in the region, as the political ramifications of Pakistan's policies intensified rather than subsided.[7] While Pakistan's nuclear strategy was narrowly directed at altering its bilateral relations with India, it had the effect of introducing, in President Zia ul-Haq's words, the "Islamic nuclear bomb."[8]

The Pakistan nuclear test also had the effect of reshaping the security balance throughout South Asia and the Middle East. The specter of Pakistan's Islamic bomb, although it was never openly described as such, could be comprehended as a *Sunni Islamic bomb*. Pakistan's changing status did not draw forth a broad Muslim coalition under the banner of Muslim solidarity. On the contrary, it led to redoubled efforts in Iran to develop a *Shiite Islamic bomb* and develop its own nuclear capability. As a member of the Non-Proliferation Treaty, Iran did have the right to develop nuclear power for non-weapon purposes, but it also had an international legal commitment not to undertake the production or maintenance of weapons-grade fissile materials. Criticism arose as it became increasingly apparent that Iran was engaged in uranium enrichment. However, Iran insisted that its actions were consistent with its rights. In July 2006, the UN Security Council passed a resolution demanding that Iran "suspend all enrichment-related and reprocessing activities, including research and development" pending the satisfaction of IAEA oversight requirements.[9] Defiant Iranian leaders continued to proceed with a nuclear weapons development program.[10] The Central Asian countries now face a situation in which they are protected by only modest conventional defense capabilities but are surrounded by states with towering strategic military capabilities.[11]

Meanwhile, new security threats in Central Asia emerged from nonstate actors consisting of extremists, terrorists, separatists, organized crime syndicates, and revolutionary fanatics. Beset by fears of terrorism, organized crime, economically motivated migration, and the loss of political control, the governments of the Central Asian region struggled to reimpose control over their peoples, their societies, their economies, and even their neighbors. In the late 1990s, all of the Central Asian countries adopted counterinsurgency programs to combat the rising influence of such revolutionary organizations as the Islamic Movement of Uzbekistan and Hizb-ut-Tahrir.[12]

Security conditions were bringing the interests of major powers in alignment with the interests of Central Asian states as they witnessed the descent into internecine warfare and lawlessness in Afghanistan. By the late 1990s, this confluence of interests even led to close diplomatic collaboration between Russia and the United States on the Afghanistan problem as the two countries jointly sponsored the adoption of UN sanctions against the Taliban government.[13] The terrorist attack on the United States in September 2001 vastly accelerated these trends. The September 11 terrorist acts quickly led back to Osama bin Laden's al Qaeda and shocked the United States into taking an active role in preventative military defense. The United States demanded that the Taliban government, the Islamic Emirate of Afghanistan, hand over Osama bin Laden and eliminate terrorist basing and training. U.S. demands were ignored by the Taliban government. In response, the United States organized and led Operation Enduring Freedom to eliminate the terrorists who had planned and carried out the September 11 attacks and to reestablish a legitimate government in Afghanistan. The United States requested and quickly received support from all the Central Asian governments in meeting the challenge from the Taliban. And, the United States spearheaded an international coalition dedicated to the normalization and reconstruction of Afghanistan and was aided by the agreement of Central Asian leaders to the deployment of Western military forces in Central Asian countries.

The risks and opportunities inherent in the political dynamics of the Central Asian region have led to increased foreign policy engagement, particularly by China, Russia, and the United States. Given the history of the region, Russia has had a long-standing influence in Central Asia. China's buoyant economic growth in the past two decades, its widening geopolitical influence, and the proximity to Central Asia imply that Chinese policy will have a permanent role in the region. The United States is widely viewed by Central Asian officials as having a dominant role in international affairs given that it is the only country that acts globally, has extensive vital interests abroad, and has military and strategic capabilities that far exceed that of other countries. For these reasons, the United States is viewed in Central Asian chancelleries as a permanent factor in Central Asian affairs, although there is considerable difference of opinion over what level of permanent presence this implies.

The resulting triangular relationships are very complicated. Russia, China, and the United States have many common interests in the region, but also have many competing and even conflicting interests. Chinese and American presence in Central Asia is a valuable counterweight for Central Asian officials in moments when they perceive Moscow's policy as reviving chauvinist Great Power hegemonic designs on the region. Central Asian officials view China not only in terms of its increased global economic role, but also in terms of its sheer size, literally dwarfing the Central Asian states and reducing their ability to negotiate as equal partners.[14] The Sino-Russian rapprochement of recent years offers Central Asian officials a countervailing force against fears of U.S. foreign policy unilateralism. For these and many other reasons, the triangular relationships are viewed by Central Asian strategic planners as both necessary and potentially hazardous. Consequently, these relationships require a certain amount of savvy diplomacy as the Central Asia countries seek to find ways to pursue their own interests, satisfy the interests of their regional neighbors and the interests of the Great Powers, and offer optimal paths to international cooperation.

How are optimal paths to such mutually advantageous cooperation found? The identification of optimal paths involves calculations on a number of levels simultaneously. In what follows, we first analyze the context of foreign policy making in Central Asia. Second, we survey the interests, values, capabilities, and policies of the major countries. Third, we briefly analyze the domestic context of foreign policy making in each of the Central Asian countries. Finally, we conclude with a discussion of some of the opportunities and risks of international cooperation in Central Asia.

CENTRAL ASIAN FOREIGN POLICIES: ENDS AND MEANS

Central Asia consists of countries with common backgrounds, common values, and many common interests. But that should not imply to outsiders that the leaders and official establishments in these countries can be expected always to perceive things identically, value things in the same way, and act in ways that are in the best interests of the region. Central Asians often perceive the same thing in very different ways. For instance, many Uzbeks supported improved relations with the United States during the period 2001 to 2005, because for them it represented recognition of the importance of Uzbekistan in Central Asia. Uzbek neighbors could see the same things differently, however. Doulatbek Khidirbekughli, a perceptive Kazakh analyst of international relations, interpreted U.S. policy in Uzbekistan in terms of the larger regional relationships, noting that "September 11, 2001 offered an opportunity for the expansion of U.S. influence in Central Asia as a part of Eurasian heartland, *of which Kazakhstan is the center.*"[15]

Motivations of policymakers in the Central Asian states are not always open to easy comprehension by outside analysts. But there are a few general principles that are applicable to the analysis of foreign policy making throughout the region. First, the Central Asian countries share a number of common traditions. These countries are occupying a common geographical space, and are closely linked in terms of mutual dependence upon the physical infrastructure for transportation and communication. Second, the countries share a common set of advantages and risks associated with the nexus between water and energy. Third, the countries are also alike in that their political systems are all marked by an extraordinary concentration of power in the hands of the executive. These common features incline the countries to act similarly. In many other respects, the countries are quite different. The Central Asian countries have differing foreign policy goals and foreign policy strategies. They have a very different set of domestic influences on foreign policy formulation. In some cases, their goals and strategies are compatible; in some cases, they are not. Even when the goals of the countries differ, there are instances of complementary exchanges that, with good leadership and a little luck, can lead to mutual gains from cooperation. But there are some issues on which the countries simply stand at loggerheads with one another.

The Central Asian states exist in a complex geographical, economic, and political context. The variegated patterns of boundaries, natural resources, fixed physical infrastructure, and foreign areas of interchange and engagement have created a complex pattern of state-to-state relations. In all situations, of course, states act. They often must act. For this reason, foreign policy is most simply conceptualized in accordance with a simple model that views the state as a purposive organization pursuing objectives through strategies. The function of strategy is to bring ends into line with means. Any country's national security strategy must be built on key assumptions about what is possible and what is desirable. What is possible is a function of the state's capabilities. What is desirable is a function of values, capabilities, and opportunities afforded by the international policy environment. Policy, in the simplest sense, is a line of action.

In theory, policymakers work toward their goals by taking specific steps along a line of action. In reality, however, the actions that are undertaken may have a variety of motives and inducements that can vary substantially from the overall objectives as the possible crowds out the desirable. The possible is often influenced by what is beneficial; but beneficial not only to the public interest, but also to the values and interests of the group that is doing the implementing. Carrying out day-to-day activities follows prescriptions about what is directed, what is required, what is permissible, what is possible, what is likely to work. On yet a different level, the strategies are carried out not only with respect to abstract public interests, but also with respect to internal divisions, competition over span of discretion (fights over turf), symbolic rather than real goals, perceptions, and timing. In Central Asia, the complex pattern of crosscutting objectives and relations among states often makes the pursuit of particular objectives difficult, requiring high-level policymakers to insist upon submissive carrying out of directives rather than risk autonomy, innovation, and the intervention of relations-based rather than directive-based implementation of government directives.

The leaders of the Central Asian states have been keenly aware of the importance of more innovative approaches to problem solving on a regional basis. Outside actors, particularly the major players, have also been keenly aware of the nexus of security and economic issues in Central Asia. But the major powers have very different perspectives on how cooperation should be structured and pursued. This reflects the interests, the perceptions, and the conceptual policy framework of the major powers. For instance, even on a single issue on which there is substantial international agreement, there are differences in nuance in approach that may have substantial effects on how cooperative actions are implemented. The terrorism issue is a good example. The United States faces an immediate danger from a large, well-financed collection of enemies with a broad, long-term agenda of hostility. China, on the other hand, faces a lower level of terror threat that is primarily focused on a single issue, separatism. Even though the United States, Russia, and China all share common interests in combating terrorism, their intentions and goals are very different. The United States seeks to maintain and reinforce its global strategic influence, while China's main concern is maintaining the stability of Xinjiang province. Russia is yet more selective, seeking primarily to interdict foreign assistance to rebels in Chechnya. Consequently, the representatives of the three governments can meet with Central Asian officials and come to rhetorically quite robust agreements about what to do, but when the articulated policy is transformed into lines of action, the outcome can be different than what was expected or desired.

CENTRAL ASIA'S INTERNATIONAL CONTEXT: CHINA, RUSSIA, AND THE UNITED STATES

Outside powers exert their influence in the Central Asian region in ways that are consonant with their interests as well as their style. Differences in style reflect differences in values and ways of understanding international affairs. The foreign policies of China, Russia, and the United States are based in different traditions, reflect different values and perceptions, and are the product of differing diplomatic, military, and economic capacities.

Chinese foreign policy consists of a synthesis of historically conditioned values and contemporary influences. Contemporary Chinese foreign policy is highly practical, goal-oriented, and materially motivated. But policy calculations of cost and benefit in China are typically not made as a result of abstract assessments of current correlations of forces. Calculations are more likely made in terms of long-term goals that are deeply rooted in Chinese historical and psychological experience. Many of the values and objectives regarding interaction with the outside world are widely believed in China to flow naturally out of the common past. As a consequence, the subject of Chinese foreign policy is simply not a matter of major debate. It is taken as a given that the People's Republic of China's foreign policy should be oriented toward creating a strong, powerful, and united China that plays a role in the international community as a Great Power and is recognized as such. Chinese strategic thinkers tend to view current international relations as a competition between states acting out of self-interest in ways similar to the historical experience of China, particularly the period of Warring States. As a consequence, Chinese calculations tend toward classical realism and regard ideological approaches, whether democratic liberalism or utopian idealism, as impractical.

China's practical orientation in contemporary policy may be attributed to a shift in policy objectives in the late 1970s under the leadership of Deng Xiaoping, when China initiated market-oriented reforms. Deng stressed that China was and would continue to be a socialist society, but the Communist Party would lead toward "socialism with Chinese characteristics." This interpretation of Chinese Marxism reduced the role of ideology in economic decision making and oriented the society toward effectiveness and accomplishment. A thaw in diplomatic relations with the Western world was followed by increasing acceleration of government policy changes aimed at opening China to foreign markets. Market-oriented reforms that were begun in China under the direction of Communist Party leaders in the late 1970s have increased to such an extent that what had previously been a state-administered bureaucratic economy has become a state-directed market economy. Opening to international trade has given rise to a dramatic growth in the private sector, the emergence of private sector enterprises, the development of a commercial banking system, and the emergence of entrepreneurial independence. China has put increasing emphasis on the practical improvement of conditions by sustaining exceptionally large annual economic growth rates for more than two decades and pulling hundreds of millions of people out of poverty.

The political organization of the state has incrementally adapted to the changes in the social fabric, but has not changed in structure. The Chinese constitution places ultimate power in the hands of the National People's Congress, the delegates of which are elected by municipal, regional, and provincial people's congresses to serve five-year terms. Chinese foreign policy has long sought to steer clear of conflicts over systemic competition, but has not avoided considerable disagreement over very practical issues such as border delineation and disputed territorial claims. In October 1962, a border dispute resulted in the Sino-Indian War. A Sino-Soviet border conflict arose in 1969, while the Sino-Vietnam War was fought in 1979. Territorial disputes include islands in the East China and South China seas, and disputed borders with India, Tajikistan, and North Korea continue right up to the present day.

China's diplomatic influence dramatically increased with the shift during the 1990s to a pragmatic, realistic foreign policy aimed at stabilizing relations with immediate neighbors and solidifying commercial relations with its major trade partners, particularly the United States. China's diplomatic and military relations steered close to a set of practical and realistic strategic goals, the so-called Five Principles of Peaceful Co-existence: mutual respect for sovereignty and territorial integrity, mutual nonaggression, noninterference in others' internal affairs, equality and mutual benefit, and peaceful coexistence in international relations. The new security concept was enunciated by the People's Republic of China in the late 1990s. The pragmatic idea is that in the post–Cold War period, nations are able to increase their security through diplomatic and economic interaction, rather than through confrontational posturing for ideological advantage. About the time that Hu Jintao took office in March 2003, the security policy increasingly came to be referred to as the doctrine of "China's peaceful rise."

The chief question on which Chinese strategic thinkers have focused involves the relationship with the United States. The dilemma is that, on the one hand, the United States may be an obstacle to China's rise to being a great power, while at the same time, the United States is also indispensable to China's rise. This forms the background for Chinese policy with respect to the Central Asian countries and Afghanistan. In the late 1970s and 1980s, Deng Xiaoping's leadership remained wary of the Soviet Union, for fear that Moscow's claim to ideological leadership in the Marxist world would amount to hegemonic control. The Shanghai Treaty of 1996 was the start of a long process that began in the 1980s and, following the collapse of the USSR, led to multilateral negotiations regarding border normalization and eventually led to the establishment of the Shanghai Cooperation Organization. Russia and China in July 2001 signed the Treaty of Good-Neighborliness, Friendship and Cooperation, bringing an end to a long-standing dispute over islands in the Ussuri River between China and Russia. After the American military presence in Central Asia arose in connection with Operation Enduring Freedom, China increasingly shifted its stance to closer alignment with Russia. China's relations with the Central Asian states are clearly in the context of relations with Russia and the United States.

The Chinese leadership's view of the country as having a limited role in the global war on terrorism is reflected in the fact that there is no official general definition of terrorism. The Chinese leadership continues to view terrorism as a law enforcement issue. The Chinese legal basis for defining terrorist acts and terrorist organizations consists primarily of the "Criminal Law of the PRC" and its 3rd Amendment (December 29, 2001) and the "National Security Law of the PRC" and its detailed rules.[16] Terrorism is also defined by a number of international agreements.[17] Generally, terrorism is regarded as the use of terror or violence as a means to harm China's national security, to destabilize society, or to jeopardize private life and property.

It is clear that various terrorist activities have been under way in Xinjiang since the 1950s. Incomplete statistics showed that from 1990 to 2001, the East Turkestan terrorist forces inside and outside Chinese territory were responsible for over 200 terrorist incidents in Xinjiang, resulting in the deaths of 162 people of all ethnic groups, including grassroots officials and religious personnel, and injuries to more than 440 people. Some of the Uighur terrorist organizations have ideological and possibly even operational links to Hizb-ut-Tahrir (the Party of Liberation) and the Hizb-i-Islami Turkestan (the Islamic Party of Turkestan). Their objective is the creation of an Islamic republic out of the five Central Asian Republics and Xinjiang. It is difficult to quantify the extent of the influence of Osama bin Laden and his International Islamic Front on the pan-Islamic elements in Xinjiang. According to Chinese official sources, before October 7, 2001, about 1,000 Uighur extremists and separatists had been trained in Afghanistan by al Qaeda. Given these challenges, China's new security concept features dialogue and cooperation as an appropriate means for confronting these threats.[18]

China's foreign policy style is considerably different than the Russian approach. Russian policy in the region has been deeply influenced by the past. Putin's public statement in late 1999 that Russia was a "Eurasian power" had already set the stage for a reexamination of Russia's strategy toward Central Asia. The "Russian National Security Strategy" of January 2000 and the "Russian Foreign Policy Strategy," adopted in July 2000 following Vladimir Putin's formal election as Russian president on March 25, 2000, formalized Russia's reassessment of its foreign policies in general and its relations with, Europe, Asia, the Middle East, and Central Asia and the Caucasus.[19] Important changes were included in the approach to the Central Asian states. It was a foreign policy statement that acknowledged and accepted Russia's much-diminished role in foreign affairs. And it was a foreign policy statement that was distinguished by its appeal to pursue mutually advantageous "partnerships" with foreign countries in lieu of the idealistic and ideologically inspired foreign policy objectives of the past.

Russia's new foreign policy received its formal initiation in an extensive round of diplomatic exchanges that took place in spring and summer 2000, as the Putin government undertook a systematic effort to articulate its new "Asia policy." Judging from the government's rhetorical statements and the content of the numerous joint communiqués signed during the May-July 2000 round of diplomatic meetings in Moscow, Tashkent, Dushanbe, Beijing, Pyongyang, and Okinawa during this period, the Putin government was seeking to reestablish its posture in Asia. Russia's new policy toward southern Eurasia—that is toward the Caucasus countries of Armenia, Azerbaijan, and Georgia and the Central Asian countries of Kazakhstan and Kyrgyzstan, Tajikistan, Turkmenistan, and Uzbekistan—was almost wholly without grandiose conceptions of Russian designs throughout the region. Once openly described as "younger brothers," the newly independent states of the Caucasus and Central Asia were regarded in the new policy formulations as "partners." More recently, Russian policy has been aimed primarily at the policy harmonization regarding customs and information sharing among agencies. A number of programs have been implemented, including educational programs aimed at higher education, physical infrastructure investment in energy and transportation, and commercial investment in energy, minerals, and banking. The Russian government has also been concerned with arms sales as both a way to reestablish one of the most important phalanxes of its previous global influence and as a way to generate jobs and revenue for Russian heavy industry. Russia's objectives in its foreign policies with respect to the Central Asian countries is closely connected to its objectives for its domestic development.

U.S. foreign policy strikes a major contrast with both China's and Russia's policy toward the Central Asian region. The United States has important interests in Central Asia, but these interests are essentially derivative of other more basic, more vital, and more global interests. They also reflect different values. The United States tends to be idealistic in consistently maintaining that the quality of government is an important antecedent to other material and geopolitical considerations.

The U.S. strategy is articulated in the National Security Strategy of the United States, which appeared in September 2002. The strategy outlines America's goals and means to pursue those goals. The strategy says that "We will defend the peace by fighting terrorists and tyrants. We will preserve the peace by building good relations among the great powers. We will extend the peace by encouraging free and open societies on every continent."[20] The "National Strategy for Combating Terrorism," which appeared in 2003 and was revised in September 2006, was more specific in outlining that the U.S. strategy in the war on terrorism sought "to integrate nations and peoples into the mutually beneficial democratic relationships that protect against the forces of disorder and violence."[21]

The United States consistently stresses that democracy and the rule of law are ends in themselves and, further, are quite apart from destabilizing, most likely to generate legitimacy and therefore stability. The United States maintains that repression, the lack of the respect for human rights and religious freedom, can be expected only to perpetuate inequality, exacerbate grievance, and radicalize the population. The lack of fundamental freedoms is likely to generate recruits for extremist organizations. For these reasons, the U.S. government has regarded assistance programs as investments in improving the conditions of government. The United States has done this through funding activities aimed at building civil society, promoting democratic and free-market reform, combating criminal activities and terrorism, and promoting regional security through counterproliferation, counterterrorism, and counternarcotics cooperation.

THE DOMESTIC CONTEXT OF CENTRAL ASIAN FOREIGN POLICIES

Kazakhstan's objectives and capabilities define its pro-globalization strategy. Kazakhstan emerged from the USSR with a deliberate goal of establishing a democratic system and a market-oriented economy. Kazakhstan's nuclear status, its oil and mineral wealth, its enthusiasm for structural reform, and its mixed Kazakh and Russian populations have been defining influences on the domestic political context of foreign policy making during the first years of independence.

Kazakhstan's integration into the fabric of institutions of the international community proceeded more swiftly and more fully than did that of its neighbors. Almaty quickly became the most significant diplomatic center in the region, home to embassies from all the major countries of the world and representatives of international organizations. During the first years of Nazarbayev's presidential tenure in Kazakhstan, his diplomatic efforts were consistently associated with the concept of "Eurasian-ness," the idea of close linkages among the peoples of the Central Eurasian landmass. Based on the idea of "Eurasian integration," Kazakhstan's foreign policy followed a careful line, balancing interests based upon many factors. Balancing interests implied not turning away from Russia, while at the same time not permitting Russia to dominate decision making for Kazakhstan. For Kazakhstan, this meant maintaining a balanced distance from Russia, remaining neither too close nor too distant. Maintaining good relations with the West and international organizations was an ideal instrument for achieving what Kazakh policymakers eventually began to refer to as Kazakhstan's "multi-vector" foreign policy. A primary motive, perhaps the primary motive, for Kazakhstan's globalization policy was the goal of preventing the reemergence of Russian domination in the region.

Kazakhstan's economic and political development since independence is indeed impressive. On an annual basis, Kazakhstan's economy has grown at a rapid clip, probably exceeding 10 percent per year for the past five years. Kazakhstan's economic success is attributable to good policy. Kazakhstan set out on a course of market reform as soon as the USSR came to an end. Kazakhstan conducted price liberalization and undertook enterprise privatization in the mid-1990s. Although the economic adjustment was not easy, Kazakhstan's political leaders persevered despite adversity. Even after the Russian economic default in 1998 sent economic shock waves throughout the former USSR, and many Central Asian advisors urged the adoption of a neo-mercantilist "Asian path" for Kazakhstan, Nazarbayev held firm to the market reform orientation, pledging "to continue the promising advances toward an independent, open and free market economy."[22] Kazakhstan's policymakers won accolades from the leadership of international financial institutions. In March 2002, Kazakhstan was listed by the U.S. government and shortly afterwards by the European Union as the first post-Soviet country to succeed in establishing a market economy.[23]

Kyrgyzstan's foreign policy was limited by the country's modest resource base and internally divided political situation. After independence, Kyrgyzstan quickly developed a reputation for being the most pro-reform country in the Central Asian region. It was the first ex-Soviet country to follow the advice of the international donor community and withdraw from the ruble zone. It was the first post-Soviet country to adopt a Western-style civil code and a modern legal and regulatory framework, to liberalize prices, to privatize industry, to open the door to foreign civic organizations, and to undertake electoral reform. It was the first country of the CIS to join the World Trade Organization. However, Kyrgyzstan's limited resources constrained Kyrgyzstan's progress. By the late 1990s the International Monetary Fund began to impose limits on Kyrgyzstan sovereign borrowing. Kyrgyzstan's reputation as the "island of democracy" in Central Asia grew tarnished.[24]

Corruption and favoritism by the leaders of the government led to intense criticism of the Akaev government and eventually to the ouster of Akaev in the so-called "Tulip revolution" in March 2005.[25] A former prime minister, Kurmanbek Bakiev, set a course for political renewal, but Kyrgyzstan's fissiparous internal politics led to scandals and internal divisions. Bakiev found that Kyrgyzstan was dependent upon foreign assistance for economic help and security protection, but also found that foreign influence often pushed in opposing directions. Rather than choose an eastern orientation over a western orientation, or vice versa, Kyrgyzstan authorities sought to support both. Russian military forces were allowed to locate at the Kant airbase not far from Bishkek, and U.S. forces were allowed to be stationed at the Manas Ganci airbase on the other side of Bishkek. Kyrgyzstan's east-west formula was balanced only in the sense that it represented a dynamic tension between two continually contending influences on the Kyrgyz government. This tension continues to be the most salient feature of Kyrgyzstan's foreign policy.

Tajikistan was the smallest, poorest, and most geographically constrained country of the Eurasian region. Tajikistan would likely have also moved swiftly in the direction of post-Soviet reform initially if the country had not fallen victim to an internal contest for power in the first year of independence. The contest plunged the country into civil war. Tajikistan is a landlocked, mountainous country lacking good transportation routes. The war resulted in a blockade by its neighbors, further compressing the already collapsing Tajikistan economy. CIS peacekeeping forces succeeded in stabilizing the country under a leadership well disposed toward Moscow. However, the Moscow-Dushanbe compact continued to be an irritant with neighboring Uzbekistan for several years, blocking improvement in relations between Moscow and Tashkent. Tajikistan's struggling economy was based almost exclusively on a few mammoth Soviet-era enterprises such as the Turzonzade aluminum smelter and the Vaksh cascade hydroelectric stations.

Tajikistan's close geographical and cultural ties with northern Afghanistan have continued to be a major factor in Tajikistan's foreign policy. The scale of the drug trade originating in Afghanistan and transiting through Tajikistan has been so large that it has continued to exert a damaging influence in Tajikistan. The UN Office for Drug Control's Annual Opium Survey for Afghanistan for 2006 showed the area under opium cultivation in Afghanistan reached a record 165,000 hectares in 2006 compared with 104,000 in 2005, resulting in nearly a 60 percent increase in opium production. The revenue produced by the production of opium, in the words of Antonio Maria Costa, "is making a handful of criminals and corrupt officials extremely rich . . . [and] is also dragging the rest of Afghanistan into a bottomless pit of destruction and despair."[26] Under present conditions, it is impossible for Tajikistan to insulate itself from the effects of the drug trade. Tajik foreign policy is struggling under these conditions to pursue diplomatic alliances that can counter these trends. Tajikistan's vulnerability to these trends is one of the reasons why the country is moving energetically in the direction of developing Tajikistan's hydroelectric potential as plans proceed to create larger, regionwide electric transmission grids in the South Asian region.

Turkmenistan's foreign policy goals since independence have been inextricably tied with the personal goals of the country's illustrious leader, who has now come to be referred to as "Saparmurad Niyazov Turkmenbashi the Great." Soon after independence, Niyazov adopted an assertive posture of national self-reliance based on Turkmenistan's gas and oil wealth. Niyazov eventually came to refer to this as Turkmenistan's policy of "positive neutrality."[27] In practice, the policy meant three things. First, Turkmenistan sought to maintain as much distance as possible from Russia without giving up the big Russian gas market and, most of all, without giving up access to Western gas markets that, by virtue of the possession of the fixed pipeline system, Russia in large measure continued to control. Second, it meant wary policies of self-interest with Turkmenistan's southern neighbors. Third, it meant drawing in foreign investment to the extent possible to revitalize the gas-related industry and build a Kuwait-style emirate in Turkmenistan.

At the beginning, Turkmenistan developed the idea of "positive neutrality" to insulate itself from being linked to Russia. The policy was used as the rationale for building new relationships with Azerbaijan, Iran, and Ukraine, outside of Russia's influence. But the Turkmen government's goal of shipping gas through Azerbaijan fell apart, the idea of the trans-Afghan pipeline was stalled, and Iranian gas sales remained, by all accounts, at a minimal level. The Turkmen government then reversed its position 180 degrees and applauded positive neutrality as the rationale for reestablishing warm relations with Russia, embodied, for instance, in a 25-year marketing contract with Russia's towering natural gas monopoly, Gazprom. Those Turkmen officials who saw the contradiction in this policy were conveniently removed from positions of influence, usually by accusations of corruption followed by prison sentences. International financial institutions discreetly withdrew from conducting many of their operations in Turkmenistan, waiting for an improvement in the governing environment.

Turkmenistan's foreign policy discernibly tilted toward Russia in the days following the death of the country's president on December 21, 2006. The Russian government considers the continuation and improvement of commercial and diplomatic relations with Turkmenistan as vital for a number of reasons. For one thing, Russia has become dependent upon the resale of Turkmenistan gas that it transports to European markets. When Russian President Vladimir Putin used his 2007 New Year's address to announce that Russia "is and will remain a dependable friend of

Turkmenistan," Putin appealed to Turkmenistan's new political leadership, headed by Gurbanguly Berdymukhamedov, to continue to observe recent agreements for commercial relations, most notably the 25-year gas export agreement signed in 2003 that gave Russia the right to market the bulk of Turkmenistan's gas exports.

Uzbekistan's pivotal role in Central Asia, given its physical location in the heart of the region as the only Central Asian country that borders all other Central Asian countries, make it the converging point for energy, water, and transportation infrastructure. Uzbekistan's leaders have aimed at recreating a largely fictional historical role for Uzbekistan as the leading country in the region. Uzbekistan quickly established itself as defiantly nationalist after independence.[28] In a few short years, the country jettisoned virtually the entire legacy of 70 years of Soviet—and thus essentially Russian—political control and cultural influence. Uzbekistan's heavy-handed president, Islam Karimov, who had been a dutiful communist in his Soviet-era incarnation, soon became an enthusiastic champion of an independent political path and an Uzbek cultural renewal.[29] In ways reminiscent of Turkey's Kemal Ataturk, Karimov engineered a determined national consolidation, a new "Uzbek path." Government, economics, culture, and essentially the entire spectrum of policy arenas were harnessed to the drive to "recover" Uzbekistan. Uzbekistan moved toward isolation from Russian influence for several years after the collapse of the USSR. Uzbekistan attenuated Russian cultural influence, disestablished widespread instruction in schools of the Russian language, suspended military cooperation, and blocked many forms of commercial interactions with Russia. The initial Uzbek neo-mercantilist strategy aggressively sought diplomatic and commercial ties with a host of countries, partially in order to increase its foreign policy options, but mainly in order to diminish the leverage of Russian diplomats and traders.

After the events of September 11, 2001, Uzbekistan formed a strategic partnership with the United States in order to aid in ousting the Taliban from Afghanistan.[30] But the U.S. partnership came with a host of conditions relating to standards of practice, governance, and civil rights. After chafing at insistent reminders from U.S. officials over civil rights and the right of free association, Uzbekistan reversed its position 180 degrees, abandoning the U.S. partnership and shifting back to closer relations with Russia.[31] The opprobrium that had been heaped on Russia for years turned virtually overnight into dithyrambs. After signing the agreement to join the Eurasec, Karimov proudly announced that the reestablishment of close relations with Russia went beyond mere cooperation. Karimov said the new relationship was akin to restoring "union relations" [*soyuznye otnoshenie*], a code word harkening back to the Soviet period.

The Central Asian states have a variety of interests and capacities and thus have bases for both disagreement and agreement. The disagreements can sometimes be alleviated by the influence of outside actors. Sometimes the disagreements are alleviated by the natural inclination of the countries to form coalitions to protect their common interests from the influence of outside actors. In other words, the relationship between internal and external influences is dynamic.

CONCLUSIONS: CONSENSUS, COMPETITION, AND CONFLICT

In the context of dynamic relationships among internal and external influences, there are areas of interaction in which a strong consensus is already apparent or at least can be evoked. In contrast, there are some issue-areas in which cooperative arrangements are likely to be mutually beneficial, but not to all parties to the same extent. These are areas of competition. Then there are some issue-areas in which interactions are likely to lead to disagreement, confrontation, and conflict, or perhaps generate enduring differences in approach. These are areas of conflict.

A number of important issue-areas in Central Asian policy interactions are already characterized by a relatively stable and enduring consensus. These areas include dealing with nonstate actors such as terrorist organizations and separatist movements. They also include nuclear security, particularly with respect to Iran. There is similar consensus regarding the prospects for the collaborative development of infrastructure for energy markets. There is widespread consensus on issues relating to the importance of international commercial and business standards.

There are also a number of important issue-areas in which disagreement over values, mechanisms, and goals among the countries is so significant that pitfalls can be expected in policy. These are the conflictual issues. This includes contrasting views on the presence of foreign military bases, contrasting views regarding monopolistic control over market access, contrasting views on military equipment procurement, and contrasting views on election monitoring and nongovernmental civic organizations. These are the key issues that potentially divide the Central Asian countries and outside powers. For example, Russia and China did not openly oppose the positioning of American military equipment in Central Asia during the initial stages of Operation Enduring Freedom, but did soon afterwards and sent a series of signals to express their dissatisfaction.[32] In October 2003, Defense Minister Sergei B. Ivanov of Russia said that Russia "expected the American military to withdraw from bases in two former Soviet republics in Central Asia once the mission in Afghanistan was completed."[33]

Surely, the jockeying for positions of influence in Central Asia by the major powers is not a new "Great Game." The nineteenth-century notions of capturing territory and resources have no foundation in, or correspondence with, the winning strategies of the twenty-first century. It is useful to leave these idealized romanticisms of the past behind. It is overly simplistic to think only in terms of friends and enemies in the contemporary international context. To argue, for instance, that Uzbekistan's expulsion of U.S. influence (and military forces) from Uzbekistan in 2005 was Russia's gain and America's loss is an oversimplification of what was lost and what was gained in this sequence of events.[34] The essence of good diplomacy is to avoid zero-sum transactions because, in the end, they are frequently less than zero. Russia's gain from pressuring for the exclusion of the U.S. military presence in Uzbekistan was not what it immediately appeared to be. But the issue of military presence continues to be a sensitive issue that requires diplomatic subtlety.

There is also a set of issues in which the Central Asian states have both advantages and disadvantages associated with the influence of outside powers. This is the category of competition. This group of issues may not effortlessly lead to cooperative arrangements but, if handled properly, can lead to virtuous circles of interaction. For instance, the promotion of democracy may be viewed within Central Asia as potentially destabilizing if it is associated with "color revolutions" that are designed to sweep governments—and the political elite, their primary beneficiaries—from power. But at the same time, there is a widespread recognition, even among elites, that good governance is inherently valuable and desirable. Kazakhstan's bid to assume the chairmanship of the Organization for Security and Cooperation in Europe (OSCE) in 2009 is a case in point. Resistance to Kazakhstan's chairmanship in Western countries is regarded among the Kazakh political elite as anachronistic and hypocritical prejudice. It undermines the very principle of self-regulating organizations that are designed to be managed by those who participate in them, not by external influences from above. Excluding Kazakhstan from a management role in the OSCE because of "Asian backwardness," Kazakh protagonists argue, would gain nothing for the authority of the OSCE and would deny Kazakhstan the critical opportunity to assume the discipline that comes with the responsibilities of a leadership role. As the case of Kazakhstan's adoption of democratic principles illustrates, the competitive interactions are the ones that are highly complex and require a great deal of subtlety. They are also the interactions that may lead to great cooperative benefits for all parties.

NOTES

1. Martha Brill Olcott, "Central Asia's Catapult to Independence," *Foreign Affairs* 71, no. 3 (1992): 108–30.

2. See Nazarbaev's speech to the Kazak SSR Supreme Soviet, December 10, 1991, "Vybor—Tsvilizovannoe demokratichskoe Obshchestvo" ["The Choice—A Civilized, Democratic Society"], in Nursultan Nazarbaev, *Pyat' let nezavisimosti [Five Years of Independence]* (Almaty: Kazakstan, 1996), 19–24.

3. Early efforts to explain the collapse of communism stressed a variety of differing approaches, primarily emphasizing transitions as the resolution of political contestation among political constituencies. One tendency was to view the postcommunist transition as a special case of a more generic phenomenon of authoritarian transition. See, for instance, Russell Bova, "The Political Dynamics of the Post-Communist Transition: A Comparative Perspective," *World Politics* 44, no. 1 (1991): 114–21. Other approaches stressed the risks and opportunities of interest groups as drivers in the political dynamic of postcommunist reform. See Philippe C. Schmitter with Terry Lynn Karl, "The Conceptual Travels of Transitologists and Consolidologists: How Far East Should They Attempt to Go?" *Slavic Review* 53, no. 1 (1994): 175–85. Yet other approaches stressed the complexity of postcommunist political development, discouraging simple linear extrapolations of common and familiar political dynamics to explain transitions. See Valerie Bunce, "Should Transitologists be Grounded?" *Slavic Review* 54, no. 1 (1995): 111–27.

4. The START I agreement was signed on July 31, 1991. See http://www.state.gov/www/ global/arms/starthtm/start/toc.html. The Lisbon Protocol was signed on May 23, 1992. See http://www.state.gov/documents/organization/27389.pdf.

5. See Rajan Menon, "In the Shadow of the Bear: Security in Post Soviet Central Asia," *International Security* 20, no. 1 (1995): 149–81.

6. Pakistan conducted a series of weapons tests involving five nuclear devices on May 28, 1998, with an additional nuclear device test on May 30, 1998.

7. See Leonard Weiss, "Pakistan: It's Déjà Vu All Over Again," *Bulletin of the Atomic Scientists* 60, no. 3 (2004): 52–59.

8. Barbara Crossette, "Who Killed Zia?" *World Policy Journal* 22, no. 3 (Fall 2005): 94–102, http://www.worldpolicy.org/journal/articles/wpj05-3/crossette.html.

9. UN Security Council Resolution 1696, July 31, 2006, http://www.un.org/Docs/sc/ unsc_resolutions06.htm. See also IAEA, "Implementation of the NPT Safeguards Agreement in the Islamic Republic of Iran," GOV/2006/53, August 31, 2006, http://www.iaea.org/ Publications/Documents/Board/2006/gov2006-53.pdf.

10. See Tutmos Tretii (pseudonym), "Iranskii yadernyi krisis" ["The Iranian Nuclear Crisis"], Center for Arms Control, Energy and Environmental Studies, Moscow Institute of Physics and Technology, June 2006, http://www.armscontrol.ru/pubs/iran060627.pdf.

11. Stephen J. Blank, *After Two Wars: Reflections on the American Strategic Revolution in Central Asia* (Strategic Studies Institute of the U.S. Army War College, July 2005), http:// www.strategicstudiesinstitute.army.mil/.

12. Gregory Gleason, "The Politics of Counterinsurgency in Central Asia," *Problems of Post-Communism* 48, no. 2 (2002): 2–14.

13. Russia and America cooperated to confront the spread of terrorism and lawlessness in October 1999 when the two states jointly sponsored UN Security Council Resolution 1267 imposing sanctions on Afghanistan. The UN resolution demanded that the Taliban put an end to harboring and training terrorists, surrender suspected terrorist Osama bin Laden, and take steps to reign in the country's opium trade. The Taliban was categorically unwilling to meet the first two UN Security Council demands—it did not agree to the extradition of Osama bin Laden and did not take steps to halt the training of terrorists. In December 2000, the Security Council adopted a harsher set of sanctions. Security Council Resolution 1333 reiterated the demands for the elimination of opium production and for the extradition of Osama bin Laden. It also required UN member states to close all offices of the Taliban and all offices of Ariana Airlines (Afghanistan's national airline company) located on their territory. Resolution 1333 reiterated the demand that all financial assets belonging to or under the control of the Taliban or Osama bin Laden be frozen. It continued to require UN member states to deny landing and takeoff rights to Taliban-owned airlines but also extended the ban to overflight rights. This essentially had the effect of grounding Afghanistan foreign air traffic. The resolution also introduced an arms embargo. Resolution 1333 forbade any UN member state from supplying, selling, or transferring arms, ordinance, arms equipment and military technical assistance to territory controlled by the Taliban.

14. Comparisons in terms of territory and population suggest some of the reasons the Central Asian officials have concerns regarding equal diplomatic partnership. China's population, as estimated by the Population Reference Bureau (http://www.prb.org), was over 1.3 billion in 2006. At the same time, China's largest immediately adjacent Central Asian neighbor, Kazakhstan, was estimated to have a population of about 15.3 million. In other words, Kazakhstan has a population of slightly over 1 percent of China's population. All five Central Asian states

have a land size of less than four million square kilometers, and a total population of about 59 million people. In other words, all of Central Asia occupies a territory over 41 percent of China's, yet has a population that makes up about 2.5 percent of China's.

15. Doulatbek Khidirbekughli, "U.S. Geostrategy in Central Asia: A Kazakh Perspective," *Comparative Strategy* 22, no. 2 (2003): 159–67, quote on 166. Italics added.

16. See http://www.china.org.cn/chinese/PI-c/92283.htm.

17. The international agreements include the "International Convention for the Suppression of Terrorist Bombings" (December 15, 1997); the "International Convention for the Suppression of the Financing of Terrorism" (December 9, 1999); and 33 separate UN resolutions related to antiterrorism made by the UN Security Council (UNSC) between 1989 and 2005. Particularly important among these are UNSC Resolutions 1267, 1333, 1373, and 1456.

18. See http://www.china-un.org/eng/xw/t27742.htm.

19. Russia's "New Foreign Policy Concept" was approved by the Russian Security Council on March 24, 2000, and approved by President Putin on July 2, 2000. The Concept was printed in *Rossiskaya gazeta,* July 11, 2000. The Concept serves as a guiding document for the Ministry of Foreign Affairs, articulating the goals and objectives of Russian foreign policy. The preceding programmatic statement, often referred to as the "Kozyrev doctrine," was adopted in April 1993 during Andrei Kozyrev's tenure as Minister of Foreign Affairs.

20. *National Security Strategy of the United States,* September 2002, i, available at http://www.whitehouse.gov/nsc/nss.html.

21. *National Strategy for Combating Terrorism,* February 2003, 3, available at http://www.whitehouse.gov/news/releases/2003/02/20030214-7.html.

22. See Nursultan Nazarbayev, "Address of the President of the Republic of Kazakhstan to the People of Kazakhstan: On the Situation in the Country and Major Directions of Domestic and Foreign Policy: Democratization, Economic and Political Reform for the New Century," *Panorama,* 38 (October 2, 1998): 1.

23. In March 2002, the U.S. Department of Commerce announced that it was revoking Kazakhstan's nonmarket economy (NME) status under the U.S. antidumping law. The Department of Commerce found that Kazakhstan had operated as a market-economy country, effective October 1, 2001. See the U.S. Department of Commerce, BISNIS Bulletin, April 2002.

24. Eugene Huskey, "An Economy of Authoritarianism? Askar Akaev and Presidential Leadership in Kyrgyzstan," in *Power and Change in Central Asia,* ed. Sally N. Cummings (London: Routledge, 2002), 74–96.

25. Erica Marat, *The Tulip Revolution: Kyrgyzstan One Year After, March 15, 2005–March 24, 2006* (Washington, DC: Jamestown Foundation, 2006).

26. *Afghanistan Opium Survey for 2006,* UN Office on Drugs and Crime, 2006, iv, http://www.unodc.org/pdf/execsummaryafg.pdf. See Svante Cornell and Niklas Swanström, "The Eurasian Drug Trade: A Challenge to Regional Security," *Problems of Post-Communism* 53, no. 4 (2006): 10–28. Also see Johan Engvall, "The State under Siege: The Drug Trade and Organized Crime in Tajikistan," *Europe-Asia Studies* 58, no. 6 (2006): 827–54.

27. See Luca Anceschi, "Positive Neutrality: The Role of Foreign Policy in the Consolidation of the Turkmen Regime (1992–2005)" (PhD thesis, La Trobe University, 2006).

28. Jim Nichol, "Central Asia: Regional Developments and Implications for U.S. Interests," CRS Issue Brief for Congress, November 16, 2006, Order Code RL33458, http://fpc.state.gov/documents/organization/76879.pdf.

29. Islam Karimov's justification of government policy is presented in his *Uzbekistan on the Threshold of the Twenty-first Century* (New York: St. Martin's Press, 1998).

30. See Shahram Akbarzadeh, *Uzbekistan and the United States: Authoritarianism, Islamism and Washington's Security Agenda* (London: Zed Books, 2005).

31. In a specific legal sense, Uzbekistan did not "abandon the U.S. strategic partnership." The Memorandum of Understanding that established this relationship still has not been officially nullified and, consequently, continues to remain in force. On the background of U.S.-Uzbek relations, see John Daly, Kurt Meppen, Vladimir Socor, and S. Frederick Starr, *Anatomy of a Crisis: U.S.-Uzbekistan Relations, 2001–2005,* Silk Road Paper, Central Asia-Caucasus Institute & Silk Road Studies Program, February 2006.

32. Andrew J. Bacevich, "Bases of Debate: America in Central Asia: Steppes to Empire," *National Interest* 68, no. 1 (2002): 39–53.

33. "Russian Official Cautions U.S. on Use of Central Asian Bases," *New York Times,* October 10, 2003.

34. A good example of this type of view is reflected by analysts in Russia who view Uzbekistan's reversal of policy in zero-sum terms. See, for instance, Andranik Migranyan's argument that "Russia does not present a direct threat to [Uzbekistan and Kazakhstan] either in the sense of a plan for military-political domination, in the sense of the restoration of an empire, or in the sense of crude dictatorial power as we have seen in the foreign relations that have come from certain political circles in the U.S. and their European allies." Andranik Migranyan, "Tashkent sdelal strategicheskyi vybor" ["Tashkent Has Made a Strategic Choice"], *Rossiskaya gazeta,* November 22, 2005, http://www.rg.ru/2005/11/22/tashkent.html.

9

Contemporary Security Challenges in the Middle East

John J. Le Beau and Mikhail Troitskiy

AMERICAN PERSPECTIVE ON THE MIDDLE EAST

John J. Le Beau[1]

It is indisputably the case that the Middle East writ large represents a critical foreign policy focal point of the United States. Although the region has held an important place in U.S. policy considerations for several decades, due in no small part to its role as an oil exporter, political and security events of the last several years starkly underline the pivotal role and herculean challenges the Middle East currently poses for U.S. interests. No other region of the world consumes as much U.S. blood, treasure, or policy attention as the Middle East. It is useful to briefly survey the various Middle Eastern issues that engage such a level of U.S. attention. U.S. interests in the Middle East are driven by two engines, one practical and one more idealistic. The first engine, as alluded to above, is a heavy reliance on world oil. The second motive force is the belief held in influential quarters of the Bush administration that democracy can be installed in the Middle East from afar and, with proper nurturing, can be expected to grow and spread in the region. With these two factors in mind, one of necessity and one transformative, it can be argued that there are at least five major issues anchored in the Middle East that occupy U.S. decision makers and the formulation of a national security strategy. These issues are Iraq, weapons proliferation, active international Jihadist or Islamist terrorism, Middle Eastern oil, and the Israel-Palestine question.

Iraq

Iraq has been since 2003 the clearest manifestation of U.S. physical engagement in the Middle East. The events leading the Bush administration to invade the country, as well as the invasion itself and its aftermath, have been well documented.[2] Now militarily occupied but by no means pacified, Iraq has arguably become a black hole for U.S. policymaking attention, drawing all into its orbit. The U.S. attempt to remake post-Saddam Iraq into a benign and democratic regional model has to date cost a huge amount of money and claimed thousands of American lives, mostly in the period after hostilities were prematurely declared over. The continuing murderous internecine strife between Sunni and Shia insurgents, combined with a deadly international terrorist presence and rampant criminality, have been a drain on U.S. resources and patience, and trying to establish the best course of future action has evolved into an overriding domestic political issue as no military engagement has since the Vietnam War.[3] As of mid-2007, the future of Iraq and its post-Saddam, U.S.-installed political system remains uncertain, but whatever the ultimate political outcome, the inability of the United States to rapidly and effectively exert hard power to pacify the country, combined with a perception of American heavy-handedness, has eroded the U.S. image internationally for years to come. The negative impact of the U.S. presence in Iraq on public attitudes is especially severe in the Middle East, and independent opinion polls strongly suggest that the United States has a massive image problem with the populations of the region. A significant portion of the Muslim world, for example, is convinced that U.S. military action in Iraq (and to some degree elsewhere, including Afghanistan) is primarily motivated by a desire to attack Islam.[4]

In strategic terms, the United States desires an Iraq that is sufficiently stable to accomplish two goals: first, guarantee the survival of a democratic and generally pro-U.S. government and, second, permit the withdrawal of American troops from the country as soon as practicable, while avoiding the appearance of having been forced out. To increase the chances of achieving these foreign policy goals, the United States has attempted to enlist the support of various "friendly" countries in the region, such as Jordan and Saudi Arabia, as buffers to insurgent support and as allies of the new Iraqi government. These efforts to utilize long-standing regional allies have arguably, to some modest extent, been successful. Saudi Arabia agreed in April 2007 to forgive 80 percent of Iraqi indebtedness, a not insignificant development. For its part, Jordan has attempted to buttress a stable post-Saddam Iraq in various ways, including through public diplomacy portraying the Iraqi government as legitimate. Still, support for Iraq by these and other players in the region has been only partial and often muted.

Effectively engaging more hostile regional powers such as Syria and Iran, as publicly recommended in late 2006 by the Iraq Study Group, has been substantially more problematic. For one thing, it is hardly transparent that either Syria or Iran necessarily regard their national interests or regional ambitions as best served by a stable Iraqi democracy enjoying strong ties to the United States. Indeed, it may well be that, in the short term at least, these two countries perceive more political advantage in a continuing atmosphere of boiling and deadly instability within Iraq as long as the violence does not leak across their borders. At the same time, Iran and, to some degree, Syria may see foreign and internal policy profit in continuing strife that whittles away at the U.S. image of omnipotence in the region. This proclivity may arguably be playing with fire, but certainly some decision-making segments in Iran and Syria view a United States tied down in Iraq as a United States that is unable to apply military force elsewhere, such as against Iranian nuclear facilities or Syrian infrastructure supportive of Hezbollah in Lebanon. At any rate, Iraq is unquestionably a major focus of American policy attention in the Middle East and will, in all likelihood, continue to be for some years. It remains unclear as to how far future U.S. administrations may be willing to go to prevent demonstrable failure in Iraq.[5] A total abandonment of Iraq seems nonetheless unlikely and, given the United States' role in setting the stage for the current Iraq troubles, we should expect any administration in Washington to attempt to find a policy solution permitting current Iraqi political institutions to survive (even if in a hollow form) and to prevent an Iraqi descent into a long night of anarchy or unbridled civil war. The widespread fear, of course, is that an implosion in Iraq will ultimately result in an explosion damaging to American interests throughout the region.

The Middle East and Weapons Proliferation

As severe as its implications are for U.S. policy interests, the continuing Iraq strife does not stand alone, however, and is connected to another issue that occupies U.S. policy concern, the theme of weapons proliferation and weapons of mass destruction (WMD). The weapons proliferation issue was originally cited by the U.S. administration as one of the primary grounds for launching the war to oust Saddam Hussein and his paladins, but the topic has a broader regional resonance as well. Although postbellum information suggests strongly that Saddam Hussein did not in fact possess weapons of mass destruction in 2003, it also appears to be true that he intended to produce an atomic bomb in the 1990s and nearly succeeded in doing so before discovery of his covert program. Separately, it is no longer disputed in reputable circles that Saddam had in fact deployed chemical weapons against domestic opposition targets. The possession of such weapons in the hands of as grand a miscalculator as Saddam would surely be recognized by most objective observers as an unwelcome development.

From the U.S. perspective, the fall of Saddam did not end the issue of weapons proliferation in a Middle Eastern context. Plagued by a history of conventional war, civil war, and brutal episodes of unconventional war, terrorism and other violence, the Middle East often seems to teeter on the edge of major instability. The introduction of nuclear weapons or deliverable biological or chemical agents into this environment could well transform a local or regional crisis into a matter of global security concern, not least from the perspective of the United States. This potential security threat did not vanish with the overthrow of the Iraqi B'aathist regime, as it was never an issue restricted to Iraq. Current focus is on the possible acquisition of a nuclear weapons capability by Iran. Opaque Iranian intentions, in turn, run the risk of sparking a nuclear arms race in the region, with the possibility of Saudi Arabia and Egypt seeking to develop their own arsenals as a Sunni counterweight to a perceived Shia military challenge; secular Turkey may harbor nuclear ambitions as well. The United States, like most Western countries, would like to prevent such a scenario from developing and has signaled with varying degrees of clarity that it is willing to go far to prevent a nuclear-weaponized Middle East.

Terrorism

Although often described as an international phenomenon, terrorism is, in point of fact, harnessed importantly to the Middle East per se, and remains a persistent challenge for U.S. interests. It is simply not true that the United States is importantly threatened by the activities of, say, the FARC in Colombia or the New People's Army in the Philippines, no matter how reprehensible the actions of these groups might be. Purely local or regional nonstatist groups that employ terrorism as a weapon of choice generally are more of a nuisance than a real challenge to U.S. interests. Terrorism as a standing threat to U.S. citizens and security policy in the present century properly refers to Islamist- or Salafist-inspired terrorism, phenomena that are perhaps best described as major export products of the Middle East. It should be recalled that the signal event of this type of terrorism, the attacks of September 11, 2001, against New York and Washington, were acts perpetrated solely by Middle Easterners, almost all of them Saudi nationals. Al Qaeda, though currently maintaining a center of gravity in the Afghan-Pakistan border area according to open sources, is fundamentally a core Middle Eastern organization measured in terms of the origin of its leadership, influences on its thinking, and major sources of its funding. The native language of Islamist terrorism is Arabic, and its motive force, while recognizing that the issue of motivation is complex, is essentially Koranic in its justifications.

Although Islamist terrorism originates in the Middle East and has a clear and chronological Middle Eastern narrative and tradition, it has a demonstrated capability to strike against U.S.-related targets internationally, both inside and outside of the Arab world. This is testified to by two massive embassy bombings in Africa, attacks on U.S.-affiliated hotels in Asia, numerous hostage-taking episodes, and the murder of Americans in various countries. Islamist terrorism—with al Qaeda as the poster child—represents a real threat to the security of American citizens; al Qaeda chief and founder Osama bin Laden has explicitly authorized the killing of U.S. civilians wherever they can be located and attacked. Thus, the arguably poorly titled "war on terror" is at root not an offensive doctrine (though often understood as such) but should more appropriately be seen as in deference to the ancient Roman maxim "The welfare of the citizens is the highest duty."[6] But—stripped of its emotion and the often breathless and superficial media coverage—precisely how much of a *strategic* threat is Middle East–rooted Islamist terrorism to U.S. policy interests?

To be sure, bin Laden and his cohorts are responsible for the deaths of thousands of U.S. citizens, most of them civilians. But if we extract from the equation the victims of 9/11 (while noting that as of 2007, a terrorist attack on that scale has not been repeated anywhere in the world) and the military deaths in Iraq and Afghanistan (which are surely more the result of an active insurgency than conventional terrorism), American deaths from Islamist terror number "only" in the hundreds. As horrendous as these deaths are, do they objectively translate into a fundamental or notable challenge to U.S. security emanating from the Middle East? I suggest that the answer must be yes, not because of terrorist events that have transpired to date but because of what could in the future transpire if Islamist terrorist networks are able to successfully harness and use weapons of mass destruction.

It is broadly accepted in the international intelligence and counterterrorist community that al Qaeda and like-minded organizations want to acquire the capability to kill large numbers of civilians in the United States, and possibly in other countries as well. Indeed, some incipient experiments with chemical and biological weapons appear to have taken place in Afghanistan before the fall of the Taliban regime. Similarly, al Qaeda appears to have had an interest in creating some sort of a nuclear weapons capability and was interested in acquiring key components such as highly enriched uranium. The available evidence suggests that they have not been at all successful in this endeavor, and the fabrication of a nuclear weapon may well be beyond their wherewithal. It is much more likely that an Islamist terrorist organization would be able to employ chemical or biological weapons or what is generally known as a "dirty bomb" or radiological dispersion device. Use of a dirty bomb, or weapons-grade anthrax, or a large chemical device, represents a credible and grave security threat. The psychological impact of such an unconventional attack, including on international financial markets, would also be severe. Accordingly, to the extent that Islamist groups are seen as anchored in the Middle East, they will continue to represent a major and perhaps overriding U.S. policy concern in the region. At the same time, the fear of an attack with unconventional weapons is likely to increase the level of U.S. cooperation with nonhostile regimes in the neighborhood in order to prevent such an event from occurring. As a direct result of this concern, bilateral and multilateral intelligence-sharing arrangements between the United States and Middle Eastern countries appear to be robust.

Oil

The importance of Middle Eastern oil to world fossil fuel supplies remains another compelling factor for the continuing criticality of the region in terms of U.S. security concerns. As has been amply demonstrated by the volatile oil prices of 2006 and 2007, the international oil market responds nervously and immediately to any evidence of tension or instability in the Middle East. Signals of chaos in Iraq, brinksmanship from Iran, and incipient signs of internal instability in Saudi Arabia have all had unambiguous and negative market impact. Not only prices are affected.

Periods of increased tension or outright hostility between the United States and Iran, for example, could conceivably result in the mining or closure of the Strait of Hormuz, a primary, exceedingly narrow, and vulnerable oil export route from the region. The collapse or degradation of rule by the House of Saud, with the attendant disruption to oil supplies and facilities in the kingdom, would also have dramatic repercussions.

Without question, the vast oil reserves in Saudi Arabia and other Middle Eastern countries are viewed by the United States as a resource of critical strategic importance upon which the U.S. national economy is dependent. Accordingly, ensuring stability in the region to permit the oil to flow without interruption is a primary and essential U.S. national security goal, as it has been for decades.

The governments of Saudi Arabia and other regional Arab powers with oil reserves are, of course, just as interested in remaining oil suppliers as Western countries (and increasingly China and India) are in remaining consumers. Yet, real potential for oil supply disruption remains. Present indicators suggest that the most likely threats to Middle Eastern oil are from international terrorist circles or a state-on-state war. Thus, a successful terrorist assault on a large refinery in Saudi Arabia could have a severe impact on oil production as well as an even more damaging psychological impact on international markets. Whereas al Qaeda had in previous times stated that Arab-owned oil facilities were not a legitimate target, that edict appears to have changed more recently. Indeed, terrorists have already plotted and attempted violent assaults on oil facilities in Saudi Arabia and Yemen, if so far without any notable success. These unsuccessful attacks may well have been intended to test the vulnerability of oil production compounds, however, and may serve to provide "lessons learned" for more refined terrorist plans in the future. The successful preemption of a major planned attack on Saudi refineries in April 2007 suggests that terrorists continue to regard attacking Saudi oil as a vital strategic goal.[7]

Again, even a partially successful attack—one causing a temporary reduction in oil supplies—would negatively impact U.S. and international security concerns. The same holds true of any conventional military conflict in the area. Iranian assertiveness resulting in a military clash with an Arab state in the Gulf would immediately threaten the unimpeded production and transport of oil. The concern of the Jordanian King Abdullah II about a burgeoning "Shia crescent" is not unrelated to fear of Iranian-sponsored attempts to alter the prevailing status quo in the region, empowering or "protecting" Shia minorities.[8] Such an Iranian intent, in precisely such a volatile regional environment, would run a risk of erupting into a major shooting war based on some unforeseen miscalculation or incident. Any U.S. administration will be guided by a strong desire to prevent disruptions of the oil supply. If war were to threaten regional stability, and with it the oil markets, the United States can be expected to intervene militarily with the goal of stabilizing and cooling the situation as rapidly as possible. This includes the possibility of preemptive U.S. action if a regional war is regarded as unavoidable.

Israel-Palestine

The United States has been a strong and reliable supporter of the state of Israel since the inception of the latter, not least because Israel is the only recognizably democratic state in the immediate area. Israel, in turn, has unquestionably been the most consequent supporter of U.S. policy in the Middle East. In spite of occasional differences, the United States is committed, at an absolute minimum, to Israel's survival, legitimacy as a nation-state, and right to exist. It is precisely this foreign policy bottom line that causes the United States so many problems with Arab actors in the Middle East, who continue to regard Israel with various degrees of fear, loathing, and contempt. The generally accepted belief that Israel is a nuclear weapons power has also not soothed Arab feelings. The issue of the Palestinians seems an epicenter of Israel's difficulties in the Arab and Islamic world. Due to its close and long-standing relationship with Israel, the United States has assumed some ownership of the Palestinian problem as well, and is widely expected by the international community to play a role in resolving, or at least defusing, the contentious issue. The level of U.S. engagement on Israel-Palestine has waxed and waned. Nonetheless, it is safe to assert that any administration in Washington would *like* to see an end to Israeli-Palestinian animosity and some sort of two-state solution, with details to be negotiated.

It is possible that the United States will be able to preside over an acceptable settlement of the Palestine issue and that a formula will be worked out to satisfy Israelis, Palestinians, and other Arab parties in the Middle East. Realistically, however, great hurdles to a lasting peace remain, and difficulties are not reduced by the mutual suspicion and, often, hatred with which Palestinians and Israelis view one another. There are reasons to suspect, however, that below the surface issue of Palestine, another problem is concealed. That is, neither most Palestinians nor most Arabs have really accepted the legitimacy of a Jewish state in the heartland of Islam. Although it is possible that widespread and often primitive prejudice against Jews would recede with a fair and equitable Palestinian solution, it is not a certainty. It is imaginable that, with the Palestinian issue resolved, Israel will remain a pariah state in the Middle East and that any acceptance of its right to exist will be grudging and provisional. Nonetheless, with or without a solution to the Palestinian issue, and even with likely future Washington–Tel Aviv disputes over the details of securing a peace arrangement, the United States will continue to be a protector of Israel's right to exist and, accordingly, a lightning rod for Middle Eastern elements who do not regard this prospect with equanimity.

U.S. Regional Interests as a Whole

In sum, the United States has a broad tapestry of interests in the Middle East at the beginning of the twenty-first century. To a notable degree, the above-mentioned five issues facing the United States in the region are interrelated. For example, Iraq, a cauldron of violence and instability, is also an important oil-producing country. Iraq is also currently a major theater of Islamist terrorism, as embodied by al Qaeda in

Iraq, and many of the terrorist exertions there are directed at U.S. troops. Islamist terrorism, in turn, threatens other oil-producing countries such as Saudi Arabia. Available information suggests that terrorist forces are engaged in a determined quest to acquire and employ weapons of mass destruction, as well. Similarly, the acquisition of weapons of mass destruction, in this case nuclear, appears to be on the Iranian policy agenda. This Iranian quest, in turn, could result in a rapid proliferation of weapons programs among a number of states in the region, adding to its overall volatility and threatening stability. Israel, a nuclear state already, is part of the equation. Threats to stability, as we have previously noted, can easily result in a disruption to oil supplies or, at the very least, skyrocketing oil prices on the international market. Thus, although we can identify five separate issues of U.S. policy focus, the issues are in fact importantly interwoven, adding to the difficulty and complexity of finding adequate policy solutions.

However, the policy difficulties for the United States are magnified by important religious issues. The United States has a long and unbroken history as a secular democratic republic with most of its citizens, like its values, rooted in the Christian tradition. Another simple historical fact is that the Middle East is the kernel of the Islamic world, which, with the exception of modern Turkey, has no secular democratic tradition. Indeed, separation of church and state is a concept foreign to Islam. Islam, Koranic verse and tradition, and Sharia law are facets of everyday life in the Middle East. In addition, centuries of violent conflict between the Islamic world and the West, literally ancient history to most Americans and Europeans, are nowhere near as remote or irrelevant to many Middle Eastern inhabitants. To many Muslims in the Middle East, the West stands stubbornly in opposition to Islam and of its nature represents a real menace and affront to the *Ummah,* the community of the Muslim faithful that recognizes no borders.

This confrontational worldview, in turn, is regarded as paranoid, exclusionary, and intolerant in the perspective of many Americans. This wide divide in basic thinking and perception between the two traditions, one broadly secular and democratic, the other generally religious and authoritarian, is a complicating factor in the ability of the United States to successfully pursue perceived national interests in the Middle East. Nowhere is this divide more apparent than in the areas of Islamist terrorism and Iraq.

The difficulties the United States has encountered in the occupation of Iraq doubtless have many fathers, but have been importantly exacerbated by the status of American troops as "unbelievers," an uninvited foreign element transplanted on Arab and Muslim territory, thus doubly offensive. One need only note the hundreds, if not thousands, of video clips from Iraq, widely available on the Internet, where an attack against a U.S. military facility or convoy is accompanied by shouts of "Allah Ahkbar" or selective verses from the Koran. Similarly, Islamist terrorist propagandists such as Al-Zawahiri and Osama bin Laden routinely justify their attacks against the United States and other Western targets strictly in Islamic religious terms; no other justification is required, and none is offered. Significantly, those Muslims who are less virulent than the Islamists are cast as heretics and apostates deserving death;

again, their crime is portrayed much more as a religious than a political transgression. This extreme message as a call to nearly indiscriminate violence may be rejected by most Muslims, but nonetheless finds resonance with a disturbingly large number in the Middle East.

This religiously and culturally motivated animosity to the West in general and the United States in particular serves as a backdrop to any U.S. policy initiative in the Middle East. Any U.S. policy activity regarding the Middle East, once known, is automatically regarded with suspicion by a considerable percentage of the region's population. Middle Eastern governments, even those generally friendly to or even profiting from U.S. positions, often publicly pander to the anti-American "Arab street" while offering private assurances to U.S. officials. All of these factors clearly serve to complicate the practice of U.S. diplomacy. The situation is unlikely to change soon.

Despite these inherent difficulties for U.S. policy in the Middle East, the United States cannot simply disengage from the region, and accordingly, it needs to forward its national policy interests as best as practicable. As long as access to oil remains an essential and, indeed, indispensable precondition of U.S. economic health, active engagement in the Middle East will continue. As long as international terrorism is active and motivated by Islamist ideology, U.S. activity, including preemptive anti-terrorist actions, will endure. As long as Middle Eastern powers and nonstate actors appear intent on engaging in the proliferation of nuclear weapons or other weapons of mass destruction programs, proactive U.S. diplomatic and, perhaps, military efforts in the region will continue. As long as Iraq threatens to explode or implode, threatening an array of negative consequences, U.S. presence in the area will remain in one degree, shape, or form.

RUSSIAN PERSPECTIVE ON THE MIDDLE EAST

Mikhail Troitskiy[9]

The Middle East is a difficult region for Russian diplomacy. It presents the country's leadership with a set of intricate dilemmas. In the Middle East, Moscow seeks to balance several priorities: coordinate security policies with regional actors, promote the interests of Russian businesses, and guard against the rise of Islamic extremism and proliferation of nuclear weapons. Given this multifaceted and sometimes contradictory set of interests, Russia has usually avoided making clear choices. Moscow prefers not to side with or put the blame on just one party in any conflict. The trademark of Russia's official perspective on Middle Eastern conflicts has been calling for multilateral solutions with due respect to the interests of all actors involved. However, should the security situation in the region deteriorate, Russian dilemmas may become more acute. As a consequence, Moscow may find itself hard-pressed to define clear-cut positions and faced with the need to take up new responsibilities for conflict management in the region.

The Shaping of Russia's Middle East Policies: Interests and Influences

Russian policy in the Middle East is informed by a combination of internal factors, regional developments, and pressures from the broader international environment. Domestically, Russia is interested in developing trade relations with the region, coordinating pricing policies for hydrocarbons exports, and fending off negative implications of the Middle Eastern conflicts for Russian internal and external security.

The ethnic composition of Russia and its internal security challenges bear directly on Moscow's stance on major Middle Eastern issues. Muslims constitute at least 12 percent of the Russian population. Some of Russia's Muslim republics, especially Tatarstan and Chechnya, successfully negotiated special deals with the federal center whereby the republican leadership enjoys more leeway than governments of other members of the Federation. Although armed separatism was by and large defeated in Chechnya by the mid-2000s, Islamist slogans continue to serve as a mobilizing tool for the various criminal and radical elements operating across the North Caucasus. In such a situation, the Russian government is cautious to avoid alienating Russian Muslims by excessive rhetorical emphasis on "combating Islamic terrorism." As a consequence, Russia has traditionally demanded that both Israel's security concerns and the Arab bid for Palestinian statehood should be equally honored by the international community.

Generally, the Russian leadership considers Israel an important ally in containing Islamic extremists in the Middle East and a promising partner for high-tech cooperation. Russia and Israel have been reported to work jointly on a reconnaissance aircraft for the Indian air force. In April 2006, Russia launched three Israeli reconnaissance satellites. Russian and Israeli security services exchange information on terrorist and other security challenges to both Russia and Israel. Contacts between the two countries are facilitated by the Russian-speaking immigrants who constitute about one-quarter of the Israeli population. However, the fact that Russian-Israeli annual trade turnover barely exceeds $2 billion and Israel's unequivocal reliance on the United States as its main ally and principal mediator in all Arab-Israeli disputes highlight the limits to Russia's engagement with Israel.

Russian arms exporters constitute a powerful domestic lobby exerting a strong influence on the country's Middle Eastern policy priorities. Russian arms sales to the Middle East are focused on the Arab states and Iran. In 2005, President Putin estimated Russian arms sales to the Middle East at a "mere" $500 million. He compared this figure to $6.8 billion worth of American arms supplies to the region.[10] Despite the relatively modest amount of Russian arms supplies, some contracts aroused political controversy both within and beyond Russia. For example, Moscow's decision to sell short-range, surface-to-air missiles to Syria was sharply criticized by Israel, which claimed that the missiles could have disturbed strategic balance in the region. As a result, Russia introduced additional measures to prevent the use of these missiles by extremist organizations, and the transaction was completed in early 2005.

However, the transfer to Syria of more advanced 900-km-range Iskander missiles was stopped by President Putin despite pressure from arms exporters. Persian Gulf states also emerged as prospective buyers of Russian arms, including fighter jets (Saudi Arabia) and surface-to-air complexes (United Arab Emirates).

Another powerful domestic interest group is the Russian atomic energy industry. Since 1996, Russian builders have been working on the completion of the Bushehr atomic power station in Iran, the whole project estimated at about $1 billion. For more than a decade, Russian policymakers were dismissing Western criticism of the Bushehr contract. Apart from being pressed by the domestic "atomic lobby," Russian leaders had reasons to believe that, should Moscow abandon Bushehr, the void will soon be filled by American and European corporations who provided Iran with valuable nuclear technology back in the 1970s.

A strong impact on shaping Russia's Middle East policies is produced by the largest Russian oil and gas corporations known for close ties with the government. Russian interest in relations with the energy-exporting countries of the Persian Gulf is two-faceted. On one hand, Russia competes with them, as members of OPEC, for the ability to influence prices on international oil markets. Russian oil exporters may lose profits if Saudi Arabia decides to employ the spare upstream production capacity Riyadh claims to maintain. On the other hand, Moscow is exploring opportunities for reaching agreements or, at least, a mutual understanding with Persian Gulf countries on coordination of oil sales strategies. In early 2007, Russia displayed enthusiasm about expanding political and economic ties with Saudi Arabia. Riyadh was fearing a decline in the U.S. commitment to the ruling dynasty and had reasons to question the reliability of Washington as a security ally.[11] Given the radical attempts at reshaping the region undertaken by the Bush administration, Riyadh could not help considering scenarios in which Washington would no longer protect the royal dynasty or the territorial integrity of Saudi Arabia. This signaled a notable change in Russia's perspective on Saudi Arabia, which had been commonly referred to by Russian analysts as a "source of funding for Islamic extremists in the North Caucasus."

Russia's Gazprom has an interest in coordinating natural gas pricing policies with the largest Middle Eastern producers, such as Qatar, Iran, and the United Arab Emirates. With the growth of a global market in liquefied natural gas (LNG), a possible emergence of an OPEC-style gas cartel is increasingly discussed among both exporting and importing countries. However, Russia's official stance on a "gas OPEC" has been cautious. Moscow values its reputation as an independent supplier of both oil and gas whose pricing policies are not skewed by any cartels.

There are at least two significant external factors influencing the Russian approach to the Middle East. In the first place, in this region, Russia stands to benefit from raising its profile as an impartial and respected mediator. Reviving Russian policy in the Middle East has become one of the manifestations of President Putin's strategy of diversifying Russian foreign policy priorities and hedging against a decline in relations with the West.

Second, Russia's leverage in the Middle East may be used to softly balance the United States as long as Washington's policies in Russia's neighborhood or on missile defense cooperation with Central European countries cause increasing concern in Moscow. However, while extending unconditional support to U.S. initiatives in the Middle East would indeed be illogical from a Russian policymaker's point of view, Moscow has tried to make sure that Russia's own security interests are not undermined by balking at American initiatives.

Under the combined influence of domestic and international factors in action since the early 2000s, Russian foreign policy makers have attributed high importance to the Middle East. During his two terms in office, President Putin traveled to the Middle East twice. His April 2005 official visit to Egypt, Israel, and the Palestinian Territories was hailed as the first trip of the Russian leader to the region for almost half a century. The Persian Gulf was covered by Putin in February 2007, when he visited Qatar and Saudi Arabia, as well as Jordan.

Assessing the Role of the United States

In the late 2000s, Middle Eastern futures are determined by external influences at least to the same extent as they are defined by internal developments. The Middle East has become a new target in the U.S. strategy of a comprehensive pre-designed restructuring of a region. Success in fostering economic and political reform in Central and Eastern Europe in the 1990s with subsequent integration of former Soviet allies into NATO gave rise, in the United States, to a new school of strategic thinking. Its adherents argued that the United States had enough determination, vision, and power to transform a whole region by means of diplomacy and military force. In fact, these two sets of tools were regarded by the first Bush administration as essentially parts of one continuum.

However, this American attempt at reforming the Middle East is seemingly running aground. One reaches such a conclusion irrespective of assessments of America's achievements in Iraq. The thrust of the U.S. approach, premised on the claim that Washington knows what the region needs better than its inhabitants, has been rejected by political elites in most Middle Eastern countries. It has frustrated American allies (such as Saudi Arabia and Turkey), destabilized "problem states" (such as Iraq and Lebanon), antagonized potential partners (such as Syria), and turned outspoken critics into open foes (such as Iran). Even some mainstream Israeli politicians have hinted that U.S. Middle East policies are being crafted with little respect for the interests of Israel as America's main ally in the region.

An influential group of Russian foreign policy experts asserted in early 2007 that "the strategy of democratizing the broader Middle East—a central foreign policy project of the Bush administration—has turned into fiasco. This can lead, in the nearest future, to Islamists seizing power in the region against the backdrop of a dramatic weakening of U.S. positions."[12] An official Russian Foreign Policy Review, issued by the Ministry of Foreign Affairs in March 2007, argued that "contemporary Islamic radicalism is essentially a strained and dangerous, but predictable reaction to the unilateral approach pursued by the United States in the post-bipolar unbalanced international system where American power is no longer checked by a global rival."[13]

American pressure on Iran with a failure to deliver on sanctions did not hamper Iran's nuclear program. Instead, it increased Tehran's determination to pursue uranium enrichment and aggravated tensions between Iran and its Arab neighbors. At the same time, mutual understanding increased between Iran and Turkey, while Ankara has been drifting away from the position of a close U.S. ally in the region. As a result, even hawkish American and European experts suggested striking a deal with Iran as soon as possible. These pundits came to realize that the longer such a deal is postponed, the worse the conditions the international community is likely to obtain.[14]

Another grand American initiative, the stabilization of Afghanistan through the removal of the Taliban, was welcomed by Russia until the U.S. and coalition forces attempted to include Afghanistan in the project of democratic restructuring of the broader Middle East. Moscow was especially critical of the United States and its allies who conducted elections in Afghanistan, but refrained from curbing opium production and using force to contain extremist elements in Afghanistan's remote areas.

Regional Points of Stress: A Russian Approach

Israel and Palestine

The Israeli-Palestinian conflict has clear prospects of continuing for many years. Developments that took place since 2001 diminished hopes for its resolution and blurred the way towards a final settlement. At the end of 2007, achieving progress along the lines of George W. Bush's road map seems problematic. Israel's unilateral disengagement policies and the outbreaks of intifada violence are now aggravated by the rise of Hezbollah in Lebanon and internal strife within the Palestinian Territories. Indeed, with the growing popularity of Hamas in Palestine and Hezbollah in Lebanon, the Israeli-Palestinian conflict has been moving away from, rather than nearing, resolution. One of Russia's most long-standing observers of the Middle East expects Israel to face a security challenge from its own Arab citizens, whose share in the country's population had grown from 11.1 percent in 1949 to 19.6 percent in 2006. In such a situation, a wall separating Israel from the Palestinian Territories is unlikely to bring the long-awaited peace. Israeli Arabs are showing signs of increased radicalization and may begin to align with Palestinian Arabs in their fight against Israel.[15] This can make prospects for a compromise even more remote.

In the presence of Arab-Israeli tensions, other conflicts in the Middle East will remain difficult to address. Some of them, such as Shia-Sunni animosity in Iraq or the factional strife in Lebanon, may prove to be manageable by means of constant financial and mediation efforts. However, other flashpoints, where at least one side is provoked by continuing Israeli-Palestinian hostilities, have considerable chances of spinning out of control. The controversy surrounding Iran's nuclear program results largely from differing readings of the Israeli-Palestinian conflict by Iran and the West. American support for Israel, as well as the massive presence of U.S. troops in the Arab world, continues to provide ideological justification and inspiration to the Islamic radicals fighting against the government of Afghanistan and seeking to use the poorly controlled areas in Afghanistan and Pakistan as a launching pad for terrorist activities across and beyond the Middle East.

Given the sources of Russia's Middle East policies outlined above, Moscow is unwilling to put most of the blame for continued hostilities between Israelis and Palestinians on one of the sides. Russia aspires to a greater role as an impartial mediator whose innovative approaches to the conflict may help to achieve a breakthrough. Although Russia does not uncritically endorse the U.S. or EU positions on the conflict, Moscow and Washington agree that the Israeli-Palestinian confrontation underlies most other conflicts in the Middle East. It constitutes a whirlpool of mutual hatred, intransigent ideas, money, and radical fighters that stirs up tensions and deepens many other divides in the region.

The Future of Iraq and the Kurdish Issue

Apart from Arab-Israeli hostilities and third parties' involvement in the Middle East, factional strife among Muslims remains a major impediment to a comprehensive conflict settlement in the Middle East. The dismal security situation in Iraq results not so much from the coalition troops' presence on Iraqi soil, than from the inability of Sunni, Shia, and Kurdish communities to forge a compromise on the governing system and division of oil revenues in Iraq.

However fierce the fighting of "all against all" may have been since the defeat of Saddam Hussein, skilled policies of the U.S.-led coalition may return southern and central parts of the country to relative stability, if not peace. A deal between the Shia and the Sunni could be hammered out and maintained through a long-term engagement of the United States with each party. Yet the Kurdish issue is likely to remain a backbreaker. Should the United States, as the coalition leader, acquiesce to the Kurdish bid for statehood, a major bout of instability will follow. Turkey may step in to squelch its own Kurdish minority. Iran will also be defending its territorial integrity with all means available and will most likely accuse Washington of trying to undermine Iran by supporting Kurdish separatism. Potentially, a concerted move of the Kurds towards independence in at least three neighboring Middle Eastern states may trigger a crisis on the scale comparable to the Arab-Israeli conflict outbreak of the late 1940s.

Iran's Nuclear Ambition

While the acute issue of Kurdish statehood has mostly regional security implications, Iran's nuclear program presents the whole of the international community with a challenge of genuinely global proportions. Quite apart from Israel's concerns about Iranian intentions, Iran's nuclear ambition may trigger a WMD arms race in the region, where the sense of rivalry is growing between Iran and its neighboring Sunni monarchies of the Persian Gulf. Such an arms race, in its turn, may exacerbate the Arab-Israeli antagonisms and push Turkey's security policy further away from its NATO allies. The multilateral regime based on the Non-Proliferation Treaty of 1968 will be completely shattered if Iran manages to get away with deploying a nuclear deterrent by the end of the decade.

The U.S. threat assessment of Iran's nuclear program was on a constant rise under the Bush administration and became surprisingly high by the end of 2006. At that point, influential analysts began questioning the conventional wisdom that the United States was not intent on attacking Iran given the challenges U.S. troops were facing elsewhere in the Middle East. Despite strong pressure, Tehran raised the stakes by making it clear that uranium enrichment would be continued and expanded.

Iran's drive towards a large-scale enrichment capacity is motivated by a complicated mix of factors, some of which appear to be inadequately assessed by major players involved in the dispute. These factors include boosting Iran's regional and global standing and defending from an external attack as well as propping up the ayatollahs' regime within Iran. In addition to that, psychologically, as some Russian observers have noted, Tehran may be vying for respect as an international player. Since the collapse of U.S.-Iran ties in the wake of the 1979 revolution, Tehran has been largely ignored and then fiercely pressured by Washington on nuclear and other issues. Iran may therefore pursue a nuclear status in order to ensure that the West, and the United States in particular, treats Iran as an equal negotiating party. Just like India was removed from the American list of countries punished for pursuing nuclear weapons, Tehran would like to be dropped out of the "axis of evil" group of pariah states. Even a rhetorical move by Washington in that direction may bring surprising benefits in terms of engaging Iran in constructive negotiations with the international community.

On its part, Russia's policy vis-à-vis Iran is based on balancing several sets of calculations. Pros for distancing from the U.S. position include revenues from launching the nuclear power station in Bushehr and weapons sales to Iran as well as an opportunity to softly balance the United States and European Union. However, as more information about the real scope of Iran's nuclear ambition was reaching the Russian leadership, Moscow became more cautious in supporting Tehran in its confrontation with the West. Russian attitudes may have been affected by fresh assessments of the threats arising from a war with Iran or a nuclear-armed Iran capable of hitting targets in Russia. In late 2006–early 2007, Moscow supported a series of UN Security Council resolutions demanding that Iran stop enriching uranium and submit all its nuclear installations to IAEA inspections. In March 2007, the Russian contractor at Bushehr accused Iran of failing to transfer payments due for the next stage of construction work and threatened to suspend further work on the ground. At the time when a military operation against Iran was considered an especially high probability, Moscow chose to avoid both an implicit endorsement of Iran's intransigence vis-à-vis the international community and any damage that may be caused to Russian personnel in Iran. The latter scenario would make it impossible for Russia to preserve neutrality and distance itself from both conflicting parties should a war between Iran and the United States become a reality.

Afghanistan

Security in the Middle East is further challenged by the continuing instability in Afghanistan. This country serves as a channel whereby South Asian security threats are projected onto the Middle East. Most Russian observers agree that the future of Afghanistan is highly uncertain and the situation may play out against Russia.[16] In the worst scenario, the United States may decide to drastically reduce its commitment to Afghan security. This could undermine the willingness of other ISAF-contributing nations to remain on the ground. Should that happen, not only Afghanistan, but the neighboring regions, including Central Asia, will be further destabilized and generate a multitude of direct threats to Russia.

At the same time, American efforts to engage Afghanistan in a network of security, trade, and social relationships with post-Soviet Central Asia were negatively received in Russia. Initiatives, such as the Greater Central Asia Partnership,[17] may export insecurity from the Middle East and South Asia straight into Russia's southern neighborhood while providing no clear benefits to Russia and its partners in Central Asia.

Russian analysts have sided with the growing number of negative assessments of the impact of Pakistani policies on the situation in Afghanistan. Russian experts were among the first to draw attention to the support provided by Pakistani security services to the Taliban and other extremist insurgents operating in Afghanistan. Given the links between Afghanistan and Central Asia, Moscow has shown interest in cooperation with NATO in the region. However, by 2007 Russia's proposals for multilateral activities with the participation of NATO, Russia, and Central Asian countries have not received positive reaction from the Atlantic Alliance. Moscow, in its turn, has ruled out any deployment of Russian contingents on Afghan soil.

Russia-NATO cooperation in Central Asia and Afghanistan may gather momentum after the Alliance deepens its partnerships with Central Asian countries. This will help NATO overcome fears about Russian domination of any multilateral cooperative arrangement in Central Asia. Both sides have already concluded that no comprehensive solution of security challenges in Afghanistan will be possible without mutual trust between Russia and NATO as well as their concerted action.

Conclusion

Russia's geographic proximity to and long-standing ties with the Middle East make it the first great power to suffer from new bouts of conflict and also the first to benefit from enhanced regional security. Multilateral comprehensive solutions, favored by Moscow, are unlikely to materialize in the foreseeable future—not only because of the unilateral inclinations on the part of Washington, but also because of the reluctance of most regional actors to achieve a final settlement. At the same time, it is becoming increasingly clear to Russia and other influential external players that the deadly threats emanating from the Middle East equally undermine both Western and Russian security. These two trends combined will be encouraging Russia and the United States, as well as EU countries, to agree on policy priorities and step up coordination of their positions on major regional issues. Only faced with concerted pressure by the leading mediators will the conflicting parties seriously consider ceasing hostilities. However undemocratic such a "Middle Eastern Concert" of nations may appear, it is a more realistic alternative to unilateral designs for a comprehensive democratization of the Middle East.

NOTES

1. The views expressed are those of the author and do not necessarily reflect the official policy or position of the George C. Marshall European Center for Security Studies, the U.S. European Command, the Department of Defense, or the U.S. Government.

2. See Tyler Drumheller, *On The Brink* (New York: Carroll and Graf Publishers, 2006). Drumheller's account is from the perspective of the U.S. intelligence community. See also Bob Woodward, *State of Denial* (New York: Simon and Schuster, 2006). Woodward explores the events leading to the Iraq war and its aftermath with a primary focus on the policymakers.

3. See Thomas E. Ricks, *Fiasco: The American Military Adventure in Iraq* (New York and London: Penguin Books, 2006).

4. Muslim attitudes to Iraq and on related issues are the subject of frequent and detailed polling by the PEW Research Center, accessible at http://www.pewresearch.org.

5. John Walcott and Jonathan S. Landay, "U.S. Maps New Course for Troubled Iraq— Again," *Seattle Times,* May 24, 2007.

6. From the Latin *"Salus populi suprema (est) lex,"* attributed to Cicero (106 BC–43 BC).

7. Andrew Hammond, "Saudi Says Qaeda Threat Not Over Despite Arrests," *Boston Globe,* April 28, 2007, http://www.boston.com (accessed May 22, 2007).

8. Ian Black, "Fear of a Shia Full Moon," *Guardian Unlimited,* January 26, 2007, www.guardian.co.uk (accessed May 2, 2007).

9. The views expressed in this chapter are the author's only.

10. President Vladimir Putin, Press Statement and Answers to Questions Following Talks with President of Israel Moshe Katsav, Jerusalem, April 28, 2005, http://www.kremlin.ru/eng/text/speeches/2005/04/28/1406_type82914type82915_87453.shtl.

11. Russian President Vladimir Putin paid an official visit to Saudi Arabia on February 12, 2007. In the course of his visit, he promoted joint Russian-Saudi projects on oil exploration and production, the building of railways and connecting Saudi Arabia to the Russian GLONASS global positioning system.

12. "Amerikanskii faktor i ego evolyutsiya" ["The American Factor and Its Evolution"], *Mir vokrug Rossii: 2017. Kontury nedalekogo buduschego [The World Around Russia: 2017. Contours of the Near Future]* (Moscow: Council on Foreign and Defense Policy, 2007), 105.

13. "Obzor vneshnei politiki Rossiiskoi Federatsii" ["Foreign Policy Review of the Russian Federation"] (Moscow: Ministry of Foreign Affairs of the Russian Federation, March 2007), http://www.mid.ru/brp_4.nsf/sps/690A2BAF968B1FA4C32572B100304A6E.

14. See Mark Fitzpatrick, "Can Iran's Nuclear Capability Be Kept Latent?" *Survival* 49, no. 1 (March 2007): 33–58.

15. Marc Khrustalev, "Blizhnevostochnyi konflikt: dinamika i perspectivy" ["The Middle East Conflict: Dynamics and Prospects"], *Mezhdunarodnye protsessy [International Trends]* 3, no. 2 (11) (May–August 2006): 17, http://www.intertrends.ru/eleventh/001.htm.

16. See, for example, Vladimir Ovchinskii, "Afganistan bez koalitsii" ["Afghanistan with a Coalition"], *Rossiya v globalnoi politike [Russia in Global Affairs]* 5, no. 1 (January–February 2007): 27–34, http://www.globalaffairs.ru/numbers/24/7042.html.

17. For one influential policy proposal, see S. Frederick Starr, "A Partnership for Central Asia," *Foreign Affairs* 84, no. 4 (July–August 2005): 164–78.

10

Managing Nuclear Proliferation: Chinese and American Approaches to North Korea

Wei Zongyou and William E. Berry Jr.

A CHINESE PERSPECTIVE: THE NORTH KOREAN NUCLEAR CRISIS AND CHINA'S RESPONSE

North Korea's announcement of a nuclear test on October 9, 2006 exacerbated the second North Korean nuclear crisis, eroding the dim hope that the crisis could be solved diplomatically, and ignited great anxiety and strong condemnation from the international community. China, as the host of the six-party talks and a neighbor and once patron of North Korea, reacted quickly and strongly. On the same day as North Korea's announcement of the test, China's Foreign Ministry issued a strongly worded condemnation.

Nevertheless, the international community did not give up trying to solve the difficult problem. After dazzling shuttle diplomacy by the concerned parties, especially China, the apparently dead six-party talk resumed on February 6, 2007. This round of talks lasted for 10 hard days and resulted in a joint document by the six parties, pulling the situation back on track. However, in view of the changed situation on the Korean Peninsula, the poor history of North Koran adherence to its international obligations, and the deep distrust and animosity existing between the United States and North Korea, whether the joint document can be fully implemented is still open to doubt. The journey toward a nonnuclear Korean Peninsula is doomed to be long and tough.

The Challenges of the North Korean Nuclear Crisis

The October 9 nuclear test by North Korea capped a decade-long nuclear crisis on the peninsula and posed a grave challenge to peace and stability in Northeast Asia and the Nonproliferation Treaty (NPT). The North Korean nuclear crisis began in 1992 when International Atomic Energy Agency (IAEA) inspectors suspected North Korea of cheating on its nuclear program and were denied special inspections of North Korea's nuclear waste sites near Yongbyon. After nearly two years of confrontation and negotiations, with numerous setbacks and frustrations, the United States and North Korea finally negotiated an Agreed Framework on the nuclear issue in October 1994.

Although the Agreed Framework greatly eased the tense situation on the peninsula and successfully froze the North Korean nuclear program, it did not end the nuclear issue. Technically, the immediate goal of the 1994 Agreed Framework was not the dismantlement of North Korean nuclear facilities and programs, but only a freeze. What is more, this seemingly moderate goal was to be reciprocated by considerable incentives offered by the United States in the form of economic, heavy oil, and nuclear energy compensations and expected political and diplomatic ties in the future. It was hoped that the implementation of the Agreed Framework would pave the way for the final dismantlement of North Korean nuclear facilities and the normalization of diplomatic relations between North Korea and the United States.

However, implementation of the framework met with great difficulties. In the United States, the framework was strongly criticized by Republicans, who controlled Congress after the 1994 elections and impeded implementation. This resulted in serious delays of the construction of the two light-water nuclear reactors and heavy-oil shipments. The promised opening of liaison offices in each capital and the final normalization of relations did not materialize, either. On the part of North Korea, while it implemented the framework literally, it is believed that it opened a second nuclear program and was engaged in secret uranium enrichment activities as early as in 1998, which breached the Joint Declaration on the Denuclearization of the Korean Peninsula signed with South Korea in December 1991. Furthermore, when George W. Bush came into office and expressed his open dissatisfaction with Bill Clinton's engagement policy toward North Korea in general and the Agreed Framework in particular, North Korea shocked a U.S. delegation to Pyongyang in October 1992, led by Assistant Secretary of State for East Asian and Pacific Affairs James Kelly, by admitting that it had opened a second nuclear program, declaring that it was justified to pursue nuclear capabilities in view of the hostile attitude of the Bush administration, and considered the agreed framework nullified.[1] North Korea's admission of its secret nuclear program and the subsequent U.S. decision to suspend shipment of heavy fuel oil to North Korea ignited the second nuclear crisis.

The nuclear crisis on the peninsula has posed serious challenges to the international community. North Korea's withdrawal from the NPT in 2003 and its subsequent nuclear test in 2006 damaged international nonproliferation efforts. North Korea is the first nation ever to withdraw from the NPT and conduct a nuclear test. It not only defied the authority of the treaty, but it also sent a wrong signal to Iran and other potential nuclear aspirants.

A nuclear North Korea poses great challenges to East Asia in particular. First, it causes a physical threat to neighboring countries. North Korea is a small country lacking strategic depth. The site where the nuclear test was conducted is only 137 km away from the border of China, 185 km from Russia, and 262 km from South Korea. If any nuclear incident happens due to mistake or technical failure, it will cause disaster not only to North Korea itself, but also to neighboring countries, especially China.

Second, a nuclear North Korea aggravates the already tense situation on the peninsula. The Korean Peninsula witnessed a bloody regional war during the Cold War, leaving millions dead or wounded. Although the 1953 armistice formally ended the fighting, no peace treaty was signed, and the Demilitarized Zone (DMZ) along the 38th parallel remains one of the most dangerous places in today's world. During the decade-long nuclear crisis, war clouds floated over the peninsula time and again, with some in the Bush administration advocating regime change in North Korea. If the nuclear issue is not settled, the confrontation between the United States and North Korea may frustrate any hope of creating a collective security regime in Northeast Asia.[2]

Third, a nuclear North Korea may ignite an arms race in East Asia. Great power competition exists between a rising China, an ambitious Japan, and a hegemonic United States. There are also lingering historical antagonisms and mutual distrust between China, Korea, and Japan, as well as territorial disputes in the region. As one scholar writes, "the persistence of lingering historical antagonisms, weakness of regional organizations, unstable relations among the great powers, and the possibility that some of the regional disputes are about to escalate into militarized conflicts— have all resulted in the widespread belief that Asia will become the most important zone of conflict in the 21st century."[3] The North Korean nuclear test may stimulate a region lacking in mutual trust and collective security regimes into a heated arms race. In fact, immediately after North Korea's nuclear test, some of Japan's high officials openly expressed their intention to review Japan's long-held "no nuclear" position.[4]

China's Policy toward the Nuclear Issue: Continuity and Change

Since 1978, when China opened up to the outside world and concentrated on economic construction, its overarching foreign policy objective has been to cultivate a peaceful and stable environment for its domestic economic development. As a close neighbor of North Korea, China pays special attention to the peace and stability on the peninsula. As history demonstrates, an unstable peninsula will inevitably affect China's security environment and domestic construction. The 1950–53 Korean War is a clear example. The war ultimately drew China in and left millions dead or wounded, greatly affecting China's development, strangling Sino-U.S. relations, and exacerbating China's security concerns.

In line with this objective, China supports a nuclear-free Korean Peninsula. In other words, it opposes a nuclear North Korea. In addition to the physical threat it will pose to China and neighboring countries, North Korea's nuclear ambition will also worsen the situation on the peninsula and perhaps even ignite a nuclear domino effect in East Asia. China first publicized its official position on the nuclear issue in an editorial in *People's Daily* on July 11, 1991, claiming that "the Chinese government supports the North Korean government's recent appeal of establishing a nuclear-free Korean Peninsula."[5] But at this phase, China's support of a nuclear-free peninsula was also directed at U.S. nuclear weapons in the South. As the United States pulled out its nuclear weapons from the South and as the nuclear crisis developed, China's nuclear-free position was gradually centered on North Korea. On February 18, 1993, China's Foreign Ministry spokesperson made this clear by declaring that "China supports the denuclearization of the Korean Peninsula, and does not support any nuclear weapons on the Peninsula, either of the North, or of the South, or from abroad. China hopes the goal set in the Joint Declaration of the Denuclearization of Korean Peninsula signed by the North and South could be fulfilled as early as possible."[6] This is the first time China publicly opposed North Korea's nuclear program. On November 1993, at a press conference held in Seattle, China's Foreign Minister Qian Qichen summarized China's position on the nuclear issue: "We've clarified our position clearly, first, the maintenance of the peace and stability of the Korean peninsula; second, the denuclearization of the peninsula, and the way to the objective is through negotiation by the relevant parties."[7]

Qian Qichen's last few words also reflect the third point of China's policy toward the nuclear issue: resolving the issue through peaceful means. In China's view, resorting to coercion, either in the form of economic sanctions or military maneuvers, is not conducive, and even counterproductive to the settlement of the problem. The basic goal behind North Korea's nuclear program is for security in view of the dramatically changed strategic environment it faces following the end of the Cold War.[8] Sanctions or military maneuvers will only exacerbate the perception of insecurity of an already paranoid North Korea and deepen the suspicion it holds of the United States. Perceiving its survival threatened, it may hold to whatever it can to safeguard its security, and nuclear weapons may prove to be the ultimate means. Dialogue, though slow and painstaking, may provide an indispensable channel for two mutually distrustful adversaries to explore the intent of the other and to alleviate misperceptions. As Madeleine Albright found after visiting Pyongyang and holding talks with Kim Jong Il, Great Leader Kim is not as irrational as she had imagined.[9]

However, an outstanding characteristic of China's position during the first nuclear crisis was that China refrained from directly involving itself in the issue and was especially unwilling to press North Korea, confining itself only to facilitating dialogue between the United States and North Korea. China's Foreign Ministry spokesperson Wu Jianming defended China's position at a press conference on April 22, 1993, stating "The problem of North Korean nuclear inspections is more of an issue between North Korea and the U.S., North Korea and the IAEA, and North Korea and South Korea. We hope the issue could be appropriately settled through dialogue and consultation by relevant parties. China will continue to play a constructive role for the settlement of the issue."[10] Nevertheless, China did lend some tacit diplomatic support to voice its displeasure with North Korea. In May 1993, when the North Korean nuclear issue was referred to the UN Security Council, China abstained on UN Security Council resolutions and helped to draft statements for the Council president urging North Korean compliance, and thus lent tacit political support to U.S. efforts. This was seen as a protest against North Korea's declaration of withdrawal from the NPT in March 1993. China even turned down a request by Kim Jong Il to see Deng Xiaoping during a visit to Beijing and canceled a high-level visit to Pyongyang on the occasion of Kim Il Sung's birthday.[11] On the other hand, when North Korea and the United States began direct dialogue, China expressed its full support.[12]

The underlying causes for China's unwillingness to be directly involved in the first nuclear crisis could be explained by three factors. First is the limited influence it has over North Korea. After China established diplomatic relations with South Korea in 1992, its relations with North Korea cooled down dramatically. The official visits between the two countries almost came to a halt during 1992–93. China's establishment of diplomatic relations with South Korea was viewed by North Korea as an act of betrayal.[13] Thus, China could not hope to exert much influence over North Korea. As North Korea repeatedly told the United States, "Forget about China. Let's make a deal."[14] Second, China itself faced tremendous diplomatic problems. In the aftermath of the 1989 incident in China and the collapse of the Soviet bloc, China's strategic environment deteriorated drastically. China faced strong economic sanctions and political containment by the West. The United States held a very negative attitude toward China's role in the nuclear issue and did not believe Beijing could be of much help.[15] Lastly, the Clinton administration showed considerable flexibility. Although reluctant, the Clinton administration did hold direct dialogue with North Korea, which helped to strike a compromise and ended the first crisis.

Although the fundamental policy objective of China toward the nuclear issue remains unchanged, China's attitude toward how to resolve the crisis has undergone considerable change since the beginning of the second nuclear crisis. China is now willing to play a much more active role than it did in the first crisis. When the second nuclear crisis broke out in 2002, the United States cut off shipments of heavy fuel oil to North Korea and even intercepted a North Korean ship in the Arabian Sea. North Korea retaliated by removing the seals at all frozen facilities, dismantling IAEA monitoring cameras, expelling IAEA inspectors, and finally withdrawing from the NPT in January 2003.[16] North Korea defended its withdrawal from the NPT by declaring that "we have no intention to produce nuclear weapons . . . After the appearance of the Bush Administration, the United States listed the DPRK [Democratic People's Republic of Korea] as part of an 'axis of evil,' adopting it as a national policy to oppose its system, and singled it out as a target of pre-emptive nuclear attack . . . it also answered the DPRK's sincere proposals for conclusion of the DPRK-U.S. non-aggression treaty with such threats as 'blockade' and 'military punishment.'"[17] In other words, North Korea thought it was forced to take actions after calls for the United States to address its security concerns through direct dialogue proved futile. In February 2003, the issue was referred to the UN Security Council, which passed a resolution formally demanding DPRK cooperation and a return to the NPT.[18]

The confrontation between North Korea and the United States coincided with the gathering war storm in the Gulf. If not handled properly, the situation on the peninsula could spiral out of control. For China, maintaining peace and stability on the peninsula is a top policy priority, which demands a nuclear-free Korean Peninsula. China must find a way to defuse the tension and, above all, to avoid military conflict on the peninsula. After tremendous diplomatic efforts, China succeeded in bringing the United States and North Korea together and held three-party talks in April 2003, thereby ending a six-month confrontational period of "no talk, no negotiation." Although the talks lasted only three days and did not produce any substantial result, they provided a platform for the two adversaries to voice their concerns directly. And the talks were themselves an indication that both the United States, which insisted on multilateral talks, and North Korea, which insisted on bilateral talks, had backed a bit from their original rigid positions. In addition, the two agreed to continue talks in the future. The next few months witnessed intensified diplomatic activities by China, which resulted in the holding of the first six-party talks in Beijing in August 2003, including China, the United States, North Korea, South Korea, Russia, and Japan. From then on, the six-party talk pattern has been accepted by all participants, including North Korea. So far, six rounds of talks have taken place despite the ups and downs of the situation, including North Korea's nuclear test.

As a mediator of the two deeply distrustful adversaries, China has to take into consideration the interests and concerns of both. While China supports a nuclear-free Korean Peninsula, in China's view, as a much weaker and isolated country, North Korea's security concerns should also be considered. Well before the Iraqi War broke out, North Korea had repeatedly voiced its concerns regarding the hostile policy of the United States and proposed to settle their mutual concerns on an equal footing. After the Iraqi War broke out, Pyongyang's worries were aggravated. As North Korea's newspaper wrote, "The Iraqi War is the consequence of the U.S. weapons inspection."[19] So from China's perspective, in order for the ultimate goal of a nuclear-free peninsula to be realized, the United States should be more flexible and show its willingness to seriously consider North Korea's security worries.[20]

In line with this position, China, along with South Korea and Russia, opposed the "Libya Model" proposed by the United States since the second round of talks. This would require North Korea to dismantle its nuclear program first, and then the United States might consider ways to alleviate the security and other concerns of North Korea.[21] In light of North Korea's deep distrust of the United States and the increasingly paranoid perception of insecurity in the aftermath of the Iraqi War, the "Libya Model" is definitely not a good prescription for the resolution to the nuclear issue. Partly due to China's quiet diplomatic efforts, and largely due to the deteriorating situation in Iraq, the Bush administration's position toward North Korea changed, which was obvious at the fourth round of talks held in Beijing from

July 26 to September 19, 2005. The United States replaced the obstructionist Kelly with a more pro-dialogue Christopher Hill as chief negotiator and showed much more flexibility and good faith in the talks, resulting in the first joint statement of the six parties in the more than two and a half years of on-and-off talks. The joint statement declared: "North Korea promises to dismantle all its nuclear weapons and existing nuclear program, return to NPT as early as possible and accept the safeguards monitoring of IAEA. The United States confirms that the United States has no nuclear weapons on the Korean peninsula, has no intention to attack with nuclear or conventional weapons or invade North Korea. . . . North Korea and the United States promise to respect each other's sovereignty, coexist peacefully and take steps to normalize their relations according to each side's bilateral policy. . . . The six parties agree to take concerted steps to implement the above listed consensus in a phased way according to the principle of 'promise to promise, action to action.' "[22]

However, China's sympathy with North Korea's security worries does not mean that it will tolerate North Korea's obstinacy or compromise China's "denuclearization" principle. When North Korea retreated from its agreed position and declared it would boycott the six-party talks days after the joint statement, China expressed its displeasure and pressed North Korea to attend the scheduled next round of talks. When North Korea announced its nuclear test on October 9, 2006, China reacted quickly by denouncing North Korea's test and supporting a UN Security Council resolution to sanction North Korea.

An interesting question is why did China become so active in the second nuclear crisis, and what are the causes leading to this change? First is the transformed diplomatic environment China faced. Compared with the first nuclear crisis, China's relations with the West in general, and the United States in particular, are much better. In addition, the relations with North Korea also were greatly strengthened. High-level visits between the two resumed, and communications between the two countries intensified. Since May 2000, Kim Jong Il has visited China more than four times, and President Hu Jintao also visited North Korea in October 2005. The relatively relaxed external environment provided much greater opportunity for China to play an active role in the crisis. Second is the "new thinking" of China's foreign policy. Since the late 1990s, and especially at the turn of the new century, China has increasingly embraced the idea of "a responsible power." China came to realize that, as a rising power, it is not enough to keep its own house in order. China must have its share in the provision of the "public good" and play an active and constructive role in the maintenance of the authority of international regimes.[23] As a result, China has been more willing to exert influence over North Korea and more outspoken about its dissatisfaction with North Korea. Third is the obstinacy of the Bush administration. Compared with Bill Clinton, Bush and his team are much harder in their attitude and policy toward North Korea. Bush himself has personal animosity toward Kim Jong Il. Encouraged by the advances in the Iraq War and the model effect of Libya's abandonment of its WMD program, the Bush administration was more willing to use coercion instead of dialogue to pressure North Korea. But North Korea is not Iraq or Libya, and its nuclear program was far more advanced than

Libya's. Thus, pure coercion will not make North Korea capitulate. China's mediation may help the two adversaries to soften their positions and deescalate the crisis.

Conclusion

As a close neighbor of North Korea, China is vulnerable to any turbulence on the Korean Peninsula. So for China, maintaining peace and stability on the peninsula is not only in the interests of both North and South Korea, but also China. Moreover, in view of the inherent danger of nuclear weapons and the threat they pose to international nonproliferation regimes and regional order, China opposes a nuclear North Korea. These two positions are inseparable. Due to its improved external environment and enhanced national power, China has played a much more active role since the second nuclear crisis. It has been the host of six rounds of six-party talks and a mediator between North Korea and the United States. It voiced its support of a nuclear-free peninsula and also lends support to North Korea's legitimate security concerns.

At present, the North Korean nuclear issue is at a crossroads. The international community has made great efforts to resolve the issue in a diplomatic way. A new joint statement has been signed and has provided enough incentives for North Korea to start the process of dismantling its nuclear program. The ball is now in North Korea's court, and it alone will take the responsibility for the decisions it will make.

AN AMERICAN PERSPECTIVE: THE BUSH ADMINISTRATION'S RESPONSES TO THE NORTH KOREAN NUCLEAR THREAT

Concerns in the United States regarding a possible North Korean nuclear weapons program began to intensify in the late 1980s and early 1990s. Although the DPRK had joined the IAEA in 1974 and became a signatory of the NPT in late 1985, it did not sign the IAEA full-scope safeguards agreement until January 1992. By the time of the IAEA safeguards signing, North Korea was believed to have a five-megawatt (MW) reactor in operation at its facilities located in Yongbyon as well as a nuclear fuel reprocessing plant with two larger reactors (50 MW and 200 MW) under construction. When the IAEA representatives arrived at Yongbyon to conduct a series of seven inspections between May 1992 and July 1993, they discovered several discrepancies that the North Koreans were not able to explain satisfactorily. Subsequently in March 1993, the DPRK threatened to withdraw from the NPT just as the Clinton administration was coming into office.[24]

During a series of negotiations in 1993 and 1994, the United States and North Korea were able to reach an accord in October 1994 that became known as the Agreed Framework.[25] Under the terms of this agreement, North Korea promised to freeze its graphite reactors, including the two under construction, and replace them with two light-water reactors (LWRs) that were to be built by the United States and other countries. In order to make up for the energy lost from the freezing on the graphite reactor, the United States agreed to provide 500,000 tons of heavy fuel oil per year. Of special importance, the DPRK pledged to remain in the NPT and to allow IAEA inspectors to monitor the freezing of its graphite reactor and other facilities at Yongbyon as well as the more than 8,000 spent fuel rods that remained in DPRK cooling ponds. In 1995, the United States, Japan, and South Korea established the Korean Peninsula Energy Development Organization (KEDO), whose primary function was to oversee the construction of the two LWRs in North Korea.[26]

The second major Clinton administration initiative toward North Korea occurred after the DPRK test fired a Taepodong 1 ballistic missile over Japan in August 1998, much to the consternation of the Japanese. After another series of bilateral negotiations, the DPRK announced in September 1999 a self-imposed moratorium on the testing of ballistic missiles that would remain in effect as long as substantive negotiations with the United States on nuclear and other issues continued.[27] The bilateral relationship improved to the point that in October 2000, Secretary of State Madeleine Albright visited North Korean leader Kim Jong Il in Pyongyang, and there was even speculation that President Clinton might also visit before he left office.[28] This visit did not occur, but the administration felt reasonably confident that it had frozen the North Korean nuclear program at Yongbyon and stopped the testing of ballistic missiles as Clinton prepared to transfer power to George W. Bush in January 2001. The best estimate was that North Korea could have reprocessed no more than 10 kilograms of plutonium prior to 1994 when the Agreed Framework went into effect. This amount of plutonium could produce only one or perhaps two small nuclear devices.[29]

Initial Bush Administration Policies Toward North Korea

Domestic issues dominated the 2000 presidential election between Vice President Al Gore and Texas Governor George W. Bush. However, the 1994 Agreed Framework did attract some attention, at least from advisers close to Bush. In March 1999, Richard Armitage wrote a critique of the Clinton administration's policy involving North Korea with a specific reference to the Agreed Framework. This critique became known as the "Armitage Report" and took on additional importance when Bush appointed Armitage to be deputy secretary of state after he became president.[30] Armitage was particularly critical of the Agreed Framework's major assumption that North Korea would terminate its nuclear weapons program under the right circumstances. For Armitage, the Agreed Framework should be viewed as the first step in a comprehensive program that would also include the DPRK's missiles, conventional military forces, and human rights violations.

After becoming president, George W. Bush initiated a North Korea policy review that took more than six months to accomplish. In June 2001, the president announced the results of this review. He directed his national security team to conduct "serious discussions" with the DPRK, but he expanded the agenda to include topics such as limitations on North Korea's missile program and a ban on missile exports in addition to nuclear weapons. Further, he added the DPRK's large conventional military forces and its human rights record as topics for any future negotiations, very similar to the recommendations Armitage made in 1999. In his concluding remarks, President Bush stated that if North Korea entered into serious discussions on these issues, the United States would expand its efforts to assist the North Korean people by easing sanctions and taking other political steps.[31]

After the terrorist attacks in New York and Washington on September 11, 2001, the Bush administration published two reports that would become extremely important in defining its policies toward North Korea. The first of these reports was the Nuclear Posture Review, released to the public in January 2002. The second was the National Security Strategy, published that September. The Nuclear Posture Review outlined plans to develop conventional and nuclear weapons that would be able to attack deep underground bunkers and specifically mentioned the DPRK as one of seven countries that could be targeted by these weapons.[32] The National Security Strategy was even more specific regarding North Korea. This document identified the very real danger that the United States and other countries confronted from terrorist organizations having global reach and support from rogue nation-states possessing weapons of mass destruction. In this context, the National Security Strategy specifically mentioned North Korea as "the world's principal purveyor of ballistic missiles" and also as a country "developing its own WMD arsenal." To counter the threats associated with rogue states and terrorist organizations, this report indicated that the more traditional forms of deterrence were no longer effective, and the United States would turn to preemptive attacks as the more appropriate means to deal with these threats.[33]

President Bush made his position even more clear in the State of the Union address in late January 2002, when he identified North Korea as a member of the "axis of evil," along with Iran and Iraq.[34] In an August 2002 interview with Bob Woodward, Bush was even more explicit when he expressed his visceral dislike and loathing for Kim Jong Il because of Kim's mistreatment of the North Korean people through starvation, the use of prison camps, and torture.[35] Based on this policy review, the positions taken toward the DPRK in the Nuclear Posture Review and National Security Strategy, and the president's own statements, it is not surprising that there was little contact between the United States and North Korea during the first two years of this administration.

The policy review was complicated because of the deep divisions within the Bush administration regarding the proper approach to be taken toward North Korea. On one side were those who voiced a more hard-line position and believed negotiations with the DPRK would be counterproductive because the North could not be trusted to comply with any agreement. Among this group of advisers were Vice President Dick Cheney, Secretary of Defense Donald Rumsfeld, Assistant Secretary of Defense Paul Wolfowitz, and Undersecretary of State for Arms Control and International Security John Bolton. Those on the other side of the debate took a more pragmatic approach and argued it was possible to reach some sort of an accord with the DPRK through negotiations and engagement. Among this group were Secretary of State Colin Powell, Deputy Secretary of State Richard Armitage, and Assistant Secretary of State for East Asia and Pacific Affairs James Kelly.[36] The point is that these divisions made formulating a consistent policy much more difficult.

In October 2002, the administration decided to send Assistant Secretary Kelly to Pyongyang for discussions with the North Koreans. This was a very important visit because Kelly presented evidence obtained by American intelligence assets indicating the DPRK was constructing a clandestine uranium enrichment facility. To the surprise of the visiting delegation, the North Koreans admitted they were developing such a facility after an initial denial. Subsequently, the North Korean negotiators would again reverse themselves by arguing that they had not developed highly enriched uranium (HEU) capability, but they had the right to do so because of what they described as the Bush administration's "hostile policies." At the conclusion of these discussions, the North Koreans announced that they no longer considered the 1994 Agreed Framework to be in effect.[37]

Although it is impossible to know for certain why the DPRK would initially admit to this HEU program, it may be that the evidence was so compelling that North Korean officials could not deny the program. Kelly made it clear that from that point forward, there was a "precondition" for any future discussions, and that precondition was North Korea's termination of its HEU program. To the DPRK's excuse that this program was a response to hostile Bush administration policies toward North Korea, Kelly retorted that U.S. intelligence indicated that North Korea had begun its HEU program considerably before Bush took office in January 2001. In fact, a Department of Energy report stated that the DPRK began to develop this program as early as 1999, if not earlier.[38] Whatever the reasons, the North Korean admission set in motion a series of events that once again increased the possibility of conflict on the Korean Peninsula.

In November 2002, the KEDO Executive Board, including representatives from the United States, South Korea, Japan, and the European Union, voted to terminate the LWR project and to suspend future heavy-oil shipments to North Korea beginning in December of that year. These shipments had been a part of the Agreed Framework and were critical to meeting the DPRK's energy needs. Reinstatement of these shipments would be contingent on the termination of the HEU program.[39] One expert on North Korean negotiating strategy has called the KEDO decision a "tactical blunder" because the DPRK then began to take a number of actions that caused even more concern in the United States and the international community.[40] In December 2002, North Korean officials once again declared the Agreed Framework to be null and void, announced the restarting of the 5-MW reactor and the continuation of construction on the 50- and 200-MW reactors, and expelled the IAEA inspectors. They also stated that North Korea intended to retrieve the 8,000 spent fuel rods that had been in cooling ponds and begin to extract plutonium from them. Finally, in January 2003, the DPRK declared its intention to withdraw from the NPT and IAEA Safeguards Agreement. This withdrawal became effective in April 2003, and North Korea is the only country to have withdrawn from the NPT to this point.[41]

Multilateral Negotiations and the Nuclear Test

President Bush believed that another problem with the Agreed Framework was that only the United States and North Korea were involved. From his perspective, the wiser course was multilateral negotiations because other countries in Northeast Asia have a stake in the North Korean nuclear weapons program, plus he was convinced it would be easier to implement a multilateral agreement. Subsequently, China agreed to host a series of discussions beginning in April 2003 that would continue through 2004. As Professor Wei Zongyou has related in the first part of this chapter, China had its own reasons for desiring to become involved in these negotiations. At first, just North Korea, the United States, and China participated, but the negotiations were expanded by the end of 2003 to six-party talks that also included South Korea, Japan, and Russia. Very little progress was made, in part because the United States and North Korea had fundamental and seemingly irreconcilable positions over what North Korean programs to include in the negotiations and how the sequencing of any agreement would be implemented.[42]

In February 2005, the North Korean Ministry of Foreign Affairs officially announced that the DRPK was a nuclear weapons country. The justification given for developing these weapons was that the United States had continued its hostile policies toward North Korea as the second Bush term began. In this statement, the Ministry of Foreign Affairs also related that the DPRK was no longer interested in participating in the six-party negotiations because no progress was possible as long as the United States maintained its current policies.[43] Despite this stated lack of interest in future negotiations, North Korean officials changed their minds by the summer of 2005. In July, the fourth round of six-party negotiations began in Beijing. The first efforts met with little success, and the talks recessed until September.

On September 19, the negotiating parties released a joint statement containing some very important provisions.[44] Among these provisions, the parties unanimously agreed that the essential goal of these negotiations was to achieve the verifiable denuclearization of the Korean Peninsula. North Korea stipulated that it was committed to abandoning all of its nuclear weapons and returning to the NPT and IAEA safeguards "at an early date." The United States provided North Korea with the security assurances it had demanded by stating that it had "no intention to attack or invade the DPRK with nuclear or conventional weapons." Both sides also stated their intentions to move toward normalizing diplomatic relations and respecting each country's sovereignty. All the parties agreed to provide North Korea with energy assistance, and the DPRK restated its position that it had the right to develop peaceful uses of nuclear energy to include light-water reactors. The other parties would only agree to discuss the LWR issue "at an appropriate time."

Despite some initial optimism, relations between the United States and the DPRK began to deteriorate almost before the ink on the joint statement was dry. The inclusion of any reference to light-water reactors caused problems for the Americans.[45] More important, the U.S. Department of Treasury, under Article 311 of the USA Patriot Act, designated Banco Delta Asia (BDA), a bank in Macao in which North

Korea had approximately $25 million on deposit, to be "a primary money laundering concern." This designation effectively froze the North Korean money in this bank and reinforced what the DPRK believed was a deliberate attempt by the Bush administration to cause financial harm to the country.[46] The next round of six-party talks, held in November 2005, lasted only briefly before adjournment because of these problems.

With negotiations stalled, North Korea performed two extremely provocative acts in 2006. In early July, the DPRK broke its self-imposed moratorium on ballistic missile tests in effect since 1999 when it launched a Taepodong 2 missile along with six other shorter-range missiles. The Taepodong flew only for less than a minute before it exploded, but the effects were immediate.[47] The United States, Japan, and other countries introduced a resolution in the United Nations Security Council that passed unanimously later in July. This unanimous passage was significant because China and Russia, two of North Korea's strongest supporters, voted in favor of the resolution further isolating the DPRK. UNSC Resolution 1695 condemned the missile launches and called on North Korea to reimpose the missile test moratorium, rejoin the NPT and IAEA safeguards regime, and continue with the six-party negotiations.[48] This resolution also applied a series of sanctions against North Korea related to its missile programs.

Unfortunately, the DPRK was not deterred and, on October 9, 2006, detonated its first nuclear device. Six days before this detonation, the Ministry of Foreign Affairs had announced that a test was imminent. The ministry stressed that this test and North Korea's nuclear capabilities were part of the country's "reliable war deterrent" and would be used only for self-defense. It pledged that the DPRK would never use nuclear weapons first and would also work toward the goal of a nuclear-free Korean Peninsula. The final part of this statement indicated that North Korea wanted to improve its relations with the United States.[49] The underground detonation of the nuclear device measured less than one kiloton (the atomic bombs dropped on Hiroshima and Nagasaki were approximately 20 kilotons). Just prior to this detonation, the North Koreans had advised the Chinese and Russian embassies in Pyongyang of the impending test. They stated the explosion would be about four kilotons, which suggests the actual detonation was less successful than the DPRK had hoped.[50] Nonetheless, there was no question, based on seismic and scientific evidence, that North Korea had tested a nuclear device.

The United Nations Security Council responded with a stronger resolution condemning the nuclear test than it had issued after the missile firings in July. UNSC Resolution 1718, dated October 14, 2006, was again passed unanimously and, under Chapter VII, Article 41 of the UN Charter, described the test "as a threat to international peace and security." Article 41 allows for the use of nonmilitary measures to enforce its provisions, including interruption of economic interchanges and the severance of diplomatic relations.[51] The resolution demanded that North Korea return to the NPT and IAEA Safeguards Agreement, not conduct any more ballistic missiles launches, and abandon its weapons of mass destruction programs (chemical, biological, and nuclear). The UN resolution banned the sale or provision of major conventional arms to the DPRK as well as luxury goods. Two experts on North Korea have referred to this resolution as "the toughest international sanctions against North Korea since the end of the Korean War."[52]

Under major pressure from China and other countries after the nuclear weapon test, North Korea began to move back to the negotiating track. In late November 2006, Assistant Secretary of State for East Asia and Pacific Affairs Christopher Hill met with Kim Gye Gwan, North Korea's vice foreign minister. In this series of meetings, Hill reportedly offered food assistance and promised help in resolving the BDA deposit problem if North Korea would agree to give up its nuclear weapons.[53] An even more important bilateral meeting took place between Kim and Hill in Berlin in mid-January 2007. According to media accounts, the two negotiators began to develop an agenda that could be used in the next round of six-party talks. In exchange for U.S. economic and energy assistance as well as relief from the BDA imbroglio, North Korea would agree to suspend certain nuclear programs to include the 5-MW reactor. These discussions were given more prominence when Secretary of State Condoleezza Rice passed through Berlin just after the conclusion of the Hill-Kim meetings and indicated her support for resuming the negotiations as soon as possible.[54]

The fifth round of the six-party negotiations occurred in Beijing from February 8–13, 2007. At the conclusion, the representatives signed the North Korea–Denuclearization Plan. This plan largely was designed to implement the September 2005 Joint Statement in a phased manner to resolve the sequencing problem that had bedeviled earlier agreements. The principle of "action for action" was to be spelled out so that all parties would know who was to do what, and when. In the initial phase that would last from 60 days of the signing, North Korea was to shut down and seal the reprocessing plant and nuclear reactors at Yongbyon and invite back the IAEA inspectors to monitor and verify these actions. The DPRK also agreed to discuss a list of all other nuclear programs with the other members of the six-party talks to include the plutonium extracted from spent fuel rods. The United States pledged bilateral talks with the DPRK to consider removing North Korea from the Department of State's state-sponsor-of-terrorism list and begin to terminate the application of the Trading with the Enemy Act to North Korea. These actions could enable the two countries to establish more normal economic relations and could lead to the DPRK gaining membership in international lending organizations such as the World Bank. To assist the DPRK with its energy requirements, the other countries agreed to supply 50,000 tons of heavy fuel oil within a 60-day initial period.

In the second phase (a specific time period was not established), the DPRK pledged to disable the nuclear facilities at Yongbyon, and provide a complete declaration of all its nuclear programs. The other countries would supply a total of 950,000 tons of heavy fuel oil in addition to the 50,000 tons in the initial phase. The February agreement established five working groups to oversee the implementation of these provisions. The first three were multilateral and would include the Denuclearization of the Korean Peninsula group, headed by China; the Economy and Energy group, headed by South Korea; and the Northeast Asia Peace and

Security Mechanism group, headed by Russia. The other two working groups were bilateral and were the Normalization of DPRK-U.S. Relations and the Normalization of DPRK-Japan Relations groups. It is unclear how the implementation of these specific agreements will transpire. In separate negotiations, U.S. Treasury officials related that the United States no longer objected if Macao authorities wanted to return the approximately $25 million to North Korea. Although this American concession appeared to clear the way for the release on the North Korean accounts, technical problems developed, and the funds were not released until June. In July, the DPRK shut down its operating nuclear reactor at Yongbyon and allowed inspectors from the IAEA back into the country to verify this shutdown. The IAEA subsequently issued a statement of verification. Later in July, the six-party talks reconvened in Beijing and basically agreed that the five established working groups would need to devise specific plans that would address the permanent disabling of the North Korean facilities at Yongbyon and the issuance by the DPRK of a comprehensive declaration of all nuclear weapons programs, among other topics.[55]

Conclusion

By almost any objective standard, the Bush administration's policies to terminate the North Korean nuclear weapon programs have been unsuccessful. President Bush and others in his administration have indicated on many occasions that nuclear weapons in the DPRK are intolerable.[56] However, in strictly quantitative terms, when Bush took office in 2001, North Korea was a member of the NPT, and IAEA inspectors were present at its known nuclear weapons sites. DPRK nuclear facilities at these sites had been shut down. Kim Jong Il had agreed to a ballistic missile test moratorium, and, at the most, had available plutonium to construct one or two nuclear bombs. Now, well into the second Bush term, North Korea has withdrawn from the NPT, expelled IAEA inspectors, restarted its nuclear reactor, and reprocessed between 46 and 64 kilograms of plutonium, of which approximately 28–50 kilograms are estimated to be in the form needed to be usable in nuclear weapons. Two experts have opined that with this amount of plutonium, North Korea is likely to have between five and 12 nuclear weapons.[57] Perhaps more worrying, North Korea has rescinded its ballistic missile moratorium, launched a Taepodong missile, and tested a small nuclear device.

From a negotiations perspective, initial divisions within the Bush administration hampered the development of a comprehensive strategy toward North Korea. Once the multilateral negotiations began in 2003, China exercised much influence over the agenda and timing of these negotiations. Finally, in the lead-up to the February 2007 negotiations, North Korea was once again able to use its brinksmanship tactics through the testing of a nuclear device to force the United States to engage in bilateral discussions both within and without the six-party context.[58] The agreement reached during the February negotiations offers promise, but the initial efforts to implement this agreement have given pause to this optimism. The North Korean shutdown of its reactor at Yongbyon and the readmission of the IAEA after five years does provide some optimism, but as Christopher Hill has stated, the really hard work of dismantling nuclear facilities and agreeing to North Korea's comprehensive list of nuclear programs remains for future negotiations.

In comparing the Chinese and Bush administration's approaches to the North Korean nuclear weapons challenge, Wei Zongyou has rightfully pointed out that China chose to play a more pronounced role in the crisis that developed after the October 2002 confrontation between the United States and the DPRK in Pyong-yang. China's diplomatic status was much improved in late 2002 and early 2003 over what it had been in the 1992–94 period. Wei also stated that China was pursuing "new thinking" in its foreign policy and acting as a "responsible power" in taking on the role of organizing and sponsoring the multilateral negotiations beginning in April 2003 and continuing to the present. Finally, he expressed Chinese frustration with what he and others saw as the obstinacy of the Bush administration's negotiating strategy toward North Korea. All of these factors have contributed to the very impor-tant roles China is playing. In addition, China is committed to a nuclear-free Korean Peninsula because this denucleariztion will foster a more peaceful and stable region, allowing China to pursue its economic modernization.

The Bush administration has been willing to accept China's increased involvement and leadership in multilateral negotiations, in part because President Bush and many of his advisers truly believe that the bilateral negotiations during the Clinton years resulted in a flawed agreement in 1994. However, the argument can also be made that the administration saw multilateral negotiations as a format whereby the Bush team could avoid bilateral contacts with North Korea or, at the least, minimize those contacts. The irony of this effort is that, late in 2006 and then early in 2007, Chris-topher Hill met with his North Korean counterpart in two separate bilateral meet-ings that set the agenda for the February 2007 six-party talks. Similarly, in early July, Hill traveled to Pyongyang as the highest-ranking American diplomat to visit the DPRK since James Kelly in October 2002. Once again, Hill and the North Kore-ans worked out the agenda for the July negotiations. The point here is that even though China is playing a much more important role in the conduct of multilateral negotiations, the North Koreans have had some success in compelling the United States to still take them seriously, as evidenced by the bilateral initiatives that have taken place and, more than likely, will continue to take place.

NOTES

1. Victor D. Cha and David C. Kang, *Nuclear North Korea: A Debate on Engagement Strat-egies* (New York: Columbia University Press, 2003), 132.

2. Wei Ling, "Dongbeiya duobian anquan jizhi jianshe: yi chaohe wenti liufang huitan weili" ("Multilateral Security Mechanism Building in Northeast Asia: Study of the Six-Party Talks"), *Waijiao pinglun [Foreign Affairs Review]* 87, no. 2 (February 2006): 44–50.

3. Renato Cruz De Castro, "Regionalism and Multilateralism: Essays on Cooperative Security in the Asia-Pacific," *Contemporary Southeast Asia* 27, no. 2 (August 2005): 331.

4. "Meiguo danxin Riben 'hewuzhang'" ("The United States Worries About a 'Nuclear Weaponized' Japan"), October 20, 2006, http://world.gansudaily.com.cn/system/2006/10/20/010160725.shtml.

5. Liu Jingzhi and Yang Huaisheng, eds., *Zhongguo dui Chaoxian he Hanguo zhengce wenjian huibian [Document Collections of China's Policies Towards North and South Korea]* (Beijing: Zhongguo shehui kexue chubanshe, 1994), 2590.

6. Ibid., 2621.

7. Ibid., 2636–37.

8. Xue Wenji, "Meichao hefengbo de shizhi yu liufanghuitan de chulu" ["The Nature of the U.S.–North Korean Nuclear Crisis and the Way Out"], *Dongbeiya luntan [Northeast Asia Forum]* 15, no. 4 (2006): 68–69.

9. Walter C. Clemens Jr., "Negotiating to Control Weapons of Mass Destruction in North Korea," *International Negotiation* 10, no. 3 (2005): 464.

10. Liu and Yang, *Zhongguo dui Chaoxian,* 2624.

11. Leon V. Sigal, *Disarming Strangers: Nuclear Diplomacy with North Korea* (Princeton, NJ: Princeton University Press, 1998), 58.

12. Jingzhi and Huaisheng, *Zhongguo dui Chaoxian,* 2652.

13. Ibid., 2599–642; Andrew Scobell, *China and North Korea: From Comrades-in-Arms to Allies at Arm's Length,* March 2004, available at http://www.carlisle.army.mil/ssi/pdffiles/00364.pdf.

14. Sigal, *Disarming Strangers,* 59.

15. Ibid., 57.

16. Cha and Kang, *Nuclear North Korea,* 133.

17. Ibid., 144.

18. Ibid., 154.

19. Qiu Haiyan, *Shixi dierci Chaohe weiji [A Study of the Second Nuclear Crisis of North Korea]* (MA thesis, Fuzhou, Fujian Normal University), 21.

20. See Xinhua News Agency, February 7, 2004.

21. James Goodby and Donald Gross, "The 'Libya Model' Could Help Disarm North Korea," *International Herald Tribune,* September 3, 2004.

22. "Disilun liufanghuitan lianheshengming" ["The Joint Statement of the Fourth Round of Six-party Talks"], September 19, 2004, http://world.people.com.cn/GB/1029/42354/3707408.html.

23. See Wei Zongyou, "Zhongguo xinwaijiao: guonei bianqian, waibu huanjing ji guojji zhixu" ["China's New Diplomacy: Domestic Changes, External Environment and International Order"], *Guoji guancha [International Review]* 82, no. 4 (2006): 33–40.

24. For more details on the Clinton administration's negotiations with North Korea on the nuclear weapons issue, see William E. Berry Jr., "The North Korean Nuclear Weapons Program: A Comparison of the Negotiating Strategies of the Clinton and Bush Administrations," in *Perspectives on U.S. Policy Toward North Korea: Stalemate or Checkmate?* ed. Sharon Richardson (New York: Lexington Books, 2006), 1–3.

25. "Agreed Framework Between the United States of America and the Democratic People's Republic of Korea," October 21, 1994. This document is available on the Korean Peninsula Development Organization Web site, http://www.kedo.org. The specifics concerning the Agreed Framework that follow are taken directly from this document.

26. "Agreement of the Establishment of the Korean Peninsula Energy Development Organization," signed by representatives of the United States, Japan, and South Korea on

March 9, 1995. Subsequently, the European Union joined KEDO. See http://www.kedo.org for the text of this document.

27. Jonathan D. Pollack, "The United States, North Korea, and the End of the Agreed Framework," *Naval War College Review* 56, no. 3 (May 5, 2003): 22.

28. International Crisis Group, "North Korea: A Phased Negotiation Strategy," Asia Report, no. 61 (August 1, 2003), 9.

29. David Albright and Paul Brannan, "The North Korean Plutonium Stock, February 2007," Institute for Science and International Security (February 20, 2007), 3.

30. Richard A. Armitage, "A Comprehensive Approach on North Korea," Institute for National Security Studies, National Defense University, Strategic Forum No. 159 (March 1999). The details that follow are from this report.

31. Statement by the President, June 11, 2001. This statement can be found on the White House Web site at http://www.whitehouse.gov/news/releases/200106/20010611-4.html.

32. "The Nuclear Posture Review Report," dated January 8, 2002, can be found at http://www.globalsecurity.org/wmd/library/policy/dod/npr.htm.

33. "The National Security Strategy of the United States of America," September 2002, 13–15. Interestingly, in the National Security Strategy published in 2006, there was much less emphasis on preemption and more on multilateral efforts. The DPRK was still listed as a tyrannical government that presented a serious nuclear proliferation challenge.

34. John Larkin, "Axis of Uncertainty," *Far Eastern Economic Review,* February 14, 2002, 12–15.

35. Bob Woodward, *Bush at War* (New York: Simon and Schuster, 2002), 340.

36. Larry A. Niksch, "Korea: U.S.-Korea Relations-Issues for Congress," Issue Brief of the Congress, Congressional Research Service (May 1, 2003), 2. See also Sebastian Harnisch, "U.S.-North Korean Relations Under the Bush Administration: From 'Slow Go to No Go,'" *Asian Survey* 42, no. 6 (November–December 2002), 856–82.

37. For a series of *New York Times* articles on the Kelly visit to North Korea in October 2002, see David Sanger, "North Korea Says It Has Program on Nuclear Arms," October 17, 2002, 1; David Sanger and James Deo, "U.S. Says Pakistan Gave Technology to North Korea," October 18, 2002, 1; and Howard French, "North Korea's Confession: Why?" October 21, 2002, 6. See also Murray Hiebert, "Still Stuck in Stalemate," *Far Eastern Economic Review,* October 17, 2002, 22–23; and Murray Hiebert, "Consequences of Confession," *Far Eastern Economic Review,* October 31, 2002, 14–19.

38. Pollack, "The United States, North Korea," 35–36; and Larry A. Niksch, "North Korea's Nuclear Weapons Program," Issue Brief for Congress, Congressional Research Service (November 27, 2002), 8.

39. KEDO Executive Board Meeting Notes, November 14, 2002 available at http://www.kedo.org.

40. B. C. Koh, "A Breakthrough or an Illusion: An Assessment of the New Six-Party Agreement," The Institute for Far Eastern Studies (March 16, 2007), 4.

41. "North Korea: A Phased Negotiating Strategy," 13.

42. Larry A. Niksch, "Korea: U.S.-Korean Relations-Issues for Congress, An Update," Issue Brief, Congressional Research Service (February 22, 2005), 5–7.

43. "DPRK FM on Its Stand to Suspend Its Participation in Six-Party Talks for Indefinite Period," Korean Central News Agency, February 11, 2005, available at http://www.kcna.co.jp/item/2005/200502/news0211.htm. See also James Brooke and David Sanger, "North Koreans Say They Hold Nuclear Arms," *New York Times,* February 11, 2005, 1.

44. "Joint Statement of the Fourth Round of the Six-Party Talks, Beijing, September 19, 2005, available at http://www.state.gov/r/pa/prs/ps/2005/53490.htm. The following information is taken from this Joint Statement.

45. Joseph Kahn, "North Koreans Insist on Demand for New Reactor in Nuclear Talks," *New York Times,* September 16, 2005, 3; and Joseph Kahn, "China Proposes a Deal to End North Korean Nuclear Standoff," *New York Times,* September 17, 2005, 4.

46. Julia Choi and Karin Lee, "North Korea: Economic Sanctions and U.S. Department of Treasury Actions 1955–September 2006," The National Committee on North Korea, 14–16, available at http://www.ncnk.org. For a critical analysis of the BDA sanctions, see Glyn Ford, "Dead Talks Walking: North Korea and Removing the Bomb," Policy Forum Online 06–104A (December 14, 2006), Nautilus Institute, available at http://www.nautilus.org/fora/security/06104Ford.html.

47. Normitsu Onishi, "6 Missiles Fired by North Korea; Tests Protested," *New York Times,* July 5, 2006, 1. For an analysis of these launches, see Arnold Kanter, "North Korean Missile Launches and Implications for U.S. Policy," PacNet 35A, dated July 21, 2006, Pacific Forum, Honolulu, HI.

48. United Nations Security Council Resolution 1695, "United Nations Security Council Condemns Democratic People's Republic of Korea's Missile Launches," July 15, 2006; available at http://www.state.gov/p/eap/rls/prs/69022.htm.

49. "DPRK Foreign Ministry Clarifies Stand on New Measure to Bolster War Deterrent," Korean Central News Agency, October 4, 2006; available at http://www.Kcna.co.jp/item/2006/news10/04.htm.

50. Richard L. Garwin and Frank N. von Hippel, "A Technical Analysis: Deconstructing North Korea's October 9 Nuclear Test," *Arms Control Today* 36, no. 9 (November 2006), the Arms Control Association, available at http://www.armscontrol.org/act/2006_11/tech.asp?print.

51. UN Security Council Resolution 1718, "UN Security Council Resolution on North Korea," October 14, 2006; available at http://www.state.gov/p/eap/rls/ot/74010.htm.

52. Ilsoo David Cho and Meredith Jung-En Woo, "North Korea in 2006: The Year of Living Dangerously," *Asian Survey* 47, no. 1 (January–February 2007): 68–73.

53. Helene Cooper and David Sanger, "U.S. Offers North Korea Aid for Dropping Nuclear Plans," *New York Times,* December 6, 2006, 11.

54. Mark Landler and Thom Shanker, "North Korea and U.S. Envoys Meet in Berlin," *New York Times,* January 18, 2007, 3. See also Jonathan D. Pollack, "North Korea's Nuclear Weapons Program to 2015: Three Scenarios," *Asia Policy,* no. 3 (January 2007), National Bureau of Asian Research, 109.

55. For more details on possible issues with the implementation of the Denuclearization Action Plan, see International Crisis Group, "After the North Korea Nuclear Breakthrough: Compliance or Confrontation," Asia Briefing, no. 62 (April 30, 2007). For more on the shutdown of the nuclear reactor and the six-party talks in July 2007, see Choe Sang Hun, "UN Inspectors Confirm Shutdown of North Korean Reactor," *New York Times,* July 17, 2007, 3; and Howard W. French, "North Korean Nuclear Talks Fail to Set Disarmament Timetable, but Yield Agreement on Goals," *New York Times,* July 20, 2007, 13.

56. For example, when Japanese Prime Minister Junichiro Koizumi visited Bush at his Crawford, Texas, ranch in May 2003, Bush stated "we (Bush and Koizumi) will not tolerate nuclear weapons in North Korea . . . and will settle for nothing less than the complete, verifiable, and irreversible elimination of North Korea's nuclear weapons program." President Bush

made a similar statement after a meeting with South Korean President Roh Moo Hyun in October 2003. For the first, see http://www.whitehouse.gov/news/releases/2003/05/20030523-4.html and for the latter, see http://www.whitehouse.gov/news/releases/2003/10/print/20031020-2.html.

57. Albright and Brannan, "North Korean Plutonium Stock, February 2007," 1.

58. For a good summary of the changed negotiating environment after the nuclear weapon test, see Don Oberdorfer, "So Far, So Fast: What's Really Behind the Bush Administration's Course Reversal on North Korea-And Can the Negotiations Succeed?" Policy Forum Online 07–024A (March 20, 2007), Nautilus Institute, available at http://www.nautilus.org/fara/security/070240Oberdorfer.html.

Index

Note: Tables are indicated with the letter *t* following the page number; figures are indicated with the letter *f* following the page number.

About the Editors and Contributors

THE EDITORS

Paul J. Bolt is Professor and Deputy Head of the Department of Political Science at the United States Air Force Academy. He received his BA from Hope College and his MA and PhD in political science from the University of Illinois at Urbana-Champaign. Dr. Bolt has taught at Zhejiang University and Baicheng Normal College in the People's Republic of China, as well as the University of Illinois. Dr. Bolt is the author of *China and Southeast Asia's Ethnic Chinese: State and Diaspora in Contemporary Asia* (Praeger, 2000) and is a coeditor of *American Defense Policy* (Johns Hopkins University Press, 2005) and *China's Nuclear Future* (Lynne Rienner, 2006). He has also published in the *Journal of Contemporary China, Asian Affairs, Issues and Studies, Diaspora, Airman Scholar,* and received research grants from the United States Air Force's Institute for National Security Studies. His primary research areas are Asian politics and defense policy.

Su Changhe is Professor of International Affairs and Executive Dean at the School of International and Diplomatic Affairs (SIDA), Shanghai International Studies University. He received his PhD in international relations from Fudan University in 1999, and then was an associate professor in the International Politics Department at Fudan University from 1999–2006. From 2000–2001, he conducted research as a Freeman Visiting Scholar at the University of Illinois at Urbana-Champaign. He joined the faculty at SIDA in 2006. He is author of *Global Public Issues and International Cooperation: An Institutional Analysis* (Shanghai People's Publisher, 2000), and is currently writing on the influence of international institutions in Chinese domestic politics.

Sharyl Cross is Professor of National Security Studies at the George C. Marshall European Center for Security Studies in Garmisch-Partenkirchen, Germany. She holds a PhD in political science from the University of California, Los Angeles. In 2004–2005, Dr. Cross was appointed Visiting Distinguished Professor in the Department of Political Science at the United States Air Force Academy. In 1999, she was awarded a Senior Fulbright Scholar fellowship to support affiliations as Research Scholar/Professor at the Institute of USA and Canada Studies of the Russian Academy of Sciences and the Moscow State Institute of International Relations of the Ministry of Foreign Affairs of the Russian Federation (MGIMO). Dr. Cross also served as Visiting Professor at the United States Air War College and was a Post-Doctoral U.S. State Department Fellowship recipient at the Hoover Institution at Stanford University. Her coedited books include *Global Security Beyond the Millennium: American and Russian Perspectives* (Macmillan Press, 1999) and *The New Chapter in United States-Russia Relations: Opportunities and Challenges* (Praeger, 1994). Her articles have appeared in *Communist and Post Communist Studies, Journal of Slavic Military Studies, Nationalities Papers, Mediterranean Quarterly, Survey, Journal of Political and Military Sociology, Presidential Studies Quarterly, Connections,* and in peer reviewed journals published by the Russian Academy of Sciences including *Social Sciences and Modernity, SShA,* and *Latinskaya Amerika.*

THE CONTRIBUTORS

Rouben Azizian is a Professor at the Asia-Pacific Center for Security Studies, Honolulu. In 1994–2002 he was a member of the Department of Political Studies of the University of Auckland, New Zealand. Prior to becoming a full-time academic, he had an extensive career in the Soviet and later Russian Foreign Service. He has edited four books and published numerous book chapters, journal articles and working papers dealing with security issues in Russia, Central Asia, and the Asia-Pacific region.

Dianne Barton is a Senior Fellow at the Institute for Science Engineering and Public Policy in Portland, Oregon. Previously she was a Distinguished Member of Technical Staff in the Evolutionary Computing Department at Sandia National Laboratories. While at Sandia, Dr. Barton led a team that built complex adaptive simulation capabilities to identify infrastructure system interdependencies and vulnerabilities. Her current research interests involve agent-based modeling, socioeconomic adaptation, and the use of advanced learning models to simulate human decision making. She received her BA in geology (1979) from Northwestern University, and her MS in geochemistry (1984) and PhD in geochemistry (1988) from the University of Arizona. Additionally, she received an advanced certificate in supercomputer applications—roughly equivalent to an MS in computer sciences (1999)—from the University of New Mexico. Dr. Barton received a 2005 NATO-Russia Collaborative Linkage Grant to conduct research in support of this publication.

William E. Berry Jr. is currently an independent consultant specializing in East Asian security issues. A career military officer, he retired from the Air Force as a colonel in 1997. During his military career, he served in Vietnam, the Philippines, Korea, and Malaysia, where he was the air attaché from 1990–93. He also taught at the Air Force Academy, the National War College, and the Asia-Pacific Center for Security Studies and was the senior military professor and chair of the Academy's Department of Political Science. Dr. Berry has been associated with the Center for Civil-Military Relations at the Naval Postgraduate School and participated on a number of the Center's mobile education teams to countries such as Papua New Guinea. He received his PhD from Cornell University, and has written and lectured extensively on topics related to U.S. security interests in both Northeast and Southeast Asia. His book, *U.S. Bases in the Philippines: The Evolution of the Special Relationship,* is generally considered to be one of the seminal works on this subject. Dr. Berry is currently writing a book for the Praeger Security International Reference Series comparing the security perspectives of the two Koreas.

Robin L. Bowman is a captain in the United States Air Force and currently an Instructor in the Political Science Department at the United States Air Force Academy. She holds a Bachelor of Arts in political science from the University of California at Berkeley, and Master of Arts in national security affairs at the Naval Postgraduate School. Her areas of interest include political violence/terrorism and U.S. foreign/national security policy in Southeast Asia.

Elizabeth C. Economy is C. V. Starr Senior Fellow and Director of Asia Studies at the Council on Foreign Relations. Her areas of expertise include Chinese domestic and foreign policy, Sino-U.S. relations, and global environmental issues. Dr. Economy has published widely on both Chinese domestic and foreign policy. Her most recent book is *The River Runs Black: The Environmental Challenge to China's Future* (Cornell University Press, 2004). *The Globalist* named it one of the top ten books of 2004, and it won the International Convention on Asia Scholars award for best social sciences book published on Asia in 2003 or 2004. She also coedited *China Joins the World: Progress and Prospects* (Council on Foreign Relations Press, with Michel Oksenberg, 1999) and *The Internationalization of Environmental Protection* (Cambridge University Press, with Miranda Schreurs, 1997). She has published articles in foreign policy and scholarly journals including *Foreign Affairs, Harvard Asia Quarterly, Survival,* and *Current History;* and op-eds and book reviews in the *New York Times,* the *Washington Post,* the *Far Eastern Economic Review,* the *International Herald Tribune,* the *Boston Globe,* and the *South China Morning Post,* among others. Dr. Economy has taught undergraduate- and graduate-level courses at Columbia University, Johns Hopkins University's Paul H. Nitze School of Advanced International Studies, and the University of Washington's Jackson School of International Studies. She serves on several China-related boards, including the China-U.S. Center for Sustainable Development and Wild Aid, and the advisory board for *Issues and Studies,* an international journal on China, Taiwan, and East

Asian affairs. Dr. Economy received her PhD from the University of Michigan, her MA from Stanford University, and her BA from Swarthmore College.

Gregory Gleason teaches international relations and public administration in the Political Science Department at the University of New Mexico, where he has been on the faculty since 1988. Dr. Gleason is the author of *Federalism and Nationalism: The Struggle for Republican Rights in the USSR* (1991), *Central Asian States: Discovering Independence* (1997), and *Markets and Politics in Central Asia* (2003) as well as scholarly articles in *Asian Perspective, Communist and Post-Communist Studies, Europe-Asia Studies, International Studies Perspectives, Problems of Post-Communism,* and other journals. Dr. Gleason has served as a consultant to Lawrence Livermore National Laboratory, Sandia National Laboratories, the Asian Development Bank, and the U.S. Agency for International Development. His research has been sponsored by the National Science Foundation and the National Academy of Sciences as well as other public and private foundations.

Graeme P. Herd is a Faculty Member at the Geneva Centre for Security Policy (GCSP), an Associate Fellow, "International Security Programme," Chatham House, London, and an Honorary Research Fellow, Department of Politics and International Relations, University of Aberdeen, Scotland. Between 2002 and 2005, he was variously Professor of Civil-Military Relations, Associate Director of the Senior Executive Seminar and Faculty Director of Research at the George C. Marshall European Center for Security Studies, Garmisch-Partenkirchen, Germany, where he also was a guest lecturer at the NATO School in Oberammergau. Prior to this he was a Lecturer in International Relations at both the University of Aberdeen (1997–2002) and Staffordshire University (1994–97) and a Projects Officer, Department of War Studies, King's College London (1993–94). His PhD examined the role of Scottish mercenary soldiers in Russia in the seventeenth century. His latest books include *The Ideological War on Terror: World Wide Strategies for Counter Terrorism* (Routledge, Taylor & Francis Group, 2006) and *Divided West: European Security and the Transatlantic Relationship* (Blackwells Publishing Ltd., 2006).

Deron R. Jackson is a major in the United States Air Force, Assistant Professor of Political Science at the United States Air Force Academy and Deputy Director of the Center for Space and Defense Studies. Major Jackson is an AFROTC graduate from the University of Illinois where he earned dual degrees in electrical engineering and political science. In 1991 he was awarded the German Federal Chancellor's Fellowship (Bundeskanzlerstipendium) sponsored by the Alexander von Humboldt Foundation. He spent a year as a guest researcher at the Stiftung Wissenschaft und Politik in Ebenhausen working on trans-Atlantic relations and the evolution of NATO and the European Union. After graduate study at the Fletcher School of Law and Diplomacy, he joined the Academy faculty in 1997. His current areas of interest include the study of terrorism, homeland defense policy, military strategy, and the impact of technological evolution on warfare and society.

Dmitri Katsy is Associate Professor at the School of International Relations, St. Petersburg State University, Russia. He received his PhD in the history of international relations and foreign policy from St. Petersburg State University in 2000 and his MA in European integration from the University of Limerick, Ireland, in 1997. He is also a graduate of the George C. Marshall European Center for Security Studies (2006). Professor Katsy's areas of interest include European security, preventive diplomacy and international negotiations. He has taught at the St. Petersburg State University School of International Relations since 1998 as well as at other universities in Estonia, Finland and the United States. Professor Katsy is a coeditor of the annual series of the School of International Relations publications, St. Petersburg State University Press. He is an author of 20 scientific articles in Russian and English and a book on International Negotiation (St. Petersburg State University Press, 2005). Dr. Katsy's selected list of publications is available at http://www.dip.pu.ru /russian/lecture/katsy.htm. His most recent publication is "North and South Cleavage: What does it Mean for Russia?" in *International Relations: From Local Changes to Global Shifts* (St. Petersburg State University Press, 2007, coauthored with Houman Sadri, Greg Gleason, and Victoria Glenn).

Konstantin Khudoley is Professor and Dean at the School of International Relations, St. Petersburg State University, Russia. He graduated from the Faculty of History, Leningrad (St. Petersburg) State University in 1973, and received his PhD in history (1978) and became a full doctor of science in history in 1988. Professor Khudoley's interest is in British politics and in relations between Russia, the European Union, and NATO. He has taught at universities in the United States, Great Britain, Germany, Canada, the People's Republic of China, the Netherlands, Finland, Sweden, and South Korea. Professor Khudoley is an author of over 80 scientific publications, many of which were published in Belgium, Great Britain, Germany, Italy, China, Slovakia, Finland, and Estonia. His recent works were published by Carnegie Moscow Center, Nomos Verlagsgesellschaft, Wisdom House and others. Professor Khudoley's list of publications can be found at http://www.sir.edu/english/lecture/ khudoleikk.htm.

John J. Le Beau is a Professor of Strategy and Security at the George C. Marshall Center for Security Studies and a faculty member of the Program on Terrorism and Security Studies. He is also Chair of the Partnership for Peace Counter Terrorism Working Group. Dr. Le Beau is a former Senior Operations Officer who retired from the Central Intelligence Agency in 2005. His intelligence community duties included assignments as chief of an operational facility in Europe engaged in counterterrorist and counter-proliferation operations and collection, and Program Manager of a human and technical collection program involving Europe and the Middle East.

Liu Jianjun is Professor and Vice Dean of the School of International Relations and Public Affairs, Fudan University. He received his BA from Qufu Normal University and his MA and PhD in political science from Fudan University. From January to May 2001, he conducted research as a visiting scholar at the University of Georgia. Dr. Liu is the author of *The Unit System in Contemporary China* and *The Development of Modern Politics in China* (Tianjin People's Press). He is also chief editor of two books: *The Logic of Ruling: Party, State and Society* and *Institution Building and State Development* (Shanghai Cishu Press).

Mikhail V. Margelov is Senator and Chairman of the Committee for Foreign Affairs, Council of Federation, Federal Assembly of the Russian Federation. He also serves as Vice President of the Parliamentary Assembly of the Council of Europe (PACE) and Chairman of the Democratic Group in PACE. In December 2000, Dr. Margelov was elected to represent the Pskov Region in the Council of Federation (the Upper House of the Russian Parliament), where he joined the Committee for Foreign Affairs. In November 2001, he was elected Chairman of the Committee. He had previously directed the Russian Information Center (Rosinformcentr) covering events in the North Caucasus and other international issues, and had headed the Public Relations Department of the Russian President during the Yeltsin period. Dr. Margelov is a graduate of the Institute of Asia and Africa affiliated with Moscow State University, and holds a PhD from the St. Petersburg State University School of International Relations. Dr. Margelov taught Arabic at the Higher School of the USSR State Security Committee, and was Senior Editor of the Arab Section of TASS News Agency. His book entitled *Russia and the Global Hydrocarbon Markets: Basic Tendencies, Contending Arguments and Perspectives,* based on his PhD dissertation, was published by St. Petersburg State University Press in 2005.

Pavel Podvig is a researcher at the Center for International Security and Cooperation at Stanford University. Before coming to Stanford in 2004, he worked at the Center for Arms Control Studies in Moscow. Dr. Podvig was a researcher at the Security Studies Program at MIT (1992–94) and the Program on Science and Global Security at Princeton University (2000–2004). His research interests include technical and political issues of missile defense, early-warning and command and control, U.S.-Russian relations, structure and capabilities of the Russian strategic forces, and Russia's defense industry and nuclear complex. Pavel Podvig was the editor of *Russian Strategic Nuclear Forces* (MIT Press, 2001), which is considered a definitive source of information on Russian strategic forces. Dr. Podvig graduated from the Moscow Institute of Physics and Technology, where he then taught physics for more than 10 years. He holds a PhD in political science from the Moscow Institute of World Economy and International Relations.

David H. Sacko is Associate Professor of Political Science at the United States Air Force Academy. He received his PhD in political science in 2003 from the Pennsylvania State University. Dr. Sacko recently coauthored *The Unipolar Dilemma: An Unbalanced Future* (Palgrave). He has published in several journals including *International Studies Quarterly* and the *Journal of Political Science Education*. Since arriving at the U.S. Air Force Academy in 2002, Dr. Sacko has researched foreign elite opinion of U.S. foreign policy and Central European security matters for the Institute of National Security Studies. His current research assesses threats to the security of Central Europe, particularly the Polish-Russian-American relationship. Dr. Sacko received a Fulbright Scholarship to lecture at Warsaw University in Spring 2007.

Mikhail Troitskiy is Associate Professor at Moscow State Institute of International Relations of the Ministry of Foreign Affairs of the Russian Federation (MGIMO), where he teaches history of international relations, Russian foreign policy and international security. He holds an MA in international relations from St. Petersburg State University (1999) and a doctoral degree in political science from the Institute for U.S. and Canadian Studies of the Russian Academy of Sciences (2003), where he also serves as senior research fellow. In August 2005–February 2006, Professor Troitskiy was a Fulbright-Kennan Research Scholar at the Woodrow Wilson International Center for Scholars in Washington, DC. In June–August 2006 he was BP Visiting Fellow at Clare Hall, Cambridge University. Professor Troitskiy has published on Russian foreign policy, U.S.-Russia, NATO-Russia, and EU-Russia relations as well as on U.S. policy within NATO.

Jennifer L. Turner is coordinator of the China Environment Forum at the Woodrow Wilson International Center for Scholars. In addition to facilitating the China Environment Forum meeting activities, she also serves as editor of the Wilson Center's journal, the *China Environment Series.* Besides meetings in Washington, DC, she has arranged several study tour activities in China, the United States, and Japan bringing together Chinese, U.S., Japanese, and other Asian experts on issues of environmental nongovernmental organizations, environmental journalism, river basin governance, water conflict resolution, and municipal financing of environmental infrastructure. Dr. Turner received her PhD in Public Policy and Comparative Politics from Indiana University, Bloomington, in 1997. Her dissertation examined local government innovation in implementing water policies in the People's Republic of China. Her current research focuses on environmental civil society and water resources protection issues in China.

Fred Wehling is Associate Professor in the Graduate School of International Policy Studies and Senior Research Associate and Education Coordinator for the Center for Nonproliferation Studies (CNS) at the Monterey Institute of International Studies, Monterey, California. In addition to teaching courses on nuclear nonproliferation, WMD and terrorism, and other topics at the Monterey Institute, Dr. Wehling organizes the Center's educational outreach projects in the United States, Russia, and other countries; and conducts research in fissile material security, exports of nuclear materials and technology from the former Soviet states, and nuclear terrorism; and develops online learning programs on terrorism with WMD. Before coming to CNS in 1998, Dr. Wehling was a consultant at RAND,

Coordinator of Policy Research for the University of California's Institute on Global Conflict and Cooperation (IGCC), and a researcher at the Cooperative Monitoring Center (CMC) at Sandia National Laboratories. After receiving his PhD in political science from UCLA in 1992, Dr. Wehling taught courses on international security and Russian foreign policy at UC San Diego. He is co-author of *World Politics in a New Era,* 3rd ed. (2003) and author of various articles and reports for *The Nonproliferation Review.*

Wei Zongyou is Associate Professor of International Relations at the School of International and Diplomatic Affairs (SIDA), Shanghai International Studies University. He received his MA in history of international relations from Nanjing University in 1998 and PhD in international relations from Fudan University in 2004. He joined the faculty at SIDA in 2004. His areas of research interest include the studies of international security, U.S. security strategy, and China's foreign policy.

Fengshi Wu is Assistant Professor in the Department of Government and Public Policy, Chinese University of Hong Kong. She specializes in China's transnational relations. She has completed substantial field research and published on transnational activism and advocacy networks related to China's environment, health, and civil society development. Her most recent publications include "International Non-government Actor in HIV/AIDS Prevention in China" (*Cell Research* 15, November–December 2005), "Environmental GONGO Autonomy: Unintended Consequences of State Strategies in China" (*Journal of the Good Society,* 2004), "Old Brothers or New Partners: GONGOs in Transnational Environmental Advocacy in China" (*China Environment Series,* 2002), and "State and Environmental NGOs in Environmental Security in Northeast Asia" (coauthor with Esook Yoon in *Environmental Security in Northeast Asia,* U.S. Institute for Peace Press, 2006). She is currently involved in the Environmental Equity in China book project funded by the Tamaki Foundation.

Yu Yixuan is Assistant Professor in the Department of International Politics in the School of International Relations and Public Affairs at Fudan University. She holds a PhD in International Relations from Fudan University specializing in the history of international political thought and foreign relations of modern China. Her publications include "How to Understand the Concept of Power—From the Perspective of Diplomacy of Modern European States," in *Diplomacy of the Great Powers: Theory, Decision-Making and Challenge,* edited by Xiao Jialing and Tang Xianxing (Shishi Press, 2003); "A Study on the North Korea Nuclear Crisis," *Exploration and Free Views* no. 1, 2003; and "Impossible 'Plan'—A Re-examination of Idealism," in *Beyond Westphalia?* edited by Chen Yugang and Yuan Jianhua (Shishi Press, 2004).

Jing-dong Yuan is Director of the East Asia Nonproliferation Program at the Center for Nonproliferation Studies, and an Associate Professor of International Policy Studies at the Monterey Institute of International Studies. A graduate of the Xi'an

Foreign Language University, People's Republic of China (1982), he received his PhD in political science from Queen's University in 1995 and has had research and teaching appointments at Queen's University, York University, the University of Toronto, and the University of British Columbia, where he was a recipient of the prestigious Iaazk Killam Postdoctoral Research Fellowship. Professor Yuan's research focuses on Asia-Pacific security, global and regional arms control and nonproliferation issues, U.S. policy toward Asia, and China's defense and foreign policy. He is the coauthor of *China and India: Cooperation or Conflict?* (Lynne Rienner, 2003) and is currently working on a book manuscript on post–Cold War Chinese security policy.

Zhang Jiadong is Lecturer of International Affairs and Assistant Director of the Center for American Studies (CAS), Fudan University. He received his PhD in international relations from Fudan University in 2004. Currently he is a researcher and lecturer in CAS, IIS, Fudan. His research areas include terrorism and counterterrorism, separatist movements, the China-U.S. security relationship, and China and U.S. counterterrorism policies. He is author of *Analysis on Terrorism* (Shishi Publisher, 2007) and *Terrorism in the Global Era and Governance* (Shanlian Publisher, 2007). He is leading a program on antiterrorism issues in China and is currently writing on the relationship between religion and terrorism in China's national security.